FREEDOM
AND PUBLIC EDUCATION

Edited by

Ernest O. Melby and Morton Puner

PRAEGER — NEW YORK

Library of Congress Catalog Card Number 52-7490

Published in 1953 by Frederick A. Praeger, Inc.,
Publishers, 105 West 40th Street, New York
18, N. Y. Manufactured in the United States
of America

Second printing, 1954

BOOKS THAT MATTER

TABLE OF CONTENTS:

vii

viii

INTRODUCTION

Ernest O. Melby

The challenges facing education today become the more serious when we see them against a backdrop of the problems surrounding the future of freedom at home and abroad. On a world-wide basis, free institutions are literally fighting with their back to the wall. We have already been involved in the Korean War and in a vast defense program. But more, the conflict has profoundly affected our life at home in America. No generation in our history as a nation has talked so much about freedom as we have; no generation has seemed as ready to abandon it as we have since World War II. It would appear that Russian Communism, through aggression and intrigue, has frightened us to such an alarming degree that we are in the process of radically modifying the character of American civil liberty, academic freedom, and the quality of American life.

If the American tradition is to be retained and preserved, education faces an almost overwhelming task. Primarily we are engaged in a struggle against materialism. The battle for the minds and hearts of men can be won only through a more effective education for freedom. Yet, at the very time when we need the most effective possible kind of education, our educational structure is being weakened by attacks on the part of its enemies, misunderstandings on the part of its friends, by the low economic and social state of the profession in our society. And we cannot even come to grips with this total social and educational problem unless we can first conquer the major ailment of the western world—fear.

You will note that fear is the subject of some of the selections in this book as well as a basic cause for the events described in others. I deeply believe that we can overcome this unfortunate fear only as we take stock of our moral and spiritual heritage, of the meaning of our free institutions, of our vast productive capacity, of the amazing creative talents of our people as well as the potential of a dynamic program of education. We need a great faith—faith in people, in freedom, in the power of love and understanding, in education—if we are to preserve our free society.

Faith—the bulwark against fear—is served directly by good education. By good education, I mean education which is practical, satisfying, and useful for effective living. It is education which helps people to become socially active and responsible—able to participate fully in democracy. This kind of education is different for different people. But its foundations are the same for almost everyone, just as the demands of living are common to nearly all of us.

To illustrate these common demands: All of us are citizens and have certain rights and responsibilities. Nearly all of us are members of a family and home. Nearly all of us are workers and earn a living by some form of production. Most of us have some leisure to use and would like to enjoy that leisure fully. All of us are members of various kinds of groups, small or large. Most of us recognize a spiritual side to our being and feel the need for some understanding of beauty, truth, goodness—for some relation of man and his education to a force greater than himself.

We need many skills and understandings to meet these common demands. They are easy to name. We need to be able to read and write and figure, to see relationships, to be able to use our hands skillfully, to understand certain ideas about time and space, to interpret data. We need to know how to rear children so that their bodies and spirits are adequately nourished. We need to have humanistic and aesthetic skills. We need to span the world in understanding the requirements of other people as well as ourselves. We need to have the skill of getting along with people of many kinds.

These skills and understandings are needed by almost all of us—these and many more. Parents, when asked what they want most for their children, often say, "We want them to learn to get along with others." This is a blanket way of saying, "We want a good education for our children so that they can be happy members of a family, of a neighborhood; so that they can earn a living and enjoy whatever time is left over; so that they can contribute to the well-being of others."

It is precisely towards these ends that good education is directed. Implicit in the answers of parents is the desire, conscious or unconscious, for better schools, better teachers, better chances for our children than we have thus far been able to give them.

How can we realize these hopes? Some of the answer is to be found in the examination of the very foundations upon which our educational system is built. These foundations consist of three momentous ideas: a democratic philosophy, a dynamic process, and a spiritual force. An appreciation of these ideas may help give us the faith that conquers fear.

A Democratic Philosophy

Education in America is rooted in a democratic philosophy. One of the most powerful ideas which came to birth with our nation was that a democratic way of life requires an educated citizenry, capable of actively participating in community affairs. This requirement is even more essential now than it was in 1776. Our problems will not yield to solution unless educational processes are employed. Education is the life-line to our free institutions; if it is destroyed or weakened, so is democracy. Good education today must have its roots sunk deeply into that kind of democratic action which is workable in our present-day society, a society marked by an increasingly urban and technological culture.

Freedom of thought and choice, freedom to express emotions, freedom of speech and the press, freedom of religion must be cherished. The responsibilities which accompany these freedoms must be learned. They can be learned through an educational program which recognizes that these qualities of living are of such supreme worth to the dignity of man that they must impregnate all teaching.

Throughout most of our national history we have taken our democratic freedoms for granted. Because there seemed to be no immediate threat, we felt that we had time to carry on an education of a pedestrian character, sometimes devoid of fervor and dedication to our way of life. We have felt that we could endure apathy from many citizens of the community. Sometimes the processes of freedom faltered but we felt that we always had time—decades or even centuries—in which to solve our problems.

Time is no longer on our side. Not only are crafty enemies allied against us. There is widespread human want and suffering in great areas of the globe. Our ideological opponents have based their hope for human betterment on materialism, denial of religious rights, and subservience of the individual to the state. Western democracy has taken its position firmly in support of the worth and dignity of all men. More than ever before, it must follow through and express that position in action.

Education must have a pervasive and vigorous purpose—the development of an intelligent and active citizenry—if it is to continue to complement democracy. After all, democracy is not an abstract philosophical idea but something to be lived in one's daily association with other men and women. A democratic community is strong and effective when its citizens participate constantly and vitally in its affairs.

How can we accomplish this in our schools? Effective education means, among other things, that children must be given a chance to make decisions daily in the areas of living in which they are capable of doing critical thinking. This process must start with kindergarten and gradually become more extensive and complex as children become more mature. Children learn to make wise choices by having the chance to choose and then living by their decisions—just as adults do. They must be taught through practice how to handle the forms of democracy— group discussion; the ballot; the referendum; the initiative; the airing of opinions; the conciliation function; the roles of business, labor, government; the functions of governing boards and councils; and so on. The rules which govern children must be arrived at in the same manner in which we hammer out our laws in adult society. Children must be aware of the need for rules governing conduct and then develop ways to meet that need.

These and other processes of participation should extend through the school and into the community so that all community policies may be developed, as far as possible, through discussion with wide community participation. There are educational problems that are tearing many communities apart today. These problems could become important activities for community education if there were more and better channels through which interested citizens could participate in the determination of educational policies.

We must evolve a program of education which is so well founded in democratic ideals that every public school citizen knows—through day-by-day practice—the citizenship skills demanded of an adult today, and understands the ideals of freedom and responsibility of living in a democracy. Thus he will be able to accept the dignity of each human being completely. By the time he is an adult, his skills and understandings based on such education should include his home, his many groups, his community, his nation, and his world. It should include his work activities as well as his play activities.

Good education—so rooted in democracy—would cause a citizen to think twice before calling his neighbor a name or defaming his character. It would cause him to question the practicing of one kind of dealings on Sunday and in church, and another kind of dealings with human beings in business transactions. It would cause him to consider the consequences of turning over the political affairs of his community and his nation to the ward politician. It would cause him to be concerned about the effect of mass media of communication upon national welfare. It would cause him, in every respect, to be a concerned and knowing citizen.

A Dynamic Process

Good education must be a growing, changing, dynamic process. This quality of education is a direct outgrowth of the fact that it is rooted in democratic beliefs. Change is as inherent to the concept of democracy as fixed supremacy of the state is to totalitarian philosophy.

In the early days of our country, the accumulated knowledge of the world changed slowly. Father could teach son his methods of business or farming and son found them adequate. The social structure of the community was relatively stable and simple. Many social forms were handed down from generation to generation in identical patterns of behavior.

As society has changed, new demands have been made upon people and education has new functions to teach. Our culture has grown tremendously; its growth presents the challenge to education. Unless education is dynamic, youth who are now being educated will eventually find they were educated for a world that no longer exists.

What are some of the new demands of the day? The most urgent is a knowledge of a fourth "R"—relationships among humans. The knowledge means learning to get along with people in a complex society in which the people we count on for food, clothing, and human wants are usually people we have never even seen. There are scores of indications of the need for learning these social skills all around us. Consider the failure of urban and rural areas to come to common agreements in state legislatures. Think of the tensions among persons of different religious, racial and nationality backgrounds. Consider the sectionalism we find in approaching many problems. Think of the misunderstandings between labor and management. In your own trade or profession think of the rivalries between departments of a single establishment.

Some of the other new demands are understanding and learning to handle the effects of mass media of communication; revamping our ideas of time, space and mobility; understanding the complexity of world economics and its effects upon political and social decisions.

This brings us to a consideration of another prong in the change process—the utilization of new knowledge. In the area of social skills, for instance, we have a science of group dynamics developed from social research. This is a new kind of knowledge which only begins to touch the classrooms of this country. Good education must take this knowledge into account.

Further, a body of knowledge concerning child growth and development has been developed during this century. It is well tested in the laboratory schools. If fully utilized, this knowledge would revolutionize many of our ideas about teaching. The emotional needs of children, for instance, have been studied extensively. The areas of mental health and psychiatry have great contributions to make to education. Good education must change and grow to encompass this knowledge.

Some people assume that if education becomes concerned with new demands and new knowledge, the established learnings are neglected. This assumption gives rise to some of the charges against the schools reported in Section III. Nothing is more absurd. The three R's were never so important as today and never has the school done so good a job of teaching them. The problem of education is not one of discarding or neglecting but rather building a new mosaic with greater strength and beauty—and one which is more useful.

Good education, constantly improving to serve a changing culture, should equip a citizen to live in the world which is now and which is emerging; not the one which has been. It should emphasize those demands which are most pressing; today these include the social skills of getting along with others. It should foster the ability of a child to adjust to new situations with the least amount of harmful tensions. It should utilize new knowledge so that each child may have the benefit of all we know about how he may best learn and develop.

A Spiritual Force

Good education in America is spiritual in nature. This idea, too, springs from the concept that education is rooted in democracy. Democracy is essentially a spiritual idea. It recognizes the dignity of the human being as supreme. We see every human as a unique organism with capacities not possessed by any other person. We, in America, have released human creative talents to a greater extent than has ever been done before in human history.

The people who founded our country were religious people. They believed in a brotherhood of man under the fatherhood of God. In recent years, it has become a little more difficult for us to deal with the religious aspects of education. Much is said of the separation of church and state; it is a principle with which most of us agree. But the principle must never be used as an alibi for failure to deal effectively with moral and spiritual values in education. We may have widely different concepts of God. But there are not many differences among us with regard to the power of love and understanding among human beings. One of the most important elements of our democracy is faith in the power of this love and understanding.

We know that children grow best—intellectually and personally—in an atmosphere of affection, security and freedom. Intellectual growth is more rapid if the child has the love and understanding of his parents and teachers. It is in this area that we may see the sharp contrast between our way of life and the collectivist one exemplified by Communism and Fascism. Communism sees the individual as mere physical organisms; it is based upon denial of God. Even the brotherhood of man, as the Communist sees it, is a materialistic, soulless concept without love or spiritual feeling.

This love and understanding is of special importance today, particularly among the various groups of our society. We need a united front against the materialism represented in the international scene by aggressive Communism. We handicap ourselves in the international scene by the manner in which we treat the Negro in our own society. We need all the churches and other social agencies which basically can unite on the worth and dignity concept of individual human beings. Yet, at this very time, religious conflict seems to be on the increase.

Every incident of this conflict produces bitterness on the part of an opposing group; tension increases from day to day.

It is a function of education to build bridges of understanding among the various groups in our society. It is our responsibility to teach the common elements of our religious and cultural heritage as they apply to human relationships and conduct in our society; to help people work together for a community which moves ever closer to a concrete expression of the American faith.

If you examine the experience of children in our schools from the time they enter nursery school until they graduate from high school, you find that moral and spiritual values are given great emphasis. Our art, music, literature, our national history, the daily life of the school, all contribute to this objective. Little children are taught to share, to take turns, to put oneself in the other's place. Older children are taught respect for property, the value of ideas and feelings, the processes for arriving at truths, the necessity for considering the welfare of all, the responsibility for using all one's ability and the appreciation of diversity.

It would be good, indeed, if the adult community gave youth a more favorable environment in which to apply the spiritual learnings acquired in the schools.

This development of a mature sense of moral responsibility is a major objective of good education. American teachers are constantly seeking improved ways to help children become more self-directive, to create an environment which requires decisions in terms of the welfare of others. In many communities, teachers and parents are working together to find ways in which the home and school may cooperate to help children become sensitive to moral responsibility. In many communities, the school program serves as the focal point for adult cooperation, thus demonstrating one of the spiritual values of American education.

The moral strength of America must be accompanied by an abiding faith that we seek a good life for all the citizens of our country. As long as education is denied to some because they cannot afford it, or because they belong to the wrong race, creed, or nationality group, we have a long way to go to realize fully the third revolutionary idea upon which good education rests.

The Problem Today

Probably no profession has as many worries as that of education today. And upon no segment of the educational profession do these concerns weigh more heavily than upon our school administrators. These men and women carry unprecedented burdens of leadership and responsibility. They have to contend with inadequate financing, out-of-date and overcrowded buildings. They have to contend with the normal difficulties of adapting education to the needs of the vast number and range of youth and adults who are to be educated. That *should* be enough. But, in recent months and years, they have had to carry their burdens in an atmosphere of widespread, bitter public criticism and anti-democratic attacks which seek to change the fundamental character of our government as well as the character and spirit of our education.

There have been casualties in this battle. Administrators have lost their jobs and suffered humiliating experiences at the hands of destructive critics. But, more important, American education has taken serious setbacks from which it will take years to recover. Teachers are afraid to deal vigorously and frankly with the issues which confront American life. The open forum qualities which once characterized our education have been damaged seriously. Freedom to criticize and dissent has, too often, been stifled.

Fortunately, the better informed, responsible sections of the public are being alerted to the hazards to the American educational system. Voluntary associations of many types—the National Citizens Commission for the Public Schools is a sterling example—are going into action. But the battle has just begun and the time is already late for educators and citizens to take careful counsel, to determine the resources to be mobilized, to build the organizational structure to maintain free education in a free society.

The first thing to remember is that the crisis in education is but a facet of the crisis in our common life. Van Wyck Brooks has brilliantly written about the period from 1885 to 1915 under the title, "The Confident Years." It was a period in the literary, artistic, political and economic history of our country when we felt secure in our freedom, in our institutions, in our religious faith. Then World War I shattered our feeling of geographical security. We had not yet accustomed ourselves to the responsibilities of a world power when the great depression shook our faith in economic freedom. Rapidly developing physical science and technology brought about a measure of overspecialization—in life and in education. The result has been that we are often unable to cope with situations outside our immediate range of knowledge. More recently, evidence of political corruption has further shaken some of our faith in government. All these have contributed to a weakening of our faith in the old religious tenets. Many of us have been left without mooring or compass in a moral or spiritual sense.

World War II made us the Number One world power. Our power has multiplied our fears and enhanced our feelings of guilt. Both the fears and the guilt are somewhat enigmatic to ourselves and to visitors from abroad. Why should the most powerful nation in the world be beset with fears. Perhaps, as John Foster Dulles thinks, we are insecure and fearful because we are over-dependent upon military and materialistic strength and not sufficiently aware of the moral and spiritual aspects of our problem.

We know that, on the international scene, our treatment of Negroes and other minority groups is our Achilles heel. We have guilt feelings about that too. We are not confident enough that we can keep our economy rolling without depressions unless that economy is stimulated by war or preparation for war. We are afraid to practice true freedom of speech and freedom of teaching because we think that the Communists or other subversives will take advantage of such freedom. So we limit our freedom and, by doing so, become more like the Communists we are fighting.

If the period from 1885 to 1915 made up the "Years of Confidence," the period in which we are now living might be called the "Years of Skepticism." The spirit of compromise and "live and let live" is not strong among us. We see unprecedented bitterness, vindictiveness—sometimes character assassination—in many phases of community life. Catholics, Protestants and Jews are often suspicious of each other. Anti-Catholicism has distressingly increased in recent years. There are many other symptoms. And the skepticism with which we view our city councils and other governmental agencies spills over into the control of education.

The loss of faith in the "Years of Skepticism" is peculiarly devastating in the field of education. There is no way of separating education from the life for which it prepares or the social structure out of which it grows. We can see this relationship by tracing the trends in local, state and national government in this country.

When I was a school superintendent in Minnesota many years ago, there were virtually no tax limitations and few other limitations on the power and functioning of the board of education. Then came a day when the state legislatures no longer trusted the local school boards. All sorts of restrictions were developed to limit their power. The spirit behind the restrictions grew and grew. Today, in California, we see a state legislative committee investigating teachers and textbooks. The committee is presumably acting on the assumption that local boards of education and school administrators cannot be trusted. How long will it be before the process extends; before Congress feels that it cannot trust the state legislatures and must, therefore, have its own congressional committee investigating education? Some sort of federal agency to police our schools may not be too remote a threat.

Good education cannot flourish within this framework of distrust. The so-called progressive education movement rested solidly on faith in freedom. It grew on the assumption that the individual child had a worth and dignity to be respected. It accepted the findings of science concerning the nature of the human organism; that the individual responds as a totality; that we cannot single out a facet of this organism for education and ignore all the rest. This type of education took the faith in the individual and in the masses—a faith which had come to us from Judaism and Christianity—and made it the basis for its educational procedures.

Now many of us have become frightened and have lost our faith both on the wider social front and in the field of education. The crisis in education is a part of the total crisis in our common life. It is a moral and spiritual crisis; a crisis in the age-long conflict between faith and skepticism, between freedom and slavery, between free government which serves people and the statist government in which people serve the state. It is illustrated in the conflict between the Judaic-Christian tradition which elevates the human spirit and materialistic Marxism in which individual human beings have neither worth nor dignity nor freedom.

If this analysis is correct, we cannot meet the current attacks on education by taking a defensive attitude—by trying to put out fires. Nor can we meet the critics on the economic, political and social fronts merely by talking about free enterprise, jailing the political scoundrels, or isolating and confining Communists, Fascists, Nativists and others in society who lack faith in the American tradition. It is not enough, for example, to know that we are against Communism. We should know what we are really for. Somehow, we must reverse the present trends of skepticism and suspicion and strive for a new age of confidence, an age of faith and achievement.

It is easy to say that we must recapture our faith. It is another matter to translate the wish into reality. Perhaps, in the "Years of Confidence," democracy could afford to be smug and complacent. It was not under militant attack. Today it is fighting for its life and cannot survive if it is characterized by inaction, by static attitudes or complacency.

Education enters here. Education for freedom must face its task with confidence and realism. Those of us who are educators must have a great faith. We must believe in the capacity of the common man to develop his own criteria of truth and value. We must have faith in all men, regardless of color, creed, or economic status. We must realize that no matter how much technical knowledge we may have we cannot be educationally effective without a great faith in people, in children, in all with whom we work. Education must itself be free or it cannot be an instrumentality for the preservation of freedom. It is the task of educational administrators to reiterate faith in educational freedom; to support, for example, teachers who deal vigorously with the controversial issues which constitute the growing edge of American society.

Education must be free to resolutely experiment to find new and better educational procedures and activities. We must discard old, ineffective procedures when newer methods prove better. Too often we have tended to adopt the new and at the same time retain the old—long after its ineffectiveness has been established. We have learned our addition but not our subtraction. In this period, we must be our own most severe, honest critics.

Education will not acquire its needed dynamism unless it can more effectively cope with the problem of incentives. We need incentives for discovery, for development, and for creative leadership. Education is, in essence, a creative endeavor. It is always a frontier undertaking. Pupils can become creative only as their teachers are free to be creative. Teachers must constantly work on the frontier of their own thought and imagination.

There are few problems more important to American education than the development of an organizational and leadership structure which will bring about the fullest release of the creative talents of teachers, pupils, and people of our communities.

The task of saving freedom is the biggest undertaking that has ever come to education. And it has become sharply clear that the problems of preserving freedom in education and society cannot be solved inside the four walls of a school building. Through education, far-reaching changes and improvements must be brought about in the thinking, feeling, and action of all who comprise our society. If our schools and colleges were many times more effective than they are now they still could not do this job alone. We cannot wait for children and young people now going to school to rescue us from our past mistakes and ineffectiveness. We must, instead, operate on a community-wide basis using every single resource that can be mobilized. Educational administration thus becomes the process of mobilizing the educational resources of the total community.

Many of us in education tend to underestimate our resources. Also, we have not learned how to work creatively with the people of our communities. We have not found ways of enabling the people of our towns to participate effectively in the processes of education. Generally speaking, we are too isolated, too exclusive, and too narrowly professional. It is important that we learn how to talk about education in language that people can understand; that we become better students and practitioners of the group process. We must be less thin-skinned when it comes to sincere criticism of what we do.

We shall not save either education or our freedom in its totality by fearful, defensive attitudes and policies. We need to conduct a vigorous positive program in behalf of both. Fear must be replaced by confidence, skepticism by faith, antagonisms and bigotry by brotherhood and understanding. We must preserve the opportunity for diversity in intellectual and spiritual directions while acquiring greater unity and common purpose in our total life. We need to oppose excessive concentration of power—in government or in any area of our living—and vitalize our democracy at the community level.

It is at this level that we stand the best chance to recapture our faith, to put love for our fellow men into practice, to learn how to understand each other—to overcome the conflicts which are now tearing us apart. It is in the more intimate relationships of the community that we can develop faith in each other.

It is here too that education can best recapture its faith in freedom, both for itself and for the nation as a whole. Finally, it is here too, that the foundation may be laid for the new age of confidence and dynamism so necessary to our free society. If we help to build those foundations, we shall ensure the future of the system of education in which we work. We shall also ensure preservation of the freedom that has given nurture to our education.

—ERNEST O. MELBY

I.

THE MAKINGS OF THE MODERN SCHOOL

A democratic philosophy, a dynamic process, a spiritual force: with these foundations our educational system has uniquely served America. What our schools have done in the past, what modern education means to the individual and the nation in the years ahead, are here defined by three men who have themselves made singular contributions to the American mainstream.

Our Schools Have Kept Us Free

By Henry Steele Commager

*(Reprinted by permission, from Life, October 16, 1950.
Copyright Time, Inc.)*

No other people ever demanded so much of education as
have the American. None other was ever served so well by its
schools and educators.

From the beginning education has had very special, and very
heavy, tasks to perform. Democracy could not work without an
enlightened electorate. The various states and regions could not
achieve unity without a sentiment of nationalism. The nation
could not absorb tens of millions of immigrants from all parts
of the globe without rapid and effective Americanization. Economic and social distinctions and privileges, severe enough to
corrode democracy itself, had to be fought. To our schools went
the momentous responsibility of inspiring a people to pledge
and hold allegiance to these historic principles of democracy,
nationalism, Americanism and egalitarianism.

Because we are a "new" nation we sometimes forget how very
old are some of our institutions and practices. The U.S.—today
the oldest democracy in the world and the oldest republic—also
has the oldest public school system in the world. The famous
Ould Deluder Satan law of 1647 which set up a system of com-
munity-supported schools in Massachusetts Bay Colony was, in
its day, something new under the sun. "As a fact," wrote Horace Mann, himself one of its later products, "it had no precedent in world history, and as a theory it could have been re-

---

Henry Steele Commager is a noted historian on the faculty of Columbia
University. He is the author of many widely-read books on American history
including "The Story of a Free Nation." Dr. Commager is now editing the
forty-volume series, "The Rise of the American Nation."

futed and silenced by a . . . formidable array of argument and experience. . . ."

What compels our interest, however, is not only the daring of that law, but the accuracy with which it reflected our national character and foreshadowed our history.

How did it happen that this little frontier colony of some 15 or 20,000 souls, clinging precariously to the wilderness shelf, should within a few years have established a Latin School, Harvard College and a system of public education? Why this instant and persistent concern for education—so great that education became the American religion? For it is in education that we have put our faith; it is our schools and colleges that are the peculiar objects of public largess and private benefaction. Even in architecture we have proclaimed our devotion, building schools like cathedrals.

None of this reflects any peculiar respect for learning or for scholarship. There has never been much of that, and there is probably less of it today than at any previous time in our history. Only in the U.S. could the term "brain trust" be one of opprobrium; only here is the college professor a stereotype of absent-mindedness and general woolliness.

Yet the paradox in all this is more apparent than real. It is not because education advances scholarship that it has been so prized in America—but rather because it promised to bring to real life the American dream of the good society. So declared the great Northwest Ordinance of 1787: "Religion, morality, and knowledge, being necessary to good government and the happiness of mankind, schools and the means of education shall forever be encouraged." And the generation that fought the Revolution had energy enough left to create a dozen new colleges, establish state universities and provide for common schools by munificent land grants. Even the Encyclopaedia Britannica could observe sourly of this generation that "notwithstanding their addiction to those occupations of which lucre is the sole object, Americans were duly attentive to cultivate the field of learning, and they have ever since their first foundation been particularly careful to provide for the education of the rising progeny." And, in our generation today, when the critical pedant of the Old World disparages American academic traditions, we are prone—and with much reason—to answer tartly: it has never been the Americans who succumbed to the evil and meretricious appeals of Fascism, Nazism or Communism.

Let us look at the specific tasks which our triumphant faith in education imposed on our schools. The first and greatest task was to provide an enlightened citizenry in order that self-government might work. Though the earliest settlers in New England used the word democracy only as a rebuke, they had in fact embarked upon an experiment in democracy. With independence the problem of self-government became urgent. It is important to remember that self-government had not been tried before on such a scale. The founding fathers confidently believed they had found the key. "To be long-lived," as Benjamin Rush observed, "republics must invest in education."

Has our investment succeeded? None can doubt that it has. Americans have, in short, made democracy work. They established a nation, held it together, and expanded the original 13 to 48 states—while steadily pursuing the grand objectives of the framers of the Constitution: their "more perfect union" *did* establish justice and domestic tranquillity, and secure the blessings of liberty. Through all their history they elected some mediocre presidents but never a wicked or a dangerous one; they never yielded to a military dictator; they avoided revolutions; they settled all problems by compromise except the greatest one, slavery, and perhaps that could not be settled by compromise; they revealed in every crisis an ability to select able leaders. Only a people taught self-government could record these achievements.

The second great task imposed upon education and on the schools—the creation of national unity—was equally difficult.

In 1789 no one took for granted the blessing of the "more perfect union"—for what, after all, was the basis for an American nation? Its geographical basis was so large as to defeat itself, for how hold together an area of continental dimensions thinly inhabited by some four million people? The historical basis was almost non-existent: differences that separated South Carolinians from Connecticut Yankees seemed to be greater than the bonds that united them.

Yet we created unity out of diversity, nationalism out of particularism. Powerful material forces—the westward movement, canals and railroads, a liberal land policy—sped this achievement.

But just as important were intellectual and emotional factors—what Lincoln called those "mystic chords of memory, stretching from every battlefield and patriot grave to every living heart and hearthstone." These were the contribution of poets and novelists, editors and naturalists, historians and jurists, orators and painters—and the medium through which they worked was the school. Through the whole 19th Century, novelists like Cooper and Sims and Hawthorne, poets like Bryant and Longfellow and Whittier, painters like Trumbull and Stuart and Peale, historians like Jared Sparks and George Bancroft, schoolmen like Noah Webster with his Spellers and the McGuffeys with their Readers—all these and scores of others created and popularized that common group of heroes and villains, that common store of poems and stories, of images and values of which national spirit is born. These men gave to Americans, old and new alike, a people's common language with which to voice a people's common heritage:

God sifted a whole nation that he might send choice grain over into this wilderness; As for me, give me liberty or give me death; If they mean to have a war, let it begin here; One if by land, and two if by sea; These are the times that try men's soul's; I only regret that I have but one life to lose for my country; I have just begun to fight; Millions for defense, but not one cent for tribute; Don't give up the ship; We have met the enemy and they are ours; Liberty and union, now and forever, one and inseparable; I propose to fight it out on this line if it takes all summer; Damn the torpedoes; Government of the people, by the people, for the people; With malice toward none, with charity for all.

And then there were the songs and the pictures, too. In

school and lyceum, children came to learn and remember at least snatches of the "Concord Hymn" or "Old Ironsides" or the "Midnight Ride of Paul Revere." From famed paintings they learned to recognize Wolfe dying on the Plains of Abraham, Penn making a treaty with the Indians, Washington crossing the Delaware, Boone pushing his way through the Cumberland Gap. Through its young eyes the young people came to see itself as one nation.

The third task imposed on education, and particularly on the public schools, was that which we call Americanism. Each decade after 1840 saw from two to eight million immigrants pour into America. No other people had ever absorbed such large or varied racial stocks so rapidly. In this, America could proclaim both its pride and its welcome in the inscription in the base of the Statue of Liberty:

Give me your tired, your poor,
Your huddled masses yearning to breathe free.
The wretched refuse of your teeming shore.
Send these, the homeless, tempest-tost to me;
I lift my lamp beside the golden door.

How, after all, were these millions of newcomers to be "Americans"—in language, in ways of life and thought, in citizenship? The nation's first and main answer was the public school. Most of the new millions, eager though they were to be Americanized, were too old for school, but their children went to the public schools, adapting themselves with children's speed to American ways, and taking home with them the idiom, the habits, the very thoughts and standards they picked up in the schoolroom and on the playground. Mary Antin tells us, in her moving *Promised Land,* what school meant to the new masses: "Education was free. . . . It was the one thing that [my father] was able to promise us when he sent for us; surer, safer than bread and shelter.

"On our second day I was thrilled with the realization of what this freedom of education meant. A little girl from across the alley came and offered to conduct us to school. My father was out, but we five between us had a few words of English by this time. We knew the word school. We understood. This child who had never seen us until yesterday, who could not pronounce our names, who was not much better dressed than we, was able to offer us the freedom of the schools of Boston! No application made, no questions asked, no examinations, rulings, exclusions; no machinations, no fees. The doors stood open for every one of us."

That magic open door imposed upon American schools such a responsibility as the schools of no other country have ever had to meet. Doutbless the necessity of teaching immigrant children even the most elementary subjects slowed up the processes of formal education in many schools. Yet those schools have done the astounding job asked of them: they have literally made millions of Americans.

There is a fourth and final service the schools have rendered the cause of American democracy. This most heterogeneous of modern societies—profoundly varied in racial background, religious faith, social and economic interest—has ever seemed the most easy prey to forces of riotous privilege and ruinous division. These forces have not prevailed; they have been routed, above all, in the schoolrooms and on the playgrounds of America. In the classroom, the nation's children have lived and learned equality—all subject to the same educational processes and the same disciplines. On the playground and the athletic field, the same code has ruled—with the reward of honor and applause heartfully given to achievements to which all could aspire equally. The roster of "foreign" names on our high school and college football teams has seemed worth a feeble joke to many an unwitty radio comedian. Who can seriously doubt that the cause of democracy is served when it is a Murphy, a Schwartz, a Groglio or a Levitsky that the cheering stands applaud? If, through the 19th and well into the 20th Century, American schools performed such magnificent service, the question remains: do they still serve the nation well? And is education still the American religion?

The evidence is conflicting. Americans in many ways still confess their faith in education, still impose upon it tasks performed elsewhere by home, church or industry. More young people are going to college and university today than went to high school only 30 years ago. Public appropriations have mounted to $5 billion annually. While the federal government has accepted a larger share of responsibility for education than even before, private philanthropy continues unabated and we still build colleges with the fervor that other ages gave only to their cathedrals.

Yet there is other evidence of a more sobering nature. The proportion of our national income devoted to education has declined in the last decades, and $5 billion for public education compares rather poorly with the $8 billion spent on liquor or the $19 billion on automobiles each year. Most school-teachers are underpaid, many buildings are antiquated, most colleges and universities are in desperate financial plight. And—even graver than the material picture—the decade that has witnessed the greatest rush to American universities has also witnessed savage attacks upon their intellectual integrity and independence.

The American mind today seems deeply worried about its school system as it never has been before. In the vast literature on education there is more discontent than complacency, more blame than praise. There is an uneasy feeling that the schools have somehow failed to do their job.

Yet no one seems very positive as to what the job of the schools is today. It is oddly ironic—to say the kindest—to hear people who rear their children on comics complain that the schools fail to instill a love of literature.

It is shocking—to say the truth—to hear the very people who support teachers' oaths and textbook censorship contend that the schools are failing to encourage greater intellectual independence.

We need to get our standards straight and clear. Many of the old purposes and criteria have disappeared, and the people have not defined new ones to take their place. The 19th Century school, for example, had an enormous job in "Americanization"—but it was a clearly defined job, universally willed by the people. Today's school faces a nice problem in deciding whether its education should reinforce nationalism—or inspire internationalism.

Two developments have further blurred the picture inherited from the 19th Century. First: schools no longer have anything like the monopoly in education they then exercised. Today they share responsibility with the movies, the radio and television and, to a far larger extent than before, with the newspapers and the magazines: for millions of Americans *Life* and the *Reader's Digest* have supplanted the McGuffey Readers.

Second: with the phenomenal growth of higher education, the new demands of industry and the professions, the government and the military, the function of elementary and secondary education has become more narrowly educational than ever before. In a day of specialization schools are called on more and more to prepare not so much for life, citizenship or democracy as for particular tasks and competences.

This means that we have placed our schools in a crossfire of conflicting demands. While we still want them to perform broad social functions, we impose upon them narrower educational functions.

The old expectation persists that schools be training grounds for democracy and nationalism. The new demands are implacable—that schools not only prepare young people for college, but somehow manage to teach domestic economy, driving, machine shop, current events, world history and typewriting at the same time.

There is a further difficulty—the one that most of us are reluctant to recognize. Schools reflect the society they serve. Many of the failures we ascribe to contemporary education are in fact failures of our society as a whole. A society that is indifferent to its own heritage cannot exepect schools to make good the indifference. A society that slurs over fundamental principles and takes refuge in the superficial and the ephemeral cannot demand that its schools instruct in abiding moral values. A society proudly preoccupied with its own material accomplishments and well-being cannot fairly expect its schools to teach that the snug warmth of security is less meaningful than the bracing venture of freedom. In all this, to reform our schools is first to reform ourselves.

For a century and a half American schools have served and strengthened the commonwealth. They provided a citizenry as enlightened as any on earth. They justified and vindicated democracy's promise. If society clearly defines the new duties it wishes our schools to fulfill and if it steadfastly supports them not only with money but also with faith, they will surely justify that faith in the future as they have in the past.

We Learn What We Live

By William Heard Kilpatrick

(Excerpted from "A Report of the Conference with Dr. William Heard Kilpatrick," Pasadena City Schools, July 13-20, 1949.)

Perhaps we can agree that the purpose of education is the achievement of the good life. But, when we say "the good life," we have to be very careful that we understand just what those words mean.

The good life is the aim, the ideal, which the wisest and best among us would choose for those whom we most love. We should like all to live the rich, full life as nearly as possible; each in himself as he enjoys it, and all together. If we leave out "each in himself," we leave out some aspects of the good life which one enjoys just himself. And we cannot leave out "all together" for no man liveth to himself.

The problem of what values go into the makeup of a good life is closely related to the kind of educational system we have. Hence, we need to distinguish carefully between the old type of education and the new. The old began in Alexandria, Egypt, during the 4th Century, B.C. Alexandria was the intellectual capital of the world. The people built the world's finest library and organized a university specializing in the sciences, and developed many new theories, such as the Ptolemaic system. In philosophy and literature, however, they could not equal the work of Athens; hence, they organized a school to teach the content of these books in an authoritative way. Later, this type of school was transferred to Rome where it was adopted by Christianity as a means of teaching its creed. During the Re-

---

William Heard Kilpatrick is professor emeritus of the philosophy of education at Teachers College, Columbia University. For more than half a century—through his thousands of students and many books—Dr. Kilpatrick has been a creative force in developing concepts of modern education and bringing them to everyday use.

vival of Learning, Dean Colet introduced this type of teaching into England, and it later spread to this country in the form of Latin grammar schools. For example, the students in the William and Mary Grammar School thought Latin, read Latin, and spoke Latin. That was their curriculum.

One aspect of this old education needs to be emphasized. The Greeks were the first people to develop the technique of critical thinking. In trying to explain why different civilizations have different customs, beliefs, and governments, they developed for the first time in history a self-conscious criticism. That is, they developed philosophy, which is one of the three great contributions which the human mind has so far made. The other two are the invention of language and the scientific method. Now the answers the Greeks gave have lasted up till the present time, and they largly determine what values we choose.

Plato reacted strongly against any kind of change, and his philosophy was devised to prove that reality is unchanging, permanent, eternal, absolute. It is our business as human beings to discover these eternal forms intellectually as being distinct from the material world which is constantly shifting and full of evil. This idea entered into theology and still controls the thought of many people.

Aristotle added to Plato's theory the idea that even the species are fixed, and this belief held sway until Darwin's *Origin of Species*. Aristotle also taught that there are natural masters and natural slaves to maintain the socio-economic setup of his culture. People today still hold onto this old idea. Those who happen to have privileges try to hold onto them on the basis of some natural right. Aristocratic privileges allowed an aristocratic intellectuality to grow such that John Dewey could describe it in this manner: 'Classic philosophy was conceived in wonder, born in leisure, and bred in consummatory contemplation.'

Modern science introduced inductive, experienced logic. The result was that it gave man new faith in himself. According to the old view, man could not hope to change things for they were eternally fixed and permanent. This experimental outlook gave man a free play of intelligence as a natural, individual right, and as a social duty. It developed slowly and culminated in the Enlightenment Movement and in the intellectual philosophy of democracy found expressed in the Declaration of Independence. It is only in this century that scientists gave up the Platonic conception of fixed laws of nature. The average person hasn't given them up yet. Thus, it is from within this framework that we must think about what our highest values are and what constitutes the good life.

Respect for personality is one of the values that must enter into the good life; hence it is a major problem in education. The world has been slow to develop a consistent respect for personality. For example, Alexander Hamilton said: 'All communities divide themselves into the few and the many. The first are the rich and well-born; the other the mass of the people. The voice of the people has been said to be the voice of God; and, however generally the maxim has been quoted and believed, it is not true to fact. The people are turbulent and changing, they seldom judge or determine right.'

In regard to children, it was a long time before the child was understood in any adequate sense. You look in any old picture book of two hundred years ago, and children are dressed just like his parents. They were in a sense small editions with emptiness inside the mind. It took a long time for us to get a place where we had any feeling that they should be respected as persons. The old Hebrews believed: 'Foolishness is bound up in the heart of a child; but correction shall drive it far from him.' Many people lived up to that doctrine, and that idea isn't dead yet. A book written for teachers in 1851 pointed out: 'The business of the teacher is strictly that of a conveyor of knowledge to the as yet unoccupied but growing mind.'

In 1945 the *Bulletin of the Association of American Professors* said: 'A dramatic dialogue by Ramus or Browning, a biblical parable, or Miltonic epic, an old Scotch song, or an American ballad can illumine more of life than a lifetime of living.'

A 1946 summer catalog of a foremost university describes a course in 'How to Study' as being the acquisition of the skill of reading and organizing assignments, note-taking, and techniques for writing term papers and examinations. That's what study meant.

How would you define study in the new and fuller sense?

Study is anticipation. It is the intellectual aspect preparatory to dealing with a situation. Study is the first part of a process, the latter part of which is doing something about a situation. Study carries through the whole thing because after you've decided what you're going to and do it, you've got to study whether it works or not. You'll have to change it if it doesn't.

Thus the essential theory of the old is that the mind is at first empty. Teaching is filling this emptiness. Plutarch says of memory: 'But we must most of all exercise and keep in constant employment, the memory of children, for that is, as it were, the storehouse of all learning. Nothing does so beget or nourish learnings as memory.' That is a perfectly clear-cut instance of the old point of view. During the Middle Ages somebody devised this sentence: 'Repetition is the mother of study.'

The old theory had the idea that there were fixed and eternal principles which man must find and obey. The new goes on the idea that we never reach perfection or fixedness except in a limited way; progress is possible, so far as we can tell, along any given line. The old used deductive logic, starting from fixed and eternal principles; the new starts where we are with facts, contradictions, and problems, and studies them with reference to control, understanding leading up to control. The old view regarded the child's mind as empty to begin with and regarded education as the filling up of this emptiness so he could think as a mature person. The new thing is that the child's progress is gradual. It begins with him today as little more than an animal. He then builds his selfhood; he grows increasingly in insight. I personally believe that intelligence is in a child from the beginning. He is to be treated as an intelligent person. He has to be respected for what he is and for what he can be. If we don't respect him we interefere with his life; we make his life unhappy, and we may damage him for the future.

The old view held that the child could not be trusted to behave on his own. We feel now that his growth depends upon what he does, what he thinks. The old view held that he mustn't be expected to think until he was old enough to know what the great minds thought. You couldn't expect him to think until after that. We now believe that the child thinks within his area of control from a very early age. Then that area will enlarge, and that skill will increase. It is a gradual process. We have him think all the time. Do you think he is going to think wisely all the time? No, but his actual thinking is the only way that can help him to think. We have to guide. How do we guide? We have to work at it the best way we know how. Do we make mistakes? Certainly, often, but if we keep working at it, we might not make the same mistakes over again. We must talk it over together, because the group ought to do better thinking than the best member of the group working alone. Even the best man can profit by what the others are thinking, and if he does a good job of thinking, the group will do better. We must listen to anybody who has any promise of something to say, consider what he says, and take it into account. If we are open-minded and let our intelligence have free play, we will do a better job of thinking. The group may make mistakes, but if we can keep working at it, we are less likely to make mistakes.

The good life is determined by group action. It can reach only as far as the people are ready to go. In this sense we are continually changing our conception of the good life to fit in with how we have grown. Each child must build for himself the highest conception that he can. As he goes about getting things done, he works with other people, and he can get them to agree or not with what his insight has been. Thus, we must work for the highest conception that the individual is capable of at the moment. Students must be trained to confront a problem and analyze it according to the most defensible method, according to the highest conception he has which will stand severe criticism. He must be constantly improving this skill. The more that people work together, the more certain will the highest and best ideals prevail. History shows that this definition of the good life is true. I don't see how any intelligent person can hold the opinion that standards for the good life will prevail for all times and for all people. This view has never been true and never will be.

I would hold up higher ideals than I'd expect the people to attain, but I would do it in such a way that they would not be discouraged or alienated. I would encourage each individual to improve himself a little each day. There is no one direction in which individuals must go in order to achieve the good life. We need to know only that if we work in a particular direction that our living can be successful and competent. For instance, we know that if all the people in the world will cooperate together, we will have a better way of life. We know that this is one directon in which to work. It might not be *the* direction. The wisest and the best are working in this direction, and our young people must study how they do it so that they too can move in the direction which intelligence indicates.

In a discussion of the good life, we can never say too much about respect for personality. We haven't said enough about the process of growth in the good life as being a gradual process. Growth in the conception and realization of the good life is a slow, gradual process. We must expect it to be so; we must not expect progress to be too rapid. Living the good life requires intelligence, the kind of thinking from which action flows. *Acting on thinking is what we want.*

In summary, we want the rich, full life for everybody. This means that education must train into all of the students the kinds of personalities and character traits which can make it possible for everyone to live this kind of life. This is the chief task of education.

SPECIFIC OBJECTIVES OF EDUCATION

I would like to suggest four principal dominating aims that ought to enter into any education wherever found. Some aims are so important that they must be sought no matter whatever else is being done.

First is *personality adjustment*. Whatever else we do, we must help children grow in personality adjustment. If personality is upset the child becomes maladjusted. It was Freud who originated and gave prominence to this conception. I reject the Freudian applications of the theory, but his view of personality adjustment is a significant contribution to education.

The importance of personality adjustment should be stressed from the lowest grade through college. In preschool, kindergarten, and first grade personality problems are fundamentally important.

A second aim which must permeate all education is *general character development*. Character which might include personality adjustment is built by what we do and how we behave. Education must build a child's character effectively.

The only way to build character is by behaving. Simply taking off to one side the intellectual aspect to look at and not carrying it through into behavior may well be to fail to build character. Much of our education gives no adequate place for behaving.

The third principal aim is the *democratic outlook*. The democratic outlook is logically included within general character, but it requires special consideration. A great many people think of democracy as being simply majority vote. I take the position that the majority vote is not even the best democracy. It may be the best we can manage under the circumstances. A consensus is more democratic than a majority vote. Even the Constitution has certain provisions whereby the majority vote cannot override certain rights. Yes, we must understand democracy believe in it, and accept it. You can't teach people to accept democracy by having them memorize it saying, 'Now I'll give you till next Monday to accept democracy, or I'll keep

you in after school.' You've got to let these children live democratically, so that they come to feel and appreciate what it
means. Then they will accept it as their way of living.

We should cultivate leadership in everybody. Some might
wonder about that a little. But if you think about it, each one
lives throughout his life many different kinds of situations.
In some of those he will not act as leader; in some others he
will. Suppose a group of people are talking. A, B, C, D, and E
are discussing what to do. E makes a proposal, but in so far as
E proposes something, E is at that time and in that far the
leader, no matter who is presiding. Suppose C criticizes. If his
criticism is constructive so that it helps them to make progress
toward a decision, C is leading at that time. If B adds something that nobody has thought of up to that time, then B is
leading. Leadership can go all around. Everybody can be a
leader in this respect.

You really haven't achieved the proper democracy until you
have developed in each person the best that is in him. That's
the aim of democracy.

Freedom and equality are essential parts of democracy, freedom, however, being limited by equality. I am free to do anything, provided anyone else can do the same thing, and I don't
interfere with them in what I do. My liberty must not interfere
with their equality.

We need to provide the opportunities for growth for the
exercise of the kinds of things that will develop character traits
and personality adjustment. These traits have to be lived or
they won't be learned. Each one has to be lived if it is going to
be learned so that it will work as needed. Learning has taken
place when the individual experiences character and personality
growth so that it stays with him thereafter. It is the child who
does the learning. Teaching exists so that the right kind of living may go on. It is the kind of living that develops character
which in turn brings the good life. That's the purpose of the
school, that this kind of living can go on.

I knew a boy once who was kept in after school to study his
lesson; when he should have been studying his lesson, he was

literally cursing that teacher for making him stay after school. How was that boy learning? Let's look at those bad attitudes. He was learning to lose respect for himself. He was learning attitudes that went along with cheating. He was building the wrong kind of character from that point. If you would ask the teacher, she would say, 'I'm upholding standards.' But the way she upheld 'standards in geography' was to destroy standards in character. If this teacher had taught geography differently, she would have gotten more geography as well as more boy.

EDUCATION FOR PROPER HUMAN RELATIONS

The fourth principal aim of education is proper *human relations*. This involves respect for personality and equality of opportunity.

A great British historian has said: 'The provision made in any state for the rights of minorities is the best test of the standard of civilization in that state.' That is a strong statement. An increasingly large number of people accept it. What the United Nations has been doing about this problem by its Declaration of Human Rights calls emphatic attention to the conscience of the world on this point. Life in any good and full sense involves participation with others on terms of mutual communication and mutual respect. We were told of old, 'No man liveth unto himself.'

Before I go further, I would like to read some quotations from a study made during the last two or three years in the city of Philadelphia under the direction of the Bureau of Intercultural Education, of which I have the honor to be chairman. The following conclusions were derived and they discredit many formerly held beliefs of education: The first is that the awareness of racial, religious and socio-economic differences may develop early in childhood and that young children do have prejudices. The second is that if children of different races, religions, and socio-economic groups work together in a friendly attitude in the schoolroom, the children will not necessarily carry these attitudes to relations outside of school. The third is that a school of homogenous population does have problems of inter-group attitudes. Many times school people say that they have no problems in a school, because they have no minority groups represented. In a way they have the problem in its worst form, because they have to learn how to respect and deal with other minority groups without having had a chance to practice it. The fourth is that young children do understand and are interested in group differences. It is true that they don't understand them as well as we do, but they notice them and act accordingly.

In a New York kindergarten, a little boy said to his mother, 'There are two Irish children in our class and I like to play with them.' This surprised the mother, for she had never said anything about the Irish. She asked the teacher, who was equally surprised. She watched the boy who had been playing with two Negro children whom he called Irish. He had noticed enough difference to comment on it, but he didn't have complete information.

The fifth conclusion is that the primary cause of prejudice is not emotional insecurity. I am very glad to see them note that. The sixth is that teaching about democracy will not wipe out undemocratic attitudes. Talking about fair play, brotherhood, and tolerance will not result in the practice of these good human relations, you've got to live good human relations.

Our next problem is to distinguish various factors which cause poor human relations. One factor is simply the fact of individual human differences. Men are markedly different from each other in mental ability and emotional poise, and we have to take into account these characteristic differences. But it is fundamental that the races of men are not innately different. The differences we see come about from different environmental conditions. In any racial group, as the Chinese, the dull members will be as dull as the dull ones in any other racial group, and the intelligent will be as intelligent. Innately the distribution will be the same for all groups. It is the difference in opportunity that makes the difference in culture. By the word culture, I mean all the things saved up from the past by which we now live.

Machines, clothes, language, customs, institutions, morals, knowledge, standards give us some idea of what the culture is and how it serves us. The individual is himself civilized through his acceptance of culture. If by some accident what the culture has given us were taken away, we wouldn't know how to conduct our daily affairs.

However, it is the culture of the past that accounts for the problem of human relations. Inadequate and evil propensities as well as good ones get built into customs. These are transmitted by our culture to the young even after the best among us have rejected them. We know what it is to have superstitions. We know people who knock on wood; we know people who are afraid of the number thirteen. More books on astrology have been sold since World War II than ever before. Thus, it is the remnants of our older culture that create this problem.

Now let's look more precisely into the factors which actually cause the problem. The first, perhaps, is human exploitation, the selfish use of man by man to enhance his own life. This is an evil that has long been with us, and in some measure it will long stay with us. It's the building of this exploitation into customs and institutions that concerns us here today. When any of these old and now undefended institutions do get interwoven with the rest, it is difficult to get rid of them. That is one way of stating the problem. Thus at various times the aristocrats have exploited peasants; men have exploited women; free men have exploited slaves; and in our own day, the haves exploit the have-nots.

The second factor at work to deny human rights is the wrong development of what I call the 'we-group'. A child soon learns that the word 'we' includes certain people and excludes others. It might be our family, our friends in the community, or people who live our way. It might exclude those who don't live our way, think our thoughts, have our religion. Now it is the hardening of the boundaries which makes for poor human relations.

The children of the out-group grow up feeling insecure as regards the in-group. The Greeks called their outsiders bar-

barians. We still use the word barbarian to refer to outsiders. A missionary in Korea saw this sign, 'If you see a stranger, kill him.' This represents the we-group attitude gone astray, and that is the heart of our problem. Notice how we use the 'we' concept. If anyone of our group does badly, we say, 'He is a bad man;' we don't say 'we' are bad. If one of that outside group does badly we say, 'Yes, they are all like that.' We tend to overlook the wrongdoing of our crowd, and we tend to emphasize the wrongdoings of the other. Exploitation and this we-group attitude work hand-in-hand.

The third fundamental factor has been mentioned; it is that culture keeps alive bad as well as good practices.

The fourth fundamental factor is the failure of communication. Effective communication makes for understanding; but ineffective, or one-sided communication makes for misunderstanding. Employers tend to communicate with their servants by telling them what they want done. They do not talk things over together. If the servants know the problems of the master's household and the employers fail to understand the problems in the servants' home, it is a one-sided understanding. That cuts pretty deep when we come to dealing with minority groups. Minorities understand the majority more than the majority understands the minority. It is hard to understand with one-way communication.

Now there are certain psychological attitudes that go along with these four factors and especially with the we-group problem. This first is the doctrine of the word 'race.' We are very ready to use the word race and assign it to different groups. It is possible, perhaps, to distinguish three races by their external features, but there is no pure race known to be in existence. However, the racial inequalities are the things that have affected our problem. Most of us grew up thinking that there were real innate racial inequalities, that our race had the best qualities and others had the worst ones, innately. It was only about twenty years ago that the scientists began seriously to question that view. Science has given it up, but it remains with us as one of the past ideas deeply rooted and very difficult for most people to give up.

It is easy to hold to some kind of a caste system if one can honestly believe that those in the lower classes belong there by native ability, that they are innately unequal, more disposed to evil. India, for example, has the hardest caste system of any country in the world, and I very soon found that the upper-upper caste didn't want to hear about equality. They didn't like it. They wanted to believe that these lower caste people belonged there by native endowment and that they themselves belonged to the top by native endowment. This idea is not limited to India.

A second escape mechanism is the attempt to generalize the weaknesses of the out-group. This has already been discussed. The third psychological ally is the selective attention. We pay attention to the weakness of outsiders, overlooking their strengths; we pay attention to *our* strengths and disregard our weaknesses. This is uncritical and unwise thinking.

Another of these hurtful psychological tendencies is rumor-mongering. Rumors seem to spread faster among the privileged when they feel their privileges are being attacked. This is a very common occurrence with regard to attempts to elevate the so-called lower groups.

Let us look at some of the results of these foregoing factors. The dominant group—that means the old-fashioned American, Protestant, white group—refuses to accept certain groups as full participants in the social process. It makes institutions that perpetuate this state of affairs. We have crystallized certain ways of treating these people into customs.

Fortunately, America has a conscience. If I were called upon to name one of the characteristics of America, it is that it has a conscience. Of course, it doesn't keep that conscience alive as it ought to be all the time. It allows it to get out of date. There is, generally speaking, a lag between the best knowledge we have and the conscience that ought to back up that knowledge. You might say that there is a two-fold lag; there is first of all, the best insight, scientific and otherwise, as to what ought to prevail; second, the conscience that ought to back knowledge up lags behind; and third, practice lags behind conscience. That is, we know what we ought to know, but we don't quite do it. I say to you that in the last ten years there has been more change in this respect, especially in America, than during any like time in the history of the world. We are beginning to feel ashamed that we don't have more Negroes on college faculties. This feeling has come within the last two years in the greatest measure.

Economic exploitations is one of our greatest difficulties. The tendency to keep certain groups down by paying low wages is especially noticeable in the South. The we-group and the out-group are very clear in the matter of religious discrimination and changes. The dominant group finds it very difficult to take in the other religious groups and give them the same rights and the same feeling of worth. The Declaration of Independence, the American Constitution, and particularly the Bill of Rights, are squarely against any discrimination. I don't know any religious group which does not oppose in theory religious discrimination. It is contrary to the teaching of Jesus. He went out of his way to take in hated peoples. Any conception of morality has to put everybody on the same basis in respect to treatment.

Perhaps the greatest single interfering factor is the socio-economic scale. Though democracy does not like to admit it, any typical community has some people at the top whom everybody looks up to, and some at the bottom, whom everybody looks down on. We are going to have that problem more or less continuously in any democracy. Our problem is not to allow people to remain at the bottom of the scale in such a way that they perpetuate their bad practices.

Now let's say a word or two about what we can do and what we cannot do. As our children grow up to be good citizens, they must accept democracy and understand it at its best, and that means equality of opportunity for all. The dominant group must learn to associate with the minority group in classrooms and be able to feel at home with them. They must learn to respect and discover their merits and accept them into their group on the basis of their merits. This is learning to live together on the basis of democracy. Children must understand that this country has been built on differences of cultural outlook, and that we are richer for having had a variety of cultural outlooks.

With respect to our schools, young people as they grow up have to understand that there is no scientific basis for innate race differences or superiorities, that all those apparent superiorities are based on the socio-economic scale. We school people have to work in the community to get the community to understand the problem. Our ministers must help.

THE NATURE OF THE LEARNING PROCESS

What does learning mean? I think we'll find that such terms as "learning," "teaching," "curriculum," "evaluation," and "subject matter," have undergone a process of remaking and redefinition, that they don't mean the same thing now that they meant a hundred years ago. They are in process of remaking.

The old method emphasized information imparted by assignments memorized under penalty. So we might say *teach* in the old days meant the imparting of textbook information by recitations assigned under penalty, the evaluation being the ability to give it back on demand. If you were to ask a teacher a hundred years ago, will a student ever use this information? 'Certainly, that is why I want him to learn it. He will keep it in his mind, and when the time comes, he'll use it.' How long before he'll use it? 'Well, I don't know—five years, maybe not till he's grown.' That was the older point of view. And they taught this type of learning by repetition, by repeating it over and over and over again.

The older point of view supposed that it was dealing with an otherwise empty mind. The business of teaching was to put something into that emptiness. If the things that were to go into that were repeated often enough and if enough things got in that way, intelligence would result and appropriate conduct would follow. Curiously enough, they thought that if you learned words, appropriate conduct would follow. Now we don't accept any of these views, except repetition in a sense. I will show you what repetition does when taken to extremes.

Some children who had been repeating the salute to the flag year after year were required to write it out, and these are some excerpts from their writings: 'I pledge allegiance... ,' 'I plague allegiance . . . ,' 'I pledge a legion to the flag . . . ,' '. . .to the Republicans one country invisable . . . ,' 'one country inavisable . . . ,' '. . . with liberty and jesters . . . .' They learned some words that didn't mean anything to them. Whether they learned any feelings toward our country or not, I don't know.

We've come a good long way. Darwin had a great deal to do with it. He made us understand as never before that behaving is the process whereby the organism comes to terms with its environment, and how everything comes out of that behaving. William James wrote his psychology on that basis. John Dewey got his psychology from William James on that same basis. Learning is an inevitable and essential part in any experience process. You wouldn't have an experience if you didn't learn. For it wouldn't be an experience if you didn't learn in connection with it.

I'd like to use a phrase which has come to mean a great deal to me: *We learn what we live.* Learning has taken place when any part or aspect of the ongoing life process remains with one. Now let's analyze the meaning of *living.* If learning is going to be lived, there are six things I'd say about it: First, it has to be a real *situation,* an actual situation. What do you mean by an actual situation? One of my students defined it this way: 'Any individual in a real situation faces the consequences of his own actions.' That is well said. As I said, first of all, it has to be an actual, real situation; second, the thing about to be learned offers itself as a *suggestion* for dealing with the confronting situation. Third, a suggestion after more or less consideration is *accepted* in a certain sense; it is accepted algebraically. Fourth *it is learned as it is accepted.* I'm riding to town A; I've never been there before. After a while I find myself in town B, not town A. As I look back, I know exactly where I took the right hand, where I should have taken the left hand. What have I learned? I learned two things: That I took the wrong road, and also, that if I ever want to go to B, I know how to get there. So I accept two things. I accept that I've done the wrong thing this time, but I've accepted that this is the road to B. I've learned them both. We learn it as we accept it. There are many things we learn not to do, because in our hearts, we are just not going to do them. Fifth, it thus stays as learned with the learner to enter the life process—you might say to re-enter the life process, as soon as, and whenever opportunity offers, to help carry on that process. Now in many cases of learning, all of this happens so immediately that we don't think of these as separate steps. Sixth, when put to use, the results tend to strengthen the original learning.

Learning is what presents itself to the child's mind as his response to the situation. He will give more or less consideration to the situation, but he finally learns that whatever he accepts is his answer, his way of dealing with it. The way he accepts it is what he learns. As he learns it, it stays with him, to come back, either in that same experience, or later or both as the case may be. Then when it's tried and put to work, that, as it were, tests the hypothesis he was previously given, namely, that this is the way to deal with the situation. When he deals with it that way, he finds out whether or not it works. He also finds out whether to approve the learning that came when he elected to try it, and whether to modify it, or whether to reject it if it doesn't work out.

The next question I want to discuss is *degrees of learning*. One item is better or stronger than another. Either it stays on longer with one or comes back into life, or it tends to come back into life more strongly. It may be either or both. There are many things we don't remember more than a day or so; many things we have forgotten as soon as they happen. There are things that we remember for a few minutes; other things we can never forget. There are some things that insist upon coming back into life. We would like to forget them but we can't. That is the definition of degrees of learning. The longer it stays to come back and the more it insists on getting there, the stronger it is.

Now this strength of learning seems to depend on two factors. The first is its greater importance to the learner. If a thing means more to him, signifies more, then it is more likely to be more strongly learned. The second is if it fits in better with what he already knows, it will be longer learned.

Another aspect of learning is what I call concomitant learnings. We know that the full organism reacts to any situation. Now since this is true, a man thinks, feels, moves, and, we believe, has internal glands of secretion acting at each time that he does any significant thing.

Let's see how it works. The teacher scolds a boy for failing to learn the fractions that have been assigned. The teacher hopes the boy will study harder next time. Perhaps he will. But he does not enjoy the scolding. He probably rejects the scolding. He feels ashamed at being scolded. He probably has less confidence in himself. He'll say to himself, 'I can't do these fractions . . . I never can learn them. In fact, I don't like arithmetic anyhow. I wish I didn't have to come to school.' Of course I don't know just what he says, but whatever he responds, that is what he learns, because it is his own feeling about it.

Related to concomitant learnings are what I call cumulative learnings. There are some learnings we get all at once. My friend died suddenly. It was reported to me. I learned it at once. I'll never forget it. I may learn more about his death, to be sure, but I know definitely that he is dead. But what I think of my friend, how I feel towards him, is an instance of cumulative learning. This learning has been built all the years that I have known him. That he is dead, I learned at once. How I felt toward him and how I valued him all the years that I'd known him is a different kind of learning.

My ideals—any ideals—are likely to be an instance of cumulative learning. My standards and behavior are cumulative learning built through many experiences. My principles of action are cumulative learnings. A habit, at least a habit on the skill side, is likely to be cumulative learning. For instance, if you are learning a new tennis stroke, you don't simply repeat the same way you've been playing, you change. You adapt, and you accumulate your adaptations until you build a new stroke. You accumulate these rearrangements until you accumulate better playing. My conception of fair play is a cumulative affair. My conception of government is a cumulative affair.

Education is cumulative learning. How does education occur? This is a good statement I found in an old book: 'In the widest sense of the word, a man is educated either for good or evil by everything he experiences from the cradle to the grave.' And that's true. It is the accumulation of all learnings. For good or evil, it is the accumulation of all his learnings. Comenius saw, foresaw in a measure, what we are talking about here as living: 'In schools, therefore, let the students learn to write by writing, to talk by talking, to sing by singing, to reason by reasoning.' That comes pretty close to it.

Responsibilities of American Education

By Willard E. Goslin

*(Condensed from an address at a general meeting of employees
of the Pasadena City Schools, September 13, 1948)*

I wish to speak as a citizen of the United States, as a freedom-loving individual who believes that his freedom and the freedom of his fellow citizens can be underwritten only through an adequate program of public education dynamic and virile enough to match the needs of our times. I want to come as close as possible to speaking for the boy who lives in the west-end, the one who lives up next to the mountains, the person still struggling at twenty dollars a week, the privileged stockholder—I want to try to speak for these and more because public education is one thing that cuts across all our lives.

Each of us has a particular part to play in this school system. I believe that we all need to understand the common purposes of the program of which we are part in order to contribute our utmost to that program. I think the man who is going to paint a classroom needs to know the kind of program of education for which he is going to paint. In the same vein, I think it is absolutely necessary for the rank and file of us to understand the main objectives of American education if we are going to nurture that program—with financial and moral support—to make that program come alive in the American scene.

Willard E. Goslin is director of school administration and community development at George Peabody College, Nashville, Tennessee. One of the nation's foremost educators, he has been superintendent of schools in Minneapolis and Pasadena and president of the American Association of School Administrators.

Education has a major responsibility in two major directions. One is the responsibility for the growth and development of an individual citizen who can stand up and carry his share of the load in our times and in our kind of society. There are at least four contributions the school must make to him. It must help make him physically strong. It must help make him emotionally stable. The school must help him acquire a kit of tools in terms of adequate information and skills—reading, writing, arithmetic, and how to run a lathe. And it must help him develop a set of attitudes and ideals that are compatible with the best that we know in a free society, deep enough to see him over those points where he is tempted to veer off.

Education also has the responsibility to help underwrite the general welfare of all the people. Life ought to be better in Pasadena, in Fresno, in Arizona, in all America, because there is a school system there. It ought to be better for all kinds of people on all sides of the tracks. To do this, I submit, education must come to grips with some of the basic problems gnawing away at the rights and privileges of citizens in this country. Three of these basic problems have to do with peace, democracy, and conservation.

There is no such thing as individual security or group security or national security other than within the framework of a world at peace. It is up to the great masses of lay people to build and keep the peace. I believe that education is by all odds the most powerful too, the most constructive single agency at the disposal of mankind with which to underwrite a world at peace.

It must be clear now after a thousand years of experience that we cannot have a world of peace by taking a group of nations on one side and neatly balancing them off with a group of nations on the other side. The world is now trying—for the second time in a generation—something else: cooperative strength. We call the current trial the United Nations, a declaration of faith on the part of some fifty odd nations. I think every American youth deserves to know what the world has and what it has not in the form of the United Nations so that he, as a youthful citizen of the world, may carry his share of the load of the world at peace. We have to help our youth understand that if the United Nations is to succeed it must have enough strength to cope with the tensions and problems which are bound to arise. We have to find a way to transfer into a common pool enough of the prerogatives of each nation of the world so that the United Nations will be strong enough to maintain peace.

Another responsibility of education is the maintenance and extension of democracy in American life. Public education was created primarily because the founders of our country came to understand that the institutions of representative government could not be sustained and made effective unless they were placed in the hands of succeeding generations of citizens who had become enlightened by education. I conceive it to be, even in a deeper sense than in the early stages of the nation, the responsibility of American education to make secure freedom and democracy. How to do it? Fundamentally, it is our duty to grow to a point as teachers in a free society where we have respect for every American child who comes to school. Short of that, we will not be able to deliver what we ought to deliver.

I would like to trail off into one simple illustration. Tomorrow morning some one of you—as a kindergarten teacher—is going to fall heir to forty little five-year-olds. They have been living around the community, rolling in the grass, pulling the pup around by the tail. Then, bang! Tomorrow morning at nine o'clock we say to all the little five-year-olds, "Now you quit all that. Get yourselves off to kindergarten. Get yourselves lined up. Keep your rows straight. Look at the back of the neck of your neighbor and keep quiet." It is no wonder that there is a story about the little youngster who came home at the end of the first day of school and said, "Mom, I don't think I'm going to like this thing called school. I can't read. I can't write. And now I can't even talk."

What are we going to do with our five-year-olds? Are we going to get them quiet as soon as possible, get rid of their mothers as soon as possible, and start taking down the vital statistics? Or are we going to take these children and sit down and live with them and talk with them? You, see, they have a problem on their hands to live in the space that society has set apart for them. Five-year-olds are citizens and I think school is a place where citizens may grow up and make decisions.

My third point is that you cannot have peace, democracy and a good life unless they are backed by those things that make it possible. If you think you can, go around the world and look at those who have been unable to lift themselves out of their poverty long enough to have an idea.

While I was in Germany recently, I had a chance to talk to a group of young Germans. The most devastating question ever asked me came at that meeting in Berlin. These young people wanted to know what kind of clothes we wore, what our schools were like, what kind of games we played. I talked to them and tried to get as close to them as any fifty-year-old can to a group of young people. There were a lot of questions but I kept thinking that the sixty-four dollar one was lurking in the background somewhere. Finally, one boy raised his hand and said, "Mister, how would you like to be young in Germany?" I didn't know the answer. I made another speech but it wasn't an answer at all.

Some way or another, we have to keep America so that it is a good place in which to be young. We can do it not only by working for its freedom and democracy but by making sure that it is possible to have a decent standard of living.

The standard of living of a people comes from only one source: the combination of the labor of the people's hands as applied to raw materials. By raw materials, I mean top soil and moisture, the products of the mines, the wells and the forests.

What has this to do with a teacher of literature? Everything, because the ideals of America are just as real as the foundation of resources that are available to the American people. We have tended to waste our topsoil, slaughter our trees, be reckless with our minerals. We have done so mainly because no one has helped us learn that you must put back what you take out of the soil, that you must use technology and the machine as assiduously to conserve and restore the resources of a nation as you do to exploit them. All of us have to understand that unless we learn to have enough of our basic wealth to maintain an adequate standard of living, America will be a poverty-ridden nation.

That is part of education for the general welfare, too.

II.

TODAY'S CHALLENGE: A SYMPOSIUM

Modern public education is an agent of our culture; its status and health are barometers of all the pressures of the day.

This is a dramatic time and, conceivably, a tragic one. Education is racked by a multitude of problems having much to do with affairs of the world; little to do with specific educational techniques.

51

The fact that education has problems is, in itself, hardly cause for alarm. But there is cause for alarm in the fact that some of these problems, in recent years, have threatened to debilitate—in some cases even destroy—the public school system.

This section deals with three of these problems; the need for federal aid to education, the matter of religion and the schools, and the general subject of academic freedom.

1. Federal Aid
The Problems Are National

By Earl J. McGrath

(An excerpt from the book, "Education: The Wellspring of Democracy," published by the University of Alabama Press, copyright 1951. Used with permission.)

It is important that we make clear to people everywhere that in this nation we are rapidly realizing our historical commitment to the idea of equal educational opportunity for all according to their talents. We must remove the remaining barriers to free schooling for all.

To help do this, changing conditions in society at large and within the world of education itself now require the federal government to extend the scope of its support of education. A general program of aid to the states is needed. For this reason certain matters related to federal responsibilities in the field of education now deserve thoughtful consideration.

The first fact to consider is the inability of states and local communities to pay the full cost of an adequate program of education within their boundaries. Productive capacity in some states is comparatively so low that they are unable to maintain an adequate program of public education. Most children of school age in some states and some children of school age in nearly every state do not get the basic education required for personal development and civic duties.

As stated in "Education—An Investment in People," "It is a fact of great significance that the states which averaged highest in expenditures per pupil in attendance at public schools in

---

Earl James McGrath is former United States Commissioner of Education.

the last thirty years are today among the states of higher educational level and of higher economic well-being."

The differences between the states in their ability to support education are great. Although no perfect measure of financial ability has yet been devised, the most commonly accepted and probably the most valid single measure of ability to support all phases of government is the average per capita income. But since the number of children in the total population varies so greatly, the per capita income probably is not as satisfactory a measure of ability to support the school program as income per child five to seventeen years of age. These figures for the various states reveal arresting differences. In 1948, for example, the income per child of school age ranged from $2,745 in Mississippi to $11,071 in New York. Thus the most wealthy state had approximately four times as much income per child of school age as the least wealthy.

A comparison of the six *most* wealthy with the six *least* wealthy states shows the average income per child of school age in the former to be $10,454, more than three times the average of $3,322 in the latter. In 1947-48, the six most wealthy states spent an average of $250.81 per pupil for current expense of education, whereas the six least wealthy states spent only $103.79.

The effort made by the respective states to support public elementary and secondary schools also varies widely. It may be measured in terms of the share of total income of the state spent for the public schools. The percentage of income allocated to the public schools in the entire United States in 1948 was 2.09. The figures for individual states, however, show that some make a much greater effort to support their school program than others. In general, the states with the lowest income per child of school age make a greater effort than those with the highest.

In 1948, the six most wealthy states spent on the average only 1.72 per cent of the income of the people for their public schools: the six least wealthy, an average of 2.49. The poorer states made 45 per cent greater effort to support their schools than the richer.

It thus becomes evident that, under present conditions, the least wealthy states must limit the advantages of education for many of their children. The alternative is to spend such a large proportion of their income for the support of education that they handicap themselves economically in competition with other states. This educational inequality among the states should concern all Americans wherever they live. Not only the wealthier communities but all the states will be handicapped by citizens with limited education, because our people do not stay where they are born.

The second factor which must be considered in reviewing the relations between the federal govenment and the local educational enterprises is the increase in the mobility of our population. Local support of education has always involved some personal inequities and social waste. But when most persons lived and died within the communities in which they were born, these matters could be considered local responsibilities. Then a community might if it wished emphasize vocational training geared to local occupations and neglect general education for the responsibilities of citizenship. While residences remained relatively fixed, the citizens of any region could consider their responsibilities discharged when they had provided education for their own children. Now, however, natives of Maine live in California; those of Mississippi in Chicago; those who spent their first twenty years in a small mining town or in a remote farm region pass their adult lives on Riverside Drive. In the face of this mobility, the nation as a whole cannot tolerate great regional differences in educational opportunity.

Social considerations are paralleled by others involving the rights and privileges of the individual. A marked relationship exists between the economic status of the family and the amount and quality of education of the children. Even in the elementary school a foreshortening of the education of children of the less privileged classes is observable. Moreover, those who leave school are not always children of low intellectual ability. Intelligence test scores show that many children who withdraw from the sixth grade to the last year of the high school are capable of further education, often more capable than those who get it. Out of every thousand children now enrolled in the fifth grade, 900 have the ability to go through high school; yet only 481 do so. Every year, the nation is failing to train 47 per cent of those who ought to finish high school. This waste of our human resources is found at all levels of intellectual capacity, and in all parts of the country.

Physical inaccessibility is another major barrier to educational opportunity. Thousands of college-age youth who cannot afford to attend a college or university away from home do, of course, enroll in a local institution. But many are not so fortunate as to live in a community rich enough to support an institution of higher education. And they cannot afford to attend a residence institution.

Throughout the United States, young people in rural areas, to whom college education is often inaccessible, have completed fewer school grades than the urban population of the same age. According to the 1940 census, the fourteen-year-old children in rural areas had completed 7.4 years of school, whereas the figures show 8.3 for urban areas. For eighteen-year-olds the disparity is even greater: 9.2 years in the rural areas as contrasted to 11.5 years in the urban.

The differences in income between urban and rural areas are so great that, even though some predominantly rural states devote unusually high proportions of their budgets to education, they cannot develop a sufficient number of quality institutions of higher education. A large proportion of America's youth is thus denied an opportunity to obtain a college education simply because of geographical accident. The areas in which they live are simply unable to provide the needed educational facilities.

When the wide differences between regions are coupled

with the fact that thirty three million Americans still do not
have access to adequate library facilities, the regional differences
for opportunities for education are all the more disturbing.

Viewed from the standpoint of the individuals' rights and
privileges in our democratic society, then, it may be stated
that financial barriers are denying many Americans their educational heritage. Viewed from the standpoint of society, such
educational privation stands as a challenge to the richest nation
on earth.

We have clearly entered an era in our history when many
local communities and states cannot provide educational opportunity for the youth who will largely determine our national
destiny. Our educational problems, particularly those of fi-
nance, are clearly not just local or sectional or regional. They
are national and they must be dealt with nationally. If existing
differences in educational opportunity are to be eliminated,
the initiative and the responsibility cannot be left solely to
individual states and institutions. The resources and the leadership of the federal government are needed. Appropriate aid
can be supplied without impairing—in any respect—local control and initiative in education, a principle to which virtually
the entire profession and the lay public are firmly committed.

2. Religion and the Schools

"Democracy is, after all, a religious ideal. A sense of relationship to God, a belief in His Fatherhood and the brotherhood of man contribute greatly to the development of attitudes that will make America safe for differences." Their goal is frequently the same as that described here by Dean Crowley of Fordham University. But many Americans have radically different methods of finding a way toward *"the development of attitudes that will make America safe for differences."* And religion, in the area of public education, seems to be a subject of continued controversy. It would be good if, amidst all the welter of discussion, this much were clear: though the origins of American education were parochial and private, the free and public school emerged as democracy grew. Today the public school is meant to serve all children, without sectarian indoctrination. And no child is to be made to feel unworthy because of what he or his family believes.

An urgent message is implied in all the following selections. There is too much conflict in the area of religion and the schools; somehow, soon, all major points of view must be reconciled lest all public education suffer. It is sad that there are areas of such strong tension—as in the matter of released-time whose main points are outlined here. Democracy's task is to find a democratic solution that will create an acceptable modus vivendi in these and other problem areas.

How Can We Teach Moral and Spiritual Values in the Public Schools?

By William G. Carr

(Reprinted from the Journal of the National Education Association, March 1951, Copyright 1951. Used with permission.)

Johnny dug from his pocket a shiny new dime, his weekly allowance. Now he stood before the candy counter trying to decide between 10 peppermints at one cent each and the chocolate bar for six cents. The chocolate bar won. After the clerk gave him four coins in change, Johnny scooped up coins and candy and ran on to school.

As he hung up his jacket, he removed his precious change and counted it—one penny, two pennies, three pennies, four— no, that's not a penny! That's a dime—not bright like the one he gave to the candy store clerk, but dull and worn, so that at first glance it looked like one of the wartime pennies. Over- joyed at his unexepted wealth, he ran to his teacher, who was correcting arithmetic papers before class. "Look," he cried, "the man at the store gave me a dime instead of a penny. Now I can have two more candy bars and one peppermint this week! Isn't that wonderful?"

What would you do in a case like that? Few teachers would say that the schoolboard employs them to teach Johnny arith- metic but not to teach him integrity. Out of thousands of such incidents and the responses that teachers and youth make to them, day by day, moral and spiritual values are taught by good schools and good teachers.

Can any kind of plan or policy be suggested to guide teaching in such an elusive area? Altho teaching of values, perhaps more than any other kind of teaching, depends on many variable

---

William G. Carr is Executive Secretary of the National Education Association.

circumstances, there are some lines of good procedure which, taken together, form a useful pattern.

First, each school system should formulate, in terms as clear as possible, its guiding moral and spiritual values. While no list should be uncritically adopted, the following may help promote discussion and reflection:

[1] *The supreme importance of the individual personality.* Public schools promote this basic moral value by trying to give every child a chance to grow to his full physical, intellectual, moral, and spiritual stature.

[2] *Moral responsibility.* Every individual should feel responsible for the consequences of his own conduct. Good schools help children develop such a sense of responsibility.

[3] *Institutions as the servants of men.* Programs of civic education train young citizens to exercise wisely their essential sovereignty.

[4] *Common consent.* Living together in harmony requires each member of a group to accept the informed judgment of the majority as the guide to group action. School experiences include many opportunities for such voluntary cooperation.

[5] *Devotion to truth.* The public schools offer young people experience in seeking truth, examining new ideas, and appealing to reason on controverted questions.

[6] *Respect for excellence.* Exceptional abilities merit respect rather than envy or ridicule. Such abilities are fostered by good schools.

[7] *Moral equality.* All persons similarly situated should be judged by the same moral standards. Good schools repudiate both special privilege and servility.

[8] *Brotherhood.* Concern for the other fellow should inspire corrective action as well as sympathy. The school helps children to outgrow selfcentered infancy and to achieve a broad humanitarianism in maturity.

[9] *Pursuit of happiness.* Children and youth learn in school that the deepest personal happiness springs from good relations with others and often requires the deferment of transitory pleasures.

[10] *Spiritual enrichment.* Individuals should cherish those aspects of human experience which transcend the materialistic aspects of life. A complete education provides experiences which enrich the life of the spirit.

Second, in this area, more than in any other, the individual teachers are the keystones of success. Their skills and energies in teaching values should be liberated from every external handicap. Too many teachers "pull their punches" in dealing with moral and spiritual values. They may fear to touch matters related to religion. The heavy and varied demands of their calling drain their time and energy. Mastery of subject-matter too often takes precedence over other kinds of learning.

Third, the education of teachers should deal explicitly with moral and spiritual values. Personal character should invariably be an important consideration in the admissions policies of institutions for teacher education. Character should weigh heavily in the employment of teachers. Teacher-educating institutions should emphasize the problems and methods of teaching moral and spiritual values.

Fourth, teaching of values should permeate the entire educational process. Character cannot be taught by simply scheduling so many minutes a day to the task. Values are best incorporated into conduct by example, experience, and observation. Such experiences must be repeated in a variety of situations to establish habits, rooted in intellectual understanding, and linked to emotional responses to provide the dynamic for action.

Fifth, all the school's resources should be used. Every teacher, every day, in every class, is dealing in values. The example he sets, the actions he approves, the way he handles his subject, his relations with students, the way he encourages consistent thought and right conduct—all have their influence. If all the teacher's questions require only facts to answer them, the students may conclude that only facts are important.

Questions which call for solutions to problems, interpretation of motives, weighing of consequences, making of comparisons, or the forming of judgments do more than help to teach usable information and skills. Such thoughtful inquiries also help the student to learn how and why and when the information and skills should be used.

Sixth, public schools need staff and facilities for wholesome personal relations. A relationship between students and teacher which avoids excessive sentimentality at one extreme and cold unconcern on the other may in itself be a fruitful source of moral and spiritual values. Such relations take time as well as skill and sympathy. Many schools today are unable to command the services of enough qualified teachers to do this part of their task adequately.

A community which complacently permits its children to be herded into crowded buildings, forced to use classrooms in converted basements, assigned to successive shifts like factory workers, and placed under the care of harried and overworked teachers, has said in effect that it does not care deeply about the moral and spiritual development of its young people. Let those who want to lift these values among American youth act now to establish educational facilities which permit constructive personal relations.

Seventh, public schools should be friendly toward the religious beliefs of their students. Altho the public-school teacher is obligated by the canons of his profession not to attempt to indoctrinate his personal sectarian creeds and opinions, the attitude of the public schools toward the religious beliefs of the children in their care should be sympathetic. The teacher's words and attitude should reassure each child that his religious beliefs are considered right *for him,* so that he will feel comfortable with his own creed or lack of a creed.

The atheist and the bigot may object to even the most objective presentation of the facts about the role of religion in American life. But such views should not deter schools from teaching a decent respect for the religious opinions of mankind.

Eighth, the public schools should continue to guard religious freedom. The Constitutional provisions which state that "no religious test shall ever be required as a qualification to any office or public trust under the United States" and that "Congress shall make no law respecting an establishment of religion, or prohibiting the free exercise thereof," are truly great achievements of the American adventure. Our society grants to every citizen the right to believe as his conscience and training dictate. The public schools should teach that this privilege means not only freedom of belief, but respect for the beliefs of others.

The public school must not dismiss religion as something to be merely "tolerated." The public school may certainly not teach sectarian religion, but teaching against religion is equally intolerant and intolerable. The science teacher, for example, who tells youth that religious faith is "unscientific" is taking unprofessional advantage of their immaturity and exhibiting his own.

Ninth, the public schools should teach about religion. This can be done without advocating or teaching any religious creed. To omit from the classroom all references to religion and its institutions is to neglect an important part of American life. Knowledge about religion is essential for a full understanding of our culture, literature, art, history, and current affairs.

That religious beliefs are controversial is not an adequate reason for excluding teaching *about* religion from the public schools. Economic and social information is taught in the schools on the sensible theory that students need to learn how to face issues and to form sound judgments. Teaching about religion should be approached in the same spirit.

Altho no one religion should be taught in the public schools, much useful information can be taught *about* the major religious faiths and their role in the story of mankind. However, although study about religion contributes to both the general and the moral education of youth, it should not be regarded by home or by church as a substitute for religious teaching.

Tenth, moral values are built by a partnership among many agencies. The school is an important source of moral and spiritual values, but it must always be a partner of the homes and the churches. The potential partners also include the Big

Four of mass communication (the press, radio, television, cinema) as well as other community institutions.

The public schools can and should increase their effectiveness in developing moral and spiritual values. Their role is one that no other institution can play as well or at all. But the public schools cannot act every part in the complex drama of personality formation. Any hope on the part of the general public that schools can do the whole job unaided is doomed to disappointment. Any attempt on the part of the teaching profession to assume such a staggering responsibility would end in frustration. The public schools need partners.

The Catholic Approach to Religion in Education

By Francis M. Crowley

(From an address originally delivered at the Institute of Religious and Social Studies under the auspices of the University of Chicago. Revised by the author especially for this volume, 1952, and used with his permission.)

Catholic education provides for the education of the whole man, "soul united to body in unity of nature, with all his faculties, natural and supernatural, such as right reason and revelation show him to be." The Catholic theory is that the effects of original sin—weakness of will and disorderly inclinations—must be corrected and good habits must be developed. This cannot be done by relying solely on the powers of human nature. The mind must be enlightened and the will strengthened by supernatural truth and the grace of God. This is the same as saying that Catholic philosophy of education is the philosophy of the supernatural; that is, it has not only a sound philosophical but a decidedly positive theological basis. The student is to be prepared for life here and hereafter. "For precisely this reason, Christian education takes in the whole aggregate of human life, physical and spiritual, intellectual and moral, individual, domestic and social, not with a view of reducing it in any way, but in order to elevate, regulate and perfect it, in accordance with the example and teaching of Christ," said the late Pope Pius XI in his great encyclical letter on the Christian Education of Youth. In order to achieve the ends of Christian education, it is necessary that the entire program be dominated by the Christian spirit, so that religion may be "the foundation and crown of the youth's entire training at every level of instruction."

Francis M. Crowley is Dean of the School of Education, Fordham University.

Many years have passed since the late Pope Pius XI published his encyclical letter. He was not the first to speak out on this vitally important question of Christian education. In his encyclical he made it quite clear that he was only repeating the instructions of Pius IX and Leo XIII, and that attendance at public schools is forbidden by Canon Law, thus making the regulation binding in conscience. "The school," he wrote, "if not a temple, is a den." A school from which religion is excluded is contrary to the fundamental principles of education. Such school in time is bound to become irreligious. The only school that is a fit school for Catholic students is a school controlled by the Church, in which religion is the foundation and crown of the youth's entire training, not only in the elementary grades but in the high school and college as well.

American bishops have been just as solicitous as the long line of Holy Fathers. Numerous pastoral letters of the American hierarchy have dealt with the subject of education, and the Decrees of the Third Plenary Council of Baltimore (1884) proclaim in forceful language that the parent must send his child to the Catholic school. The language is quite to the point—in its strictest interpretation the Bishop alone can approve sending a Catholic child to a public school. In the hurly-burly existence which we lead, it is impossible for the average Catholic parent to care for more than the normal demands made on him by his occupation and his home. For those who have been fortunate enough to secure an education under Catholic auspices, the instruction of their offspring in the teachings of the Church is a comparatively easy matter; but we must remember that a great number are only possessed of a rudimentary knowledge of the teachings of the Church, usually secured through Sunday school instruction, released time programs, desultory reading and attendance at missions or Sunday services. Thus, the Catholic Church has been obliged, for the sake of principle, to establish a separate system of schools. The chief purpose of these schools is to give to the Catholic child the Catholic training which is his baptismal birthright. Educational institutions functioning under the aegis of the Church in America today provide training adapted to all stages of the student's educational growth.

The Third Plenary Council decrees influenced the growth of parochial schools, since many Catholics were quite dissatisfied with public schools and only needed such counsel to undertake the task of organizing a separate school system. In 1883, the year preceding the Baltimore Council, there were 6,241 churches and 2,491 schools; that is, forty per cent of the churches reported schools. By 1933, the numbers had grown to 12,537 and 7,462 respectively, showing that sixty per cent of the parishes offered education at the elementary level. While this represents a twenty per cent increase during the fifty-year period (1883-1933) in the number of parishes with schools, it falls far short of the ideal set by the Baltimore Council—a school in every parish.

The elementary division of the Catholic school system includes three types of schools: parochial, private and institutional. The parochial school is controlled by a parish, a private school by a religious order, and an institutional school by a diocese, a religious order or a private foundation. Of the 8,589 Catholic elementary schols in operation in 1950, 7,831 were parochial, 495, private; 263, institutional. Parochial schools are now functioning in every State and in each of the 122 archidioceses and dioceses. Episcopal jurisdictions, bearing the names of American cities, provide extensive facilities such as: Chicago, 376 schools; Philadelphia, 348; New York, 286; St. Louis, 259; Pittsburgh, 237; Brooklyn, 223; Milwaukee, 200. The schools in most jurisdictions are administered by a school board and a diocesan superintendent of schools empowered to appoint teachers, approve the curriculum, supervise instruction, prepare reports, direct building programs, and promote public relations. The superintendent and the board are directly responsible to the bishop of the diocese, who in turn is entirely free to adopt policies and practices which fit the peculiar needs of the schools of his jurisdiction. In other words, each diocese is autonomous since there is no national head of the Catholic school system. The unifying principle is the philosophy of education to which all subscribe, since it promotes a common belief in the efficacy of religious instruction, obedience to episcopal authority, and sound principles and methods. This is especially evident in the uniformity in policy and practice characteristic of approximately 150 Religious Orders which supply the 59,698 Sisters required to care for the instruction of 2,560,815 pupils in 8,589 elementary schools. In addition, there are 2,080 priests and brothers and 4,747 lay teachers (1950.)

The Catholic Church cares for approximately sixty per cent of all Catholic children in parochial schools. It has not been possible to live up to the ideal set by the Third Plenary Council of Baltimore—a parochial school near each church. Poverty, indifference, widely scattered Catholic groups and the shortage of religious teachers may be cited as some of the reasons for inability to achieve the ideal. Many Catholic parents have been obliged, therefore, to send their children to public schools. The religious instructions of these pupils must be cared for in the home, in Sunday schools or in released time programs, in keeping with the tradition of the Catholic Church.

The Sacred Congregation of the Council in Rome issued a decree in 1935 on Catechetical Instruction. It provided for a special series of lessons in religion for better and more advanced instruction of those who teach Christian Doctrine to public school children, and instructed the Bishops to supply able catechists of both sexes to help the pastors. The Confraternity of Christian Doctrine, whose establishment is obligatory in every parish in the world, is the chief agency employed by bishops and pastors to organize Sunday schools, religious vacation schools, and week-day religion schools to provide instruction during released time or during out-of school hours. Most of the dioceses now have Directors of the Confraternity of Christian Doctrine who are responsible for the organization and direction, under the bishop's supervision and with the pastors' aid, of proper programs of instruction. The experience of such officials shows beyond doubt that released time programs may be operated successfully. Such programs provide the best form of religious education for public school children, especially when supplemented by attendance at religious vacation schools. It is a matter of record that Catholic children attending public schools frequently transfer to parochial schools after experiencing the advantages of organized religious instruction. The Catholic Church is in favor of any plan which makes it possible to provide for the religious education of Catholic children attending public schools and looks on released time programs with special favor. Even the perfect program of supplementary instruction, however, would not be considered as a substitute for the Catholic school.

The use of released time makes weekday religious education possible. Children are released during school hours to attend classes in religious education held by the different denominations in churches, schools or halls. The schools thus cooperate with church and home in providing religious education. In the pioneer days programs were conducted before and after school hours. The advantages of using released time have become so evident that the present swing toward this practice is decidedly marked. In 1937, it is reported that released time schools were conducted under various legal provisions in forty-five states, in more than 2,000 centers, with an estimated enrollment of 265,000 pupils. Returns for 1945 showed a sharp increase. In January of that year 1,500,000 elementary and high school children were participating in the released time plan. The programs for these students were offered in approximately 2,000 communities in all but two states. In 1952, approximately 2,000,000 students were using the released time privilege. Since in the better plans, provision is made for qualified teachers, proper equipment, attendance reports, proper grading, standard examinations and activity programs, school leaders have been willing to cooperate, and in many instances have taken the initiative in recommending the adoption of the plan.

The released time program leads the student to see that religious instruction is an integral part of education. More time is provided for religious instruction, thus making continuity possible. The instruction is unquestionably vested with a certain amount of dignity and higher standards are established. Providing for the instruction elsewhere does away with the criticism of bringing sectarian influence into the public school, and removes entirely any possibility of friction or legal action. The weekday religious education program does as much as any plan can to make the religious attitude a part of the learning process. The cooperation of home, Church and school makes education one to the child. The ideal set-up is the denominational school, such as the Catholic parochial school; but funds are not forthcoming for support of a still greater number, so we must do the best we can for the great number of Catholic children now in public schools, and we can do so through the weekday religious education program.

There are some who claim that released time for religious instruction creates a divisive influence in the public school. They hold that group antagonisms are thus promoted with all of their ugly consequences. But the record does not support this claim: in fact, the contrary seems to be true, in the sense that common planning for a worthy purpose promotes cooperation based on sympathy and understanding—the only true basis of tolerance. But we may not with impunity shut our eyes to a growing degree of intolerance which has become so manifest of late in sporadic outbreaks on a national scale. All agencies engaged in educating American youth must view the promotion of tolerance as a very real and pressing obligation. In promoting tolerance, however, we must do so within the limits prescribed by truth and the principles of free government.

It is rather unfortunate that so many sources of group antagonisms have a European origin. How the course of history might have been changed if such antagonisms, by some magical process, could have been sublimated or destroyed at the moment of taking the oath of citizenship. But that might have been only a partial solution, chiefly because the economic, social, political and religious stresses of American life would in time have produced other conflicts in more virulent form. What I am trying to say is that no formula will do away with group antagonisms altogether. The most unpredictable of all animals is man. He is still "Mr. X" when you have used your formula to solve the problem.

The solution is largely a matter of education of the right kind. The school can contribute something but not so much as some expect. The home, the community and religious groups must also shoulder the burden. All face great handicaps because there is so little to work with. Training or appeals based on love of one's fellowman because he is an American or a good citizen do not care for the problem. Campaigns and conferences serve a very useful purpose. But the work of any agency is headed for failure unless there is a direct appeal to conscience, so shaped as to develop an intelligent understanding of man's relationships with man and of the duties and responsibilities that flow out of these relationships. "Thou shalt love thy neighbor as thyself." Children must be taught that they have a common Father in heaven and that they must love one another as God also loves them. Many Americans are so little concerned over God and the things of God that the concepts of the fatherhood of God and the brotherhood of Christ have little meaning for them. Yet it is these concepts alone which give rise to belief in the sacredness of the human personality. It is the only basis for the American way of life. The wise man makes sure that his fellow enjoys the same rights that he holds sacred. Personality is sacred for all or for none.

The home is the first and holiest school. The attitude of the young toward most of life's activities is determined by the home environment. The prejudices of childhood often shape the thinking of the man. Justice and charity must function in the home training of youth or the promotion of tolerance is a lost cause. Family education of the right sort is then of the very essence. It must have a foundation in the supernatural, for religion is necessary to give social charity form and sanction. This prerequisite gives second place to the church. The third should go to the school and community agencies functioning on a cooperative basis. This order is somewhat at variance with that commonly accepted by the public, calling for the school in first place; the community, second; the home, third, and the church, last. All of the foregoing implies that better homes mean better men. We must strengthen the homes by increasing its responsibilities. "Its protection and improvement and, where necessary, its rehabilitation, is a challenge to our intelligence, our courage, and our high resolve." Religious instruction in any form promotes this high purpose. Any form of activity which protects and strengthens the American Way of Life is not divisive in character. Released time for religious education may be considered as an effective means of promoting this end.

One of America's most pressing problems is the lack of religious instruction in public schools, since the Church and the home are unable to cope with the problem single-handed or through joint action. School officials must be concerned more and more with the moral enlightenment of the masses, since there has been a sharp increase in juvenile delinquency, and the home has broken down as an agency for religious instruction because of parental indifference or ignorance. Surveys show that the majority of children receive only a modicum of moral and religious preparation, yet modern complex social conditions submit even the well-molded character to temptations and stresses undreamt of a generation ago. Religious education is necessary for protection, clarity of purpose, and progress in terms of social welfare. Society can only be transformed through the individual. At the very moment our problem is "to make America safe for differences." Democracy is after all a religious ideal. A sense of relationship to God, a belief in His Fatherhood and the brotherhood of man contribute greatly to the development of attitudes that will make America safe for differences.

Religion and Public Education
By Jerome Nathanson

There are many reasons for the present-day attack on progressive education. There is the pressure to conformity, affecting education as it does so much else. There is the insistence that progressivism in education undermines American values, teaching cooperation to children and failing to prepare them for a competitive society. There are the habits and vested interests in social stratification along class and race lines, as against increasing democratization in the schools. There is the fact that good education costs money and that some taxpayers emphasize the old-fashioned educational techniques, not because they are better, but because they are cheaper. By no means the least important of the influences at work is the religious. Religious inroads on the integrity of our public school systems are among the most serious of all.

What is the background of these present religious forays on public education? On the one hand, despite the rapid development of the Sunday School movement in recent generations, the churches have not been satisfied with the results. On the other hand, with respect to those groups which have developed parochial schools, existing facilities are inadequate to existing needs.

One consequence of this has been the rise of the released-time movement. The Supreme Court in the McCollum case ruled that it was unconstitutional to give such religious instruction on public-school premises. The question of released time which does not involve the use of public buildings has not yet been decided. Aside from the question of constitutionality, however, the degree to which children are divided along sectarian lines under the released time system is highly undesirable.

Nevertheless, religious institutions are increasingly insistent on their own essential role in the educational process. They

Jerome Nathanson is leader at the Ethical Culture Society and chairman of Federal Aid to Education.

are making much of the contention that when the schools ignore religion they are actually loading the dice against religion. So they have been making various proposals for dealing with this state of affairs.

One of the major propositions presented is that, despite differences among the various religious sects, there is a common core of belief among them. Much as Protestants, Catholics, and Jews may differ in other respects, they all believe in one God, accept the Old Testament, and share such ethical emphases as are made in the Lord's Prayer. Accordingly, protagonists of this proposal urge that we give a "common-core" religious education in the schools. On examination, however, what does this talk about a common core come to? As a matter of fact, differences among religious sects exist, not because they hold things in common, but because they insist on the supreme importance of the theological differences which separate them. But even if there were a common core of religious belief acceptable to the three groups mentioned, to teach it would do violence to the beliefs of millions of other Americans who do not share them.

The other major proposition is that we should teach about religion just as we teach about science and literature, for acquaintance with religious traditions and beliefs should be as much part of everyone's cultural equipment as anything else. It would be a good thing to teach about religion in the schools if it were feasible to do so. But is it feasible? Do the churches really want a critical reading of the Bible, an objective and scientific examination of their respective denominational tenets? Obviously, whatever might someday happen, they do not wish this to happen now. Insofar as Bible reading, recitation of the Lord's Prayer, and religious instruction in more general terms are actually indoctrinations, they have no place in the public schools.

Where does this leave us? Avowedly, the whole drive for religious education starts from the fact of moral delinquency. But taking this avowed concern at its face value, what does it mean? In the first place, moral delinquency at the present time, as contrasted with other times, is probably exaggerated, and it is well that we keep this perspective for the sake of our own sound judgment. However that may be, the general moral condition of the present day is certainly not one about which anyone should feel complacent.

The question is, what is responsible for man's moral condition? If it were true, as some of the churches contend, that morality is contingent upon theology, then mankind would be in an infinitely worse condition than it is. For the lack of theological belief in our time is due, not to sinfulness in man, but to the lack of credibility in the light of scientific insights. If morality were exclusively dependent upon theology, when theological beliefs are corroded it would lead inevitably to moral relativism, to nihilism, or to totalitarianism—as has actually happened in some instances. Fortunately, it can be shown both in theory and in practice that the moral life is not dependent upon any one theology or metaphysics.

Since our educational concern at the moment is with the moral life, our solution will not lie in indoctrination along traditionally religious lines, but in developing increasingly sensitive attitudes in human relations. Actually, our public schools have done far more than they are nowadays credited with doing. But still more can and should be done. The human-relations inquiries which are being conducted in so many places, the insights which come from the social sciences, and the experiences of the Ethical Culture Schools over the past seventy-five years all point in desirable directions.

The drive for religious education in the public schools can lead only to increasing difficulties, divisiveness, and tensions in American life. The place for religious education is in the home and the church. Once we clarify the distinction between our religious and moral concerns, we can concentrate fully on the ethical education of our children and youth. For as religious sectarianism divides people, so ethics can unite them. The continuing development of a democratic ethics as an indispensable part of democratic education is the common stake we have in a common future.

The Clerical Challenge to the Schools

By Agnes E. Meyer

(Reprinted from The Atlantic Monthly, March, 1952. Copyright 1952. Used with permission of the author.)

It is no mere vagary of taste that has brought about in this period of revolution a rediscovery of Thomas Jefferson and a reappraisal of him as the outsanding scholar and humanitarian and the most creative mind of our first Revolution.

What were Jefferson's greatest achievements? He himself told us when he wrote the epitaph for his tombstone: "Here was buried Thomas Jefferson, author of the Declaration of American Independence, of the statute of Virginia for Religious Freedom and Father of the University of Virginia."

The Virginia act ranked high in Jefferson's mind because he considered that in this act for civil and religious freedom he had hoped eventually for the nation, the "wall of separation between Church and State" which the First Amendment read into the Constitution. The State should neither support nor oppose any particular form of Church. It should leave the Churches strictly alone and the Churches should leave the State and all its institutions strictly alone. In the course of time this became the official American position and, as Jefferson foresaw and James Bryce confirmed, it saved our nation all the bloodshed, cruelties, and intolerance which have defaced the history of religious strife in Europe.

The separation of Church and State is not merely a principle of our democracy but a body of experience that we have lived for a hundred and fifty years. The written law became so thoroughly accepted as a commonplace of our American culture that recent historians have taken it for granted. As a result the

---

Agnes E. Meyer is education writer for the Washington Post.

man in the street has forgotten the immense contribution it has made to all of his freedoms, not only of religion, but of thought, speech, and press. Jefferson evolved this principle because he hated every form of tyranny over the mind, but unless the average person has some awareness of this he can scarcely share the passionate conviction of the late Justice Rutledge's statement: "We have staked the very existence of our country on the faith that complete separation of church and state is best for the state and best for religion."

Today the Protestant and Catholic Church leaders are giving ample proof that they have both forgotten what a profound debt they owe to the "wall of separation." It was the Protestant Churches which first breached this wall when, just before the First World War, they introduced the released time program for religious education in the public schools. The Protestant clergy had become alarmed on reading the report of the United States Office of Education that "only a small proportion of the children throughout the country have even brief contact with church influence." Instead of asking themselves whether this failure may not have resulted from their own inadequacy, they decided that they must invade the schools with methods of education not powerful enough to attract American families to their churches. Nor have they ever explained why teaching that was ineffective in the churches would be more effective in the schools.

The released time program was of two types. In some communities the clergy entered the schools to teach their sectarian creeds; in others the children were dismissed from school attendance to go to a church of the parents' choice for religious instruction. The former plan, whereby the clergy enter the public schools, was declared unconstitutional by the Supreme Court in the McCollum decision. Did this make an impression on the clergy? On some, yes. On others, no. "It must be said to the shame of Protestantism," says the Reverend Charles Clayton Morrison, "that in too many cases and communities the Protestant churches still carry on the released time practice and, in some cases, even more flagrant forms of violation, in defiance of the Supreme Court's mandate. I contend that all Protestants should have hailed the Supreme Court's decision with deep satisfaction and immediately withdrawn from every semblance of continuing the released time practice. Protestantism has an incomparably greater stake in the separation of church and state than it could possibly have in the trivial religious education toy called released time." The scholarly Dr. Morrison is a Protestant voice calling in a wilderness of religious confusion. One of the few resolutions passed unanimously by the National Council of Churches in the U.S.A. at its recent meeting in Atlanta stated that the Council would support the New York plan of released time whereby pupils leave the public schools an hour early, when the appeal is argued before the Supreme Court.

Yet simultaneously the Council has issued a strong manifesto opposing the appointment of an ambassador to the Vatican on the ground that such an appointment fuses government with religion and is therefore an infringement of the separation of Church and State. When the Protestants bring up the First Amendment in this question, they themselves admit that they are on dubious ground.

It is irresolute Protestant thinking such as this which endangers the wall of separation far more than the outright declaration of war upon the First Amendment which the Catholic Bishops made in their official statement of 1948, "The Christian in Action."

Protestant leadership must begin to realize that its position on the First Amendment is painfully ambiguous, whereas the position of the Catholic Church on this vital problem is crystal clear. The Administrative Catholic Bishops boldly declared the American principle of separation of Church and State a "novel" interpretation of the Constitution, "a shibboleth of doctrinaire secularism" which was recently invented by the Supreme Court in the McCollum decision. They attacked that decision as unconstitutional and announced their determination to work "peacefully, patiently and perseveringly" for its reversal.

Since the Catholic Bishops intend to reverse the McCollum decision, they must necessarily bring to bear all the arguments they can muster in favor of the New York released time legislation when it comes before the Supreme Court. This is a logical consequence of their position.

Yet nobody has spoken more frankly against the 1948 pronouncement of the Catholic Bishops than certain Protestant leaders and publications. They have pointed out what American experience has confirmed—the dependence of democracy on freedom of religious conscience and the impossibility of assuring this without complete separation of Church and State. Thus the Bishops' statement places the Catholic hierarchy in permanent hostility to American democratic principles. Some Protestant authorities claim that the Bishops' statement does more than that. It challenges the very meaning of America, the whole Jeffersonian doctrine of civil and religious freedom, and our very philosophy of life, our belief in human progress, our hopeful concept of man and his ability to govern himself. Thus, unless the Bishops' pronouncement of 1948 is retracted, their challenge is bound to precipitate a division in this country, of whose intensity the present religious hostilities are merely a foretaste.

But how, I should like to ask the Protestant Churches, can they logically defend the First Amendment if their own position on the separation of Church and State remains as ambiguous, vacillating, and contradictory as it is today?

At present the Protestant Churches are conducting a violent campaign against Catholic ambitions for Federal aid to their parochial schools, for the extension of bus transportation for parochial school pupils, and other services which the Catholic prelates minimize as "incidental." "It [the Catholic Church] seeks to crack the Constitutional principle of separation of Church and State," said the Reverend Charles Clayton Morrison before the Convention of the Disciples of Christ, "at some point where the average citizen will not discern that it is being cracked and where even the courts may find a way of rationalizing their approval." But that is precisely what the Protestants did when they first introduced religious training on public school time—they cracked the First Amendment at a point where neither the average citizen nor they themselves discerned that it was being cracked. And now they are trying to persuade the Supreme Court Justices to find a way of rationalizing their approval. How can the Protestant Churches oppose with a good conscience the Catholic campaign to break down the wall between Church and State when they themselves have for years been breaching that wall by other methods?

Our American schools, like those of Europe, were founded by the Churches. But when our schools were finally secularized toward the middle of the last century, under the leadership of Horace Mann, that movement was not anticlerical or antireligious. To be sure, the sectarian conflicts of that period and their destructive influence on the schools played an important part in the movement. But there was nothing negative or hostile about the agreement to adhere to separation of State and Church in public education. The secularization of our schools was a positive movement to embody in American education the interaction of the real and the ideal, upon which both democracy and active Christianity depend. Whenever a human being strives upward toward self-development, goodness, and concern for others, there the divine will is active.

The educational program, moreover, has never excluded instruction about religion. It banished only instruction *in* religion when the schools were secularized. If we bear in mind that the whole future of our democracy depends upon moral solidarity, freedom of conscience, and freedom of inquiry, the secularization of our schools becomes an act of sublime courage and of sublime loyalty to the American faith that our institutions should be of the people, by the people, and for the people.

Although the Supreme Court in the McCollum decision has declared unconstitutional a form of released time program which permits the clergy to enter the public schools to teach sectarian creeds, the New York plan, which proposes the public school pupils leave school an hour before the general dismissal to receive religious instruction, remains in a realm of doubtful legality.

The crux of the McCullum decision lies in the following extract from Justice Black's opinion for the Court:—

The foregoing facts, without reference to others that appear in the record, show the use of tax-supported property for religious instruction and the close co-operation between the school authorities and the religious council in promoting religious education. The operation of the state's compulsory education system thus assists and is integrated with the program of religious instruction carried on by separate religious sects. Pupils compelled by law to go to school for secular education are released in part from their legal duty upon the condition that they attend the religious classes. This is beyond all question a utilization of the tax-established and tax-supported public school system to aid religious groups to spread their faith. And it falls squarely under the ban of the First Amendment (made applicable to the States by the Fourteenth.)

Three elements are held illegal by the court:—

1. Although the use of tax-supported property does not enter into the New York released time program, the use of tax moneys does. The New York City Board of Education alone provides a million dollars' worth of educational opportunity which is not used by the 102,705 released time students in that city and is consequently wasted. But it is not only the small proportion of children who are dismissed that lose an hour of instruction. The education of the majority who remain in school comes to a halt in order that the dismissed children shall not fall behind in their school lessons. Thus the whole class, and in some cases the whole elementary school, together with the teaching staff is deprived of one hour of educational opportunity per week. The total waste of taxpayers' money is incalculably large.

2. The close cooperation between school authorities and

religious groups in promoting religious education, which the Supreme Court condemns, also exists in the New York plan. The ultimate responsibility for the administration of the program rests wholly with the public school teachers and principals. On them also falls the burden of interpreting the policy of the Board of Education and of executing the mandates of the law. Whether the religious instruction is given within the school or without, the operation of the State's compulsory education system assists and is integrated with a program of religious instruction carried on by separate religious sects.

The third point made by the Supreme Court, that "pupils compelled by law to go to school for secular education are released in part from their legal duty upon condition that they attend the religious classes," is an exact description of what also happens under the New York program and therefore "falls squarely under the ban of the First Amendment," as Justice Black put it. This point is reinforced by the Everson decision of the Supreme Court, which states: "The prohibition [of the First Amendment] broadly forbids state support, financial *or otherwise*, of religion in any sense, form or degree."

These and other quotations from the McCollum and Everson decisions apply so clearly and forcibly to the released time plan of religious instruction that many states and localities have already canceled this type of program. In St. Louis, Missouri, when the local board of education decided to disregard the opinion of the State Superintendent of Public Instruction and continue classes on released time outside of the school buildings but without the enforcement of attendance by the public schools, the Circuit Court enjoined the practice, stating in part:—

> The differences [between the St. Louis case and the McCollum case] are inconsequential. The controlling fact in both cases is that the public schools are used to aid sectarian groups to disseminate their doctrines. Whether these sectarian classes are conducted in school buildings or elsewhere can make no difference, since attendance upon them during compulsory school

hours is deemed attendance at school. Failure to exercise supervision over the instruction of religion and to require the keeping of proper attendance records does not make the school program legal; it merely indicates laxity on the part of the school authorities. The fact that any sect may participate in this program is immaterial; the public school cannot be used to aid one religion or to aid all religions.

Have the Protestant Churches ever asked themselves whether their intrusion into the schools is, in itself, a moral act?

They advance the argument, for example, that there is no compulsion on the children to take advantage of released time religious training, that parents are free to decide whether their children are to participate, and that therefore the program does not infringe upon the freedom of religion guaranteed by the First Amendment. A scientific survey of the New York City released time program made by the Center for Field Services of New York University reports evidence "that resistance of children released for religious instruction presents a problem." Frequently the children refuse to go because they prefer to stay in school. Some teachers interpret the word "dismiss" as permissive and let the children do as they please. Others interpret "dismiss" to mean pressure, and force the children to go.

I have, personally, experienced the pressure, the unhappiness, the rancor, created by the program, especially in small communities, not only among children but among their parents. I have known teachers to use their influence to force children into these programs, and others who burned with silent rage because they resented the tensions the program creates but lacked the freedom to condemn it. In fact, the pressure on the teachers and school administrators is just as wicked as the pressure on the children. Would a teacher who values her position dare to oppose or even criticize the Churches openly? What irony that a program to teach Christian love should create acute conflicts, confusion, and hatred!

Justice Frankfurter had the psychological insight to realize the cruel situations the program would create when he said in his McCullum brief: "That a child is offered an alternative may reduce the constraint; it does not eliminate the operation of influence by the school in matters sacred to the conscience and outside the school's domain. The law of imitation operates and non-comformity is not an outstanding characteristic of children. The result is obvious pressure upon children to attend."

Some adherents of the program profess to see an improvement in the children's morals. Yet is it a commonly known fact throughout the country, and the report on New York City confirms it, that the released time is an invitation to truancy. Reliable statistics show that about 40 per cent of the children who leave their schools never arrive at the religious centers. Often the children play in the school yard and disturb the school session. Others start out but never arrive. Principals realize that this trend will grow because the Churches cannot control attendance and the teachers are forbidden to do it. Some Churches try to prevent truancy by sending escorts to conduct the children from school to church. Most do not take this precaution. The escorts sometimes fail to appear. Often the religious centers call off their program at the last minute, for lack of personnel. If the children have already left school, they can all play hooky. As the children are caught in an equivocal situation, they lie their way out of their difficulties. Since the object of the released time training is the betterment of character and conduct, the truancy and dishonesty to which it tempts children negate its objectives.

The children often travel so far to arrive at the religious center that there is but a small part of the hour left for instruction. The belief that children can benefit from a half hour or even forty-five minutes of oral instruction once a week, especially if their parents have no church affiliation, indicates a superficial concept of religion.

The released time program is unjust because it penalizes the majority of the children who remain in school. If the public school teachers carry on worth-while activities during this hour, the clergy denounce them for unfair competition. In Chicago, when less than 10 per cent of the pupils were enrolled in the released time program, the principals received orders that "nothing significant shall be taught the children not taking religious instruction." In one elementary school in Westchester County, ten children out of some five hundred use the released time program. As they come from various classes, the whole school loses an hour of work. The indignant parents asked the principal whether the regular curriculum could not be restored. The principal was so terrified of the clergy that he refused to take up the question with them. On the slightest challenge of clerical omniscience, a teacher's whole future may be—and often is—ruined by accusations of atheism. As a result, sabotage of public education and intimidation of schoolteachers, principals, and parents are taking place all over the country. This is tyranny.

It was demonstrated in December, 1950, at the last session of the White House Conference on Children and Youth, that the vast majority of the American people are determined to protect the freedom of their public schools. The 4620 delegates to this Conference were outstanding local leaders in the fields of religion, education, health, welfare; of women's and service clubs; of the labor unions, fraternal organizations, and other major groups.

The committee on religion had submitted to the Conference a report of four paragraphs, one of which recommended that the students of public educational institutions throughout the nation should be allowed to go during school hours to any neary-by religious foundation for religious instruction and receive credit toward graduation for such courses. This plan, if it had been accepted, would have wrecked the curriculum and the discipline, the moral integrity and the independence, of our whole public school system. It indicates to what extremes the released-time program would be carried by some of the clergy if they are not promptly denied all access to the public schools by the courts.

One of the delegates proposed that the whole religious section be struck out and the following resolution substituted:—

> Recognizing knowledge and understanding of religious and ethical concepts as essential to the development of spiritual values and that nothing is of greater importance to the moral and spiritual health of our nation than the works of religious education in our homes and families and in our institutions of organized religion we nevertheless strongly affirm the principle of separation of church and state which has been the keystone of our American democracy and declare ourselves unalterably opposed to the use of the public schools directly or indirectly for religious educational purposes.

After long and heated debate this resolution was carried by a majority of about two to one.

This was an epoch-making event because it was the first time that the released time program for religious instruction was democratically debated and submitted to the test of public opinion in a gathering whose delegates represented, conservatively estimated, three fourths of our total population. The overwhelming popular vote indicated that the majority of our people are willing to fight to maintain the independence of our schools.

I, too, believe that the child is robbed of its full development if it receives no guidance in early years toward recognition of the religious aspects of life. But this teaching, to be effective, must originate in the home and family life with the cooperation of the Churches. The child's whole character and spontaneous sense of right and wrong are largely determined before it goes to school. Before school age the responsibility for the child's development lies with the family and the Church. It is the weakness of these two institutions and their failure for several generations to develop the character of the pre-school child that have now created acute moral problems. Having failed in their primary mission to strengthen the family and reach the children during their most impressionable and formative years, the Churches now seek a short cut, through the released time program, which will cure overnight the moral defects of children who have been neglected throughout infancy.

A very forthright German Catholic Bishop told me last year that he was pessimistic about the future of the family in that country. "And if the family goes, the Church goes," he added gloomily. This is an accurate appraisal of the predicament in which organized religion finds itself. Therefore, if the Churches are honestly concerned about the future of Christianity they should spend all their efforts upon saving the family instead of wasting them upon a futile and ineffective released time program. Why invade the public schools to do a superficial job, when the Churches need all their energy, money, and spiritual fortitude to do a more salutary job right in their own parishes?

The school needs all of its time to improve the education of our children and to center upon the task of developing the morality and strength of character that are ideals common to men of all religious faiths. This task is made difficult when the Churches force the school to engage in programs that generate divisiveness. The children are in school only five or six hours a day, about two hundred days of the year. That leaves the Churches ample time to teach religion.

Now that freedom is threatened as never before, Protestantism has a special responsibility to live up to its sublime traditions as the guardian of individual rights, human liberty, and democratic solidarity. If the Protestant leaders will review the effects of the released time program, they will find that it destroys everything that Protestantism has always cherished as its highest ideals. For it is oppressive, unjust, and disruptive of moral discipline. It undermines the legitimate and the unique task of the public schools to establish an integrated program of education that will bind our American children as comrades in a common life.

Protestant publications, notably the *Christian Century,* have often expressed their fear of "pluralism," the division of our citizens into separate isolated religious groups. Nothing encourages pluralism more than breaking up public school children into separate released-time groups. Either the wall of separation between the school and the sectarian groups must be kept invulnerable or the walls between the sectarian groups will become impassably high.

Moreover, the Churches will only weaken themselves if they use the school as a policeman and teach the children to associate religious instruction with the school rather than the church. By leaning on the schools, the Churches are postponing the time when they must face their real task—of developing religious depth and imparting this sense of depth by educational methods in tune with the needs of the day. The Churches should long ago have discarded their outworn authoritarian verbalism for educational methods based on experience such as our schools have developed. The outmoded methods of instruction of the Churches can only lead to contempt for religion, especially when placed in close juxtaposition with the more vital methods of education that prevail in our best schools.

3. Freedom and Education

John Foster Dulles calls for a renewal of dynamic faith—in our God, ourselves, our nation. William O. Douglas and others warn that fear and lack of faith are "driving more and more men and women . . . either to silence or to the folds of the orthodox." Others enunciate principles by which a person dedictated to civil liberties must live. And in the columns of a weekly newspaper of a small New Jersey city, a concerned citizen and a college professor come to grips on a most acute problem facing education today—academic freedom in a time of fear and tension.

Three Propositions

By John Foster Dulles

(Excerpted from an address given at a meeting of the National Alumni of Princeton University, February 22, 1952. Used with permission of Mr. Dulles.)

My *first* proposition is this: The dynamic usually prevails over the static, the active over the passive.

As between stone and water, which will prevail? The answer is: whichever is in motion. Water in motion will wear away stone that is still; but a stone that is thrown will penerate the water.

The United States, however massive be its material might, can be destroyed by forces that, in themselves, seem weak, if these forces are active and if we are passive.

My *second* proposition is this: In human affairs, the non-material or spiritual element is more important than the material.

I do not ignore the importance of military and economic power at this time, but Napoleon, who was no dreamy-eyed idealist, said that in war the non-material is to the material as 3 is to 1.

It is primarily through social ideas that Soviet Communism has achieved its victories. Almost no part of its expansion has been due to the old-fashioned method of open military aggression. The successful weapon has been political warfare, with the main reliance placed on revolutionary slogans which arouse the masses to Soviet-directed violence.

The free world has failed to draw strength from ideas. We, more than the communist world, think and work in material terms. The United States has given and loaned abroad almost $40 billion since the end of the fighting and that is a great

John Foster Dulles has long been the Republican Party's leading expert on foreign policy and is now Secretary of State.

deal of money. We are spending $60 billion a year on armament and that, too, is a great deal of money.

But, today, a revolutionary spirit grips over half of the human race. There are passions that cannot be allayed by oil royalties or suppressed by foreign guns.

It would seem that the non-material forces are principally serving the opposition.

My *third* proposition is this: There is a moral or natural law not made by man which determines right and wrong and conformity with this law is in the long run indispensable to human welfare.

Our nation was founded by the men who believed that there was a Divine Creator who endowed men with unalienable rights. They believed, as George Washington put it in his Farewell Address, that religion and morality are the great pillars of human happiness and that morality cannot prevail in exclusion of religious principles.

Our Federal and State Constitutions, our laws and practices reflect the belief that there is a Being superior to ourselves who has established His own laws which can be comprehended by all human beings and that human practices should seek conformity with those laws.

Seeking first the Kingdom of God and His righteousness many material things were added to us. We developed here an area of spiritual, intellectual and material richness, the like of which the world has never seen. What we did caught the imagination of men everywhere and became known everywhere as "the great American experiment." Our free society became a menace to every despot because we showed how to meet the hunger of the people for greater opportunity and for greater dignity. The tide of despotism, which at that time ran high, was rolled back and we ourselves enjoyed security.

That mood seems to have changed. Professor Arnold Toynbee, surely one of the greatest historians of our time, finds that the crisis of our civilization is due to the fact that our practices have been divorced from their Christian context, so that we have "been living on spiritual capital. Practice unsupported by belief is a wasting asset, as we have suddenly discovered, to our dismay, in this generation."

So, on my third proposition, while Soviet communism wholly fails to invoke moral principle, we ourselves are not doing much better.

There comes a time in the life of every great people when their work of creation ends. They lose their sense of purpose and of mission in the world, seeking only to conserve what they have. Material things begin to seem more important than spiritual things and security seems more a matter of military defense than of a spiritual offense.

Surely that hour has not struck for us. We have, to be sure, become rich and, in worldly terms, we are reckoned among the great. Our economic productivity is 3 or 4 times that of Soviet Russia. Our deficit is in the non-material things. We should, however, be able easily to make good that deficit. We are not an old and decaying nation. We are still young in terms of national life expectancy. We are still imaginative and creative and our people are still imbued with religious faith. There is no reason whatsoever why we should stand frightened and on the defensive in the face of Soviet communism. On any impartial appraisal of our relative capabilities, it should be the despots, not we, who do the trembling.

The Black Silence of Fear

By William O. Douglas

(Excerpted from an article in The New York Times Magazine, January 13, 1952. Used with permission of The New York Times and the author.)

There is an ominous trend in this nation. We are developing tolerance only for the orthodox point of view on world affairs, intolerance for new or different approaches. Orthodoxy normally has stood in the path of change. Orthodoxy was always the stronghold of the status quo, the enemy of new ideas—at least new ideas that were disturbing. He who was wedded to the orthodox view was isolated from the challenge of new facts.

The democratic way of life rejects standardized thought. It rejects orthodoxy. It wants the fullest and freest discussion, within peaceful limits, of all public issues. It encourages constant search for truth at the periphery of knowledge.

We as a people have probably never lived up to that standard in any of our communities. But it has been an ideal toward which most of our communities have strived. We have over the years swung from tolerance to intolerance and back again There have been eras of intolerance when the views of minorities have been suppressed. But there probably has not been a period of greater intolerance than we witness today.

Fear has driven more and more men and women in all walks of life either to silence or to the folds of the orthodox. Fear has mounted—fear of losing one's job, fear of being investigated, fear of being pilloried. This fear has stereotyped our thinking, narrowed the range of free public discussion, and driven many thoughtful people to despair. This fear has even entered universities, great citadels of our spiritual strength, and corrupted them. We have the spectacle of university officials lending themselves to one of the worst witch hunts we have seen since early days.

William O. Douglas is an Associate Justice of the United States Supreme Court.

This fear has affected the youngster. Youth has played a very important role in our national affairs. It has usually been the oncoming generation—full of enthusiasm, full of idealism, full of energy— that has challenged its elders and the status quo. It is from this young group that the country has received much of its moral power. They have always been prone to question the stewardship of their fathers, to doubt the wisdom of traditional practices, to explode cliches, to quarrel with the management of public affairs.

Youth—like the opposition party in a parliamentary system— has served a powerful role. It has cast doubt on our policies, challenged our inarticulate major premises, put the light on our prejudices, and exposed our inconsistencies. Youth has made each generation indulge in self-examination.

But a great change has taken place. Youth is still rebellious; but it is largely holding its tongue. There is a fear of being labeled a "subversive" if one departs from the orthdox party line. That charge—if leveled against a young man or woman— may have profound effects. It may ruin a youngster's business or professional career. No one wants a Communist in his organization nor anyone who is suspect.

And so the lips of the younger generation have become more and more sealed. Repression of ideas has taken the place of debate. There may not be a swelling crowd of converts to the orthodox, military viewpoint. But the voice of the opposition is more and more stilled; and youth, the mainstay in the early days of the revolt against orthodoxy, is largely immobilized.

This pattern of orthodoxy that is shaping our thinking has dangerous implications. No one man, no one group can have the answer to the many perplexing problems that today confront the management of world affairs. The scene is a troubled and complicated one. The problems require the pooling of many ideas, the exposure of different points of view, the hammering out in public discussions of the pros and cons of this policy or that.

The great danger of this period is not inflation, nor the national debt, nor atomic warfare. The great, the critical

danger is that we will so limit or narrow the range of permissible discussion and permissible thought that we will become
victims of the orthodox school. If we do, we will lose flexibility.
We will lose the capacity for expert management. We will
then become wedded to a few techniques, to a few devices.
They will define our policy and at the same time limit our
ability to alter or modify it. Once we narrow the range of
thought or discussion, we will surrender a great deal of our
power. We will become like the man on the toboggan who can
ride it but can neither steer it nor stop it.

The mind of man must always be free. The strong society is
one that sanctions and encourages freedom of thought and
expression. When there is that freedom, a nation has resiliency
and adaptability. When freedom of expression is supreme, a
nation will keep its balance and stability.

Our real power is our spiritual strength, and that spiritual
strength stems from our civil liberties. If we are true to our
traditions, if we are tolerant of a whole market place of ideas,
we will always be strong. Our weakness grows when we become
intolerant of opposing ideas, depart from our standards of
civil liberties, and borrow the policeman's philosophy from the
enemy we detest.

That has been the direction of our drift. It is dangerous to
the morale of our people; it is destructive of the influence and
prestige of our country, of our resiliency, much of our inventive
genius. The demands of orthodoxy already have begun to sap
our strength—and to deprive us of power. One sees it from
far-off Asia. From Asia one sees an America that is losing its
humanity, its idealism, and its Christian character. From Asia
one sees an America that is strong and rich and powerful, and
yet crippled and ineffective because of its limited vision.

When we view this problem full face we are following the
American tradition. The times demand a renaissance of freedom of thought and freedom of expression, a renaissance that
will end the orthodoxy that threatens to devitalize us.

Fear Gnaws Away at Freedom

By Marquis Childs

*(Reprinted from the Nashville Tennessean, November 15, 1951.
Used with permission of the author.)*

Anyone traveling through the country with even half an
eye for what is happening in America today must be struck
with one phenomenon in particular. That is the cloud of fear
and suspicion generated around the American educational
system.

The obvious symptoms are the loyalty oaths applied to
academic faculties by suspicious boards of trustees. Such an
oath has had far-reaching repercussions at the University of
California, with some prominent and highly reputable members
of the faculty resigning in preference to signing the oath. Gov.
Earl Warren and President Robert Sproul of the university have
stood out against the oath and it seems likely to be permanently
withdrawn.

At the University of Oklahoma a loyalty oath more broadly
phrased is said, in effect, to exclude any but native-born Americans from teaching. Here, too faculty members resigned and
particularly several with outstanding reputations who were
invited to other institutions.

But these are only the most obvious manifestations. The
repressive influence extends down to the secondary school
system, with community suspicion directed at teachers, often,
it would seem, because of the very fact that they are teachers.

Sometimes this takes the form, as in Pasadena, California, of
an attack on progressive methods, with the pressure behind it
not too thinly concealed of forces seeking to cut the cost of
education. The link with "communism" is readily made for
those who fear anything new and untried.

The reason for this fear and suspicion are not hard to find.

Marquis Childs is the author of a nationally syndicated column, "Washington
Calling."

With the development of the intercontinental bombers, atomic fission and the jet engine, the United States is open to the perils of a deadly attack. This has been a discovery deeply upsetting to many who have come of age in the belief that we were secure and isolated behind the ocean barriers.

This alteration in the geography of our world has in itself, had profoundly disturbing effect. In addition, there is the realization of the intent of the Communist conspiracy to dominate or take over everywhere by force or treachery. And related to that is the knowledge that a few Americans—a very few—betrayed their country to become part of this conspiracy.

Demagogues have played on resulting fears for their own ends. They have exaggerated and distorted the threat of communism from within until it sometimes seems that a great, proud, productive nation lives in fear of its own shadow. This basic fear has been turned against the teachers, as the timid and the fearful and the demogogic long ago turned against the philosopher, Socrates, in ancient Athens.

Few have stopped to think about the harm this does. They assume that while it may do an injustice to some in the teaching profession, it will do little damage even though it produces nothing in the way of positive good.

Actually, it strikes at the right of free inquiry, and that right is at the base of not merely intellectual freedom but the whole structure of scientific development. Some individuals and even some groups seem to believe that you can put the right of inquiry in blinders and yet go on with the kind of high scientific achievements this country has known. That is a dangerous fallacy.

Some evidence exists to show that German scientists, after the whole structure of Germany's intellectual life was shattered by nazism, had neither the will nor the capacity to pursue research. They were outdistanced in the race to discover atomic fission while exiles who had fled from Germany contributed to American progress.

In Russia history is what Stalin says it is. Science is what Stalin decrees it to be. That is the inevitable end of suppression. . . .

Charges of Freedom Curbs Rising *

By Benjamin Fine

*(Condensed from the New York Times, May 29 and 30, 1949.
Used with permission of the author.)*

Many leading American educators are concerned at the threat
to academic freedom caused by the dismissal of college teachers
because of their political activities. However, they are virtually
unanimous in upholding the ouster of Communist party members from their faculties.

Representative college and university presidents questioned
in a survey believe that there are limits beyond which academic
freedom should not extend. Any teaching of subversive doctrines, it is generally held, cannot be permitted to use the
cloak of academic freedom. A man who belongs to the Communist party disqualifies himself from the teaching profession,
many educators assert.

The dismissal of communist teachers will not impair our
traditional principles of academic freedom, leading college and
university heads maintain. The use of the protection of academic freedom by those who are opposed to the American form
of government is dishonest and hypocritical, many contend.

It is necessary, although it may be more difficult, to maintain
the principles of academic freedom during the present "cold
war," according to the educators. Unless the pattern of free
inquiry and expression is continued the entire concept of
democratic education in this country may collapse, they warn.

Typical of the comments is that made by Dr. Edmund E.
Day, president of Cornell University. Although academic free-

---

Benjamin Fine is education editor of the New York Times.

* Institutions of higher learning are generally discussed in this section because,
in the opinion of the editors, they offer clear illustrations of a phenomenon
threatening all schools. The fact that elementary schools have precisely the
same problem is, we believe, amply shown in the following chapter of this
book.

dom has been under attack during recent months it has not been seriously impaired, Dr. Day said. The elimination of avowed members of the Communist party from our educational institutions is fully warranted and does not weaken academic freedom, he declared.

"The faculty of any college or university should be made up of free, honest, competent, inquiring minds, seeking to find and disseminate the truth," Dr. Day held. "The mind of a member of the Communist party is enslaved to the party line. It cannot possibly claim to be either free or honest. It is manifestly disqualified for membership in a faculty of higher learning in a free and freedom-loving society such as ours.

"But in undertaking to eliminate these traitors to the American academic tradition we must be careful not to sacrifice free and inquiring minds that are honestly engaged in the pursuit of truth, however disturbing this truth may appear to be. The untrammelled pursuit of truth, wherever it may take us, is an indispensable part of any long-range defense of freedom."

Many educators agree with Dr. Clarence R. Decker, president of the University of Kansas City, that the ouster of Communists will not impair academic freedom but "the ouster of left-wing or liberal teachers would." Similarly, Dr. Stewart H. Smith, president of Marshall College, Huntington, W. Va., said that his faculty showed little concern over the ouster of Communists, except that "there was some concern that a program of ouster tactics might make teachers timid in expresing their beliefs."

Taking an opposite view, Chancellor Robert M. Hutchins of the University of Chicago declared that Communist or "left-wing" activities of teachers might or might not influence their qualifications as teachers. This is a matter for their fellow members of the faculty to determine, as a matter of their competence, Chancellor Hutchins said.

"Disqualification of teachers for their political beliefs alone, by boards of regents or trustees, is an attack on academic freedom," he stated.

Most of the educators reached in the study expressed opposition to loyalty oaths or to laws that require teachers to stay out of "subversive" groups. Chancellor Hutchins observed that the means by which most organizations are designated as "subversive" groups are generally not subject to legal safeguards or determinations. Since virtually any organization can be termed "subversive" by its opponents, he pointed out, teachers may be subjected to penalty without adequate safeguards or recourse.

Dr. Ludd M. Spivey, president of Florida Southern College, declared that laws requiring teachers to take loyalty oaths tended to endanger academic freedom. He added that "it would be difficult for a group of human beings to make a general and final statement as to what is subversive."

"I think that the passing of laws requring teachers to take loyalty oaths and stay out of subversive groups is quite dangerous and unfair to the teaching profession," Chancellor J. D. Williams of the University of Mississippi declared. "In order to be fair it seems that all citizens should be included, not just teachers. Why not require lawyers, doctors, research workers, industrialists and all other groups to take loyalty oaths and to stay out of subversive groups?"

Dr. Theophilus S. Painter, president of the University of Texas, asserted that the state laws requiring faculty members to take loyalty oaths did not endanger academic freedom.

"The trouble with such legislation," he added, "is the difficulty of defining what groups are subversive and what are not, and this is likely to lead to witch-hunting which will impair academic freedom."

But it has not been solely on the higher levels that the issue of academic freedom is being challenged today. Many states have passed legislation or now have bills before them that would bar Communists or subversive teachers from the classroom. In most instances the teaching profession has lined up against such proposed measures, charging that by singling out one group the measures were of a discriminatory nature.

Three new trends in legislation have become apparent in the last year or two:

370.973

MeL

Dismissal of teachers on grounds of disloyalty is now authorized by Kansas, Massachusetts and Pennsylvania.

Teachers are forbidden to join certain organizations, usually designated as subversive, in Maryland, New Jersey and New York.

Investigations or check-ups of the loyalty of teachers are authorized in Maryland and New York.

Many school leaders see in this trend the forerunner of the type of "witch hunt" that took place after World War I. They fear that the freedom of teachers to express themselves or to be free citizens of the community may be endangered by restrictive legislation. Many who oppose the measures are known anti-Communists; they maintain that the teaching profession is endangered by the action taken against teachers generally.

The National Commission for the Defense of Democracy Through Education, an influential group within the National Education Association, deplored "the constantly increasing legislation appearing in the various states which impugns the integrity of the teaching profession by requiring teachers to take oaths other than those required by all officeholders." In a recent resolution the commission said:

"We view with alarm the danger to the many loyal teachers resulting from the investigations of teachers by committees of the state legislatures. These are reminiscent of the witch-hunting of the 'Twenties. These legislative enactments are loosely drawn, and are frequently used to curb the proper rights of teaching which the democratic processes demand."

At its meeting in Chicago last month the Department of Higher Education of the NEA likewise condemned the legislation that has been passed limiting the teachers' activities and singling them out for special investigation. The academic discipline of a teacher suspected of subversive behavior or "adherence to organizations which might corrupt his integrity," the department said, should be undertaken by the profession itself.

"The Department of Higher Education of the National

Education Association condemns legislative actions which restrict freedom of learning and freedom of lawful association and by implication make the American teacher suspect by virtue of his calling," the educators declared.

Under the Feinberg law, passed by the recent session of the New York State Legislature, the Board of Regents is requested to draw up a list of subversive organizations, membership in which would be cause for dismissal from the teaching position. The board has appointed a special committee to develop the administrative plans necessary for this action. In announcing this action, Chancellor William J. Wallin commented:

"The Board of Regents is fully alive to its responsibilities under the Feinberg act dealing with subversive activities of those in the public school system and is determined in carrying out the law not to tolerate any so-called witch hunt."

The Illinois Legislature is considering a bill that would amend the school code concerning teachers. Any teacher could be dismissed for "advocating in his teaching any doctrine to undermine the form of government of this state or of the United States by force and violence."

Vigorous opposition has been voiced in Illinois to the school measures under consideration. Many top-flight educators in that state have warned that the academic freedom of the teaching profession would be seriously curtailed if the bills were passed.

On the college and university levels, the number of cases involving the question of academic freedom has grown to a record height. The American Association of University Professors serves as the clearing house for the higher education profession. This association, founded thirty-five years ago, has a membership of 35,000. Although it does not have any actual authority to force a college to reinstate a teacher judged to be dismissed unjustly, it does have tremendous influence through its power to put the administration of an institution on the censured list, or "blacklist." Such a listing is considered to be a smirch on the good name of the institution.

The association does not reach its conclusions hastily. It

usually takes three to six months, sometimes longer, to reach a decision. At present the association has under investigation, or is preparing to investigate, the eight colleges that are charged with dismissing faculty members because of political grounds.

Other cases, in the general fields of tenure and academic freedom, are expected to reach the association soon. In some instances the faculty member does not appeal to the association, but puts up a fight himself, or, to avoid publicity, resigns and gets a post on another campus.

Case History of a Failure

By Dan Fowler

(Reprinted from the January 29, 1952, issue of Look Magazine. Used with permission of the Cowles Syndicate.)

Three years ago, the regents of the University of California forced their faculty members to take oaths denying that they were Communists. A group of teachers refused to sign, precipitating a bitter academic conflict which is just now being resolved. The affair furnishes a good case history on fear-inspired oath-taking.

The imposition of the oath had these results:

The university lost directly—by firing, protest resignations or refusal of appointments—more than 100 scholars, including some widely described as "among the illustrious minds of our generation."

The university was forced to drop 55 courses from its curriculum for lack of instructors. Entire departments were crippled.

The university lost an enormous amont of professional prestige. Some 1,200 members of the faculties of 40 other colleges and universities condemned the action. Twenty-three illustrious learned societies condemned the loyalty oath and recommended that their members refuse appointments at California. And from all this wreckage of reputation, morale and intellectual power were dredged exactly two people who could be labeled as Communists. One was a piano player employed in dancing classes. The other was a part-time graduate student working as a teaching asistant.

In short, the action of the regents followed the pattern of hysteria-induced actions—it came dangerously close to destroying the thing it was supposed to save.

Dan Fowler is a member of LOOK's West Coast Bureau.

The avowed purpose of the oath was to root Reds and Red influence out of the California faculty. The suspicion naturally followed that there must be a great many Communists among the faculty to justify such action. This suspicion, vigorously fanned by a few ambitious state politicians, greatly damaged the university's fine reputation.

Within the institution itself, the results were even worse. Members of the faculty were forced to meet secretly, suspect each other, examine each others' records and motives and even censor their own telephone conversations on the campus.

Ironically, the University of California's loyalty oath was never even intended to be the weapon for ousting Reds which it was advertised to be. It was, actually, a device by which the school's administration hoped to preserve its appropriations in lobbying before the legislature.

The University of California loyalty oath dates back to 1948 and to Jack Tenney, then a state assemblyman. Tenney was a politician who rode to office on a program of fear psychology and he introduced a broadside of anti-subversive bills in the legislature. One of these bills would have required a loyalty oath from the faculty of the university, although its disloyalty never had been proved nor even seriously questioned.

Since the legislature controls the school's appropriations, the university's lobbyist became fearful that Tenney's move might effect the amount of revenue. He decided that the wisest course would be to beat Tenney to the punch. President Robert G. Sproul agreed with this reasoning and the university's own loyalty oath—not one adopted by the legislature—was drawn up and on Sproul's recommendation was adopted by the regents on March 25, 1949.

So the oath was born. Not to combat communism, but to protect the university's source of revenue.

One obvious question which became a political issue and a subject of great newspaper comment was this:

"Why should any patriotic American—if he has nothing to hide—object to taking an oath that he is not a Communist?"

It seems a reasonable question to many people, but the

faculty members who objected to it insisted they had reasonable answers.

Originally, when it still masqueraded in a cloak of anti-Communist respectability, the oath was resented by faculty members as a completely unjustified reflection on their loyalty and integrity. One retort colorfully expressed this resentment. "We'll deny we are a subversive group," it ran, "if the regents will take an oath that they are not homosexuals." The meaning is clear: Compel any group, however respectable, to swear that it is *not* something and suspicion is born that it is—where there's smoke there's fire, etc., etc.

Some of the teachers maintained that the oath of allegiance to the constitutions of the United States and the State of California, signed by all faculty members when they entered the university, was oath enough. They argued that any Communist who would take these oaths of allegiance would be the first to sign any additional oath; that instead of trapping any real Communist the new oath would serve only to conceal him better.

Opposition to signing the loyalty oath was led by Edward C. Tolman, former professor of psychology at California, considered one of the country's foremost psychologists. Among his many honors is a doctorate bestowed by Yale University after he refused to sign the oath and left the university.

Another leader of this group was Professor Ernst H. Kantorowicz, a political refugee from Nazi Germany and a distinguished historian, now a member of the Institute for Advanced Study at Princeton.

"This is the way it always begins," he warned a faculty meeting. "The first oath is so gentle you can scarcely notice anything at which to take exception. The next oath is stronger. The first oath demanded of German teachers by Hitler was to keep faith with the Fatherland and to honor the constitution and laws. But the next," he reminded his colleagues, "demanded allegiance to Adolf Hitler."

Among others who refused to sign were Ludwig Edelstein,

professor of Greek, now with the department of philosophy at John Hopkins University, John L. Kelley, now with the department of mathematics at Tulane, Harold W. Lewis, now a research physicist for Bell Laboratories at Princeton, John M. O'Gorman, now with the Department of Commerce, Brewster Rogerson, now visiting English department lecturer at Princeton, Hubert S. Coffey, now lecturer in social relations at Harvard and Gian C. Wick, internationally known expert on atomic energy, now with Carnegie Tech.

Thus, the principle of academic freedom was injected into the controversy. Although it is perhaps not too well understood outside the teaching profession, academic freedom is a precious thing to educators. In its most idealistic meaning, academic freedom is complete freedom to seek and teach the truth. It means to a bio-chemist, for example, freedom to prove that some nostrum is harmful witout fear of reprisals by the manufacturer. To a professor it means freedom to think and talk and write without political pressure or atempts to have him discharged.

Finally, the oath was opposed by those who believed that keeping the university free of Reds was the faculty's job and not the regents'. And the question raised by this opposition, "Who's running this university, the faculty or the regents?" became the real battle line in the three-year fight.

Angered by a challenge to its power, the regents pulled a gun. "Sign or get out," they told the faculty, in effect. And, as happens when a gun is drawn, the regents were forced either to use it or back down.

The showdown came when, in a last attempt to settle the dispute, a committee of alumni was authorized to seek a compromise. In an effort to appease both sides, the alumni group worked out a plan whereby faculty employment contracts would contain a non-Communist statement. Then a clause was added to the contract giving non-signers the right to a hearing before the faculty's Committee on Privilege and Tenure. Although the regents previously had accepted recommendations of this committee, they inserted a clause of their own into the compromise: "It is recognized that final determination of each case is the prerogative of the regents."

Forty-nine faculty members refused to sign the non-Communist contracts and appeared before the Tenure Committee for hearings. Six refused to answer questions and their discharge was recommended—not, of course, because they were Communists but because they refused to live up to the terms of the compromise agreement worked out by the alumni committee.

The other 43 non-signers spent four weeks testifying before the committee and their retention on the faculty was strongly recommended. A transcript of their testimony was delivered to the regents along with this statement:

"It is this committee's deliberate judgment that the refusal of non-signers as a group to accept the contract of employment is not based upon sympathy with communism as an active and destructive force but upon a variety of opinions and feelings which have no relation to revolution or destruction of any kind. They are valuable members of the university faculty."

The committee report also included testimony showing that 26 of the non-signers had previously been screened by Federal Bureau of Investigation agents or Army authorities and cleared for war or defense work.

To clarify its position, the faculty adopted a policy statement opposing the hiring of Communists as teachers. And at a regents' meeting which considered the faculty committee recommendations, the question of communism was once more disposed of. C. J. Haggerty, an anti-oath regent, declared, "There is no longer an impugning of these individuals (the non-signers) as Communists." To which Governor Earl Warren, also an anti-oath regent, added: "We are discharging these people because they are recalcitrant and won't conform." According to those present, the pro-oath regents also agreed that communism was no longer an issue, that the only issue was discipline. Thus, the fight had gone far from its original framework.

The first vote on the committee's recommendations was in favor of re-instating those who testified but refused to sign. But advocates of the oath, led by John F. Neylan, a regent, delayed final action to the next meeting, mustered their forces and fired the non-signers by a two-vote margin.

They had used their gun to prove who was running the university. They were.

At this point the Board of Regents appeared in a rather awkward position. They had committed themselves to a policy of "Let's give 'em a fair trial and then hang 'em." And they had fired—for refusing to sign a statement that they were not Communists—men who had been officially screened and found completely free of taint.

But that wasn't all. When they refused to renew the contracts of those who would not sign the non-Communist statement they violated academic tenure.

Academic tenure is the thing which guarantees academic freedom in a university; in some it is a written guarantee. It is a respected tradition that a faculty member cannot be discharged except for proved incompetence or moral turpitude. This is the professor's guarantee of security, his assurance of the kind of life for which a fine scientist will pass up a high-salaried post in industry for a lifetime of classroom and research.

The violation of this principle at the University of California brought the full weight of America's academic world down on the regents' heads.

Robert Penn Warren, now at Yale, a Pulitzer Prize winner, the author of *All the King's Men,* declared in declining an offer to teach at California. "It seems to me that the regents of the University of California would reduce the academic community, both faculty and administration, to the level of hired hands serving at the whim of a group of men whose acquaintance with intellectual life and its responsibilities is, in some cases at least, of the most rudimentary order."

Rudolph Carnap of the University of Chicago, regarded as one of the three leading philosophers alive today, wrote, "I regard the pre-emptory dismissal of eminent scholars, without regard to their tenure rights and their long distinguished service to the university, as a shocking violation of academic freedom. I wish my refusal to accept any honor from this university to be regarded as a protest against the violation of the principle that scholarship, teaching ability and integrity of character should be the only criteria for judging a man's fitness for an academic position."

Howard Mumford Jones, Harvard English professor and poet, playwright and author of distinction as well as scholar, declined an invitation from California as follows: "Until your board of regents ceases to violate the ordinary principles of academic tenure and honest agreement between parties to a contract I cannot in good conscience accept."

Among other eminent scholars who declined to accept appointments at California were Joseph R. Strayer, Princeton history professor and delegate to the American Council of Learned Societies, and Henry Scheffe, Columbia professor of mathematical statistics and former consultant to the Office of Scientific Research and Development. Others who declined did not make their actions public.

One of these, who asked that his name be withheld, recalled the attacks on intellectuals in Hitler's Germany and Stalin's Russia and concluded: "In all conscience I cannot feel that I would be loyal to our country if I abet the adoption of methods used by ideological systems antipathetic to those of our democracy."

Among the distinguished scholars who signed protests or sent sympathy messages to the faculty were Albert Einstein; J. Robert Oppenheimer, director of the Los Alamos laboratory when it produced the atom bomb; Sumner H. Slichter, Harvard professor known at one of America's most influential industrial economists; Walter Stewart, trustee and chairman of the board of the Rockefeller Foundation and Reinhold Niebuhr, outstanding clergyman and professor of Applied Christianity at Union Theological Seminary.

The 1,200-odd other protests came from such schools as Harvard, Princeton, Stanford, John Hopkins, Boston University, Ohio State and Ohio University, Yale, Dartmouth, Vassar, Bryn Mawr, Sarah Lawrence, Minnesota, Virginia, Utah, Wisconsin, Michigan, Franklin-Marshall and Duke Divinity School.

The 23 learned societies whose members were advised not to accept California appointments included the Modern Language Association, American Historical Association, American Psychological Association, American Mathematical Society, American Anthropological Association, Phi Beta Kappa, American Philological Association, Far Eastern Association and the American Oriental Society.

The regents' vote which crammed the oath down the faculty's throat subsequently was held by a California Appeals Court to be unconstitutional and invalid.

In attempting to justify their action, regents who approved the oath maintained (and still do) that they possessed power to fire any faculty member and were not bound by law to follow any committee's recommendations, even after they implicitly agreed to honor faculty recommendations when they adopted the alumni compromise.

In further defense of their action some pro-oath regents have made much of the fact that an overwhelming majority of faculty members signed the non-Communist contracts. They blame the whole thing on "a dissident minority," the handful of non-signers.

This defense is weak, for in every vote in which the oath issue was clearly drawn the faculty condemned it and the list of those who signed under protest is lengthy. Also, a "sign, stay and fight" movement developed which encouraged many to sign.

What, then, brought about this remarkable vote?

It has been charged that politicians among the regents sought to embarrass Governor Warren, who fought the oath as unlawful and impractical from the beginning. It was blamed on another group "out to get" President Sproul for getting them into the mess and then changing his mind. And it was blamed on a third faction out to get Sproul because he stands for university unity while they favor greater autonomy for the University of California at the Los Angeles campus.

All of these things may have influenced the vote, but the best guess would be that the pro-oath faction, angered and determined to show who was boss, maneuvered themselves into an impossible position and wouldn't admit it.

This case history in oaths is almost ended. The appeals court which declared the oath unconstitutional has ordered reinstatement of the non-signers.

The complexion of the Board of Regents has changed. Term expirations depleted the old majority and Governor Warren has replaced pro-oath regents with men who share his view. The November, 1951, meeting of the board finally rescinded it officially.

In doing so, the new majority did save face for the old guard: It held that a recent legislative act compelling all state employees to take non-Communist oaths had made the special regents' oath unnecessary. Despite this hedge, the new majority seems firmly dedicated to the theory that the faculty is best suited to settle faculty problems.

A certain atmosphere of suspicion and distrust is bound to overhang this great school for a time, but the general feeling now is one of optimism. Academic tenure seems secure again. Sproul, who admitted the oath was a mistake and changed belatedly to the faculty's side, appears to be as strong as ever. After this trial, the university which split the atom, produced six Nobel Prize winners, and has many other notable achievements, seems strong and well. The court which held the regents' oath invalid declared:

"We are keenly aware that, equal to the danger of subversion from within by force and violence, is the danger of subversion from within by the gradual whittling away and the resulting disintegration of the very pillars of our freedom."

Freedom in Education

By James P. Baxter III

*(Condensed from the book, "Civil Liberties Under Attack,"
edited by Clair Wilcox. Copyright 1951 by the University
of Pennsylvania Press and used with permission of the
publisher and author.)*

The recent attack on freedom at the University of California
concerns not only the citizens of that great state but you and
me. It was a former regent of that university, the late Chester
A. Rowell, who described freedom in education as "the central
liberty of civilization without which no other liberty could
long survive or would be worth keeping."

Freedom in education is supremely important because of its
genetic relationship to the other freedoms. Totalitarian rulers
have paid a high tribute to the educational world by moving
rapidly, as soon as they grasp the helm of state, to get their
hands on universities and thereby dam up the spirit of liberty
and its fountainhead. Any manual for dictators would lay stress
on seizing the educational system as promptly as the central
power stations and the arsenals. All three of these targets are
essential in both the defense and the overthrow of freedom.

The tradition of academic freedom is an ancient one. The
teachers of America, like the teachers of France or Great
Britain, are the spiritual descendants of the companies of scholars who, in the late Middle Ages, constituted the great dynamos
of our western culture. These scholars were free to seek truth
and to teach and publish it, because without freedom their
function would be meaningless.

"Truth is great," declared Thomas Jefferson, "and will prevail if left to herself. She is the proper and sufficient antagonist
of error and has nothing to fear from the conflict unless, by
human interposition, disarmed of her natural weapons, free

James P. Baxter III is president of Williams College, Williamstown, Mass.

argument and debate; errors ceasing to be dangerous when it is permitted freely to contradict them."

As the coping stone of his life work, Jefferson founded the University of Virginia, dedicated to the advancement of truth by the free use of the human reason. The first appointment to the Virginia faculty provoked an outburst of criticism in the state legislature, for the eminent scholar, Dr. Thomas Cooper, had been prosecuted under the Sedition Law, and had also been denounced as a Unitarian.

Under pressure from certain religious leaders, Dr. Cooper lost his job. But, as time went on, the battle for Jefferson's ideas of freedom in education continued to gain ground.

During the first World War and directly following it, there developed an hysterical attack on teachers and on history textbooks that reminds one of the jitters from which many Americans have been suffering since 1939. Our entry into war with Germany made us acutely aware of the dangers of hyphenism and suspicious of the loyalty of our German-American citizens. Other scapegoats were also around; the American people were fearful, intolerant, and too often guilty of conduct that now seems shameful and ridiculous in the strongest and most secure of great democracies. A visiting British journalist described the American public mind of 1919 as "hagridden by the specter of Bolshevism . . . Property was in an agony of fear, and the horrid name 'Radical' covered the most innocent departure from conventional thought with a suspicion of desperate purpose. 'America,' as a wit of the time said, 'is a land of liberty—liberty to keep in step."

Suspicion turned against teachers just as it turned against Americans of foreign extraction. In 1921-22, I taught history part-time in a well-known small college in Colorado. My wife came back from a luncheon one day and told me that her hostess had delivered a tirade against teachers in general. "But shouldn't teachers be allowed to say what they think?" Mrs. Baxter inquired.

"Of course they should, my dear," replied the hostess. "They should be encouraged to do so. Then, if they're not thinking properly, they can be discharged."

As a Republican from Maine, I happened to be above suspicion. But I had a first hand opportunity to see what damage a denial of freedom can do to an outstanding small college. There were a number of resignations arising from a controversy after the Trustees had dismissed—without a hearing—the dean of the college who had served with distinction as chairman of the English department for the past twenty five years. These resignations were serious blows to the college but not so serious, perhaps, as the decline in morale of the teachers who remained.

Having seen with my own eyes the damage to a fine Colorado college by an attack on academic freedom, I could better appreciate how much the championship of freedom by Presidents Lowell and Conant did to strengthen the Harvard faculties, help them to attract outstanding scholars, and hold them against competing offers. When I became a college president myself, in 1937, these lessons were fresh in my mind. In my induction address I pointed out that freedom in education had been destroyed in Russia, Italy, and Germany, and had been attacked too often in our own country. The true course seemed to be that indicated by Justice Holmes in the U.S. vs. Schwimmer case: "If there is any principle of the Constitution that more imperatively calls for attachment than any other, it is the principle of free thought—not free thought to those who agree with us but freedom for the thought we hate."

Recent history has colored our thinking about thought control. Because we saw despotism triumph in Italy, Germany, and Russia, many of us have come to fear the power of the big lie more than the power of the big battalions. The advances in the art of lying during my lifetime are as potentially dangerous as the advances in nuclear physics. Recent developments in two widely different research fields, psychology and electrical communications, have stepped up the power of propaganda. The psychologist showed how rumors, innuendoes, half truth and the grossest falsehoods could be used to stampede men like cattle headed for a precipice. At the same time, the physicist and the communications engineer magnified his power a thousand fold.

We made no mistake in fearing the skill of the Nazis and of the Communists in psychological warfare. While I served as deputy director of the Office of Strategic Service in 1941 and 1942, I saw many of the intercepted instructions which were sent from the director of German apparatus within this country to his agents here. I marveled at the skill with which the flaws in our democratic life, anti-Semitism, anti-Catholicism, anti-Negroism, were turned to enemy advantage.

Where we have erred, it seems to me, is in understanding and misjudging the means at our disposal to combat communism. The idea of protecting society against dangerous thoughts by the imposition of teacher's oaths is an unfortunate outcome of the jittery state of public opinion in the past two decades. The oath required of teachers in public and private institutions in Massachusetts runs as follows: "I do solemnly swear (or affirm) that I will support the Constitution of the United States and the Constitution of the Commonwealth of Massachusetts, and that I will faithfully discharge the duties of the position of . . . in . . . according to the best of my ability."

Educators objected to it because they saw no reason why it should be exacted of them as a class but it has done little harm, and presumably very little good, in the years I've watched it operate. Against communists it is less effective than a toy pistol. Indeed, a Communist Party member might get the same zest from false swearing that a Boy Scout gets from his good deed of the day. In such a group of idealistic individualists as a college faculty, however, there is always the risk that someone completely free from any suspicion of radicalism may have conscientious scruples about a required oath, and thereby be lost to the teaching profession.

I have long maintained that there should be no place for Communists on a college or university faculty. My argument turns on the fact that the *minimum* requirements for Communist Party membership disqualify them from belonging to the company of scholars. They join a party of conspirational character which has at times advocated, and perhaps still does advocate, forcible overthrow of the government; which systematically practices falsehood and deceit; and which destroys free speech and other civil rights wherever it triumphs. It seems to me idle to argue that a man might be a Communist on part time or on a basis of limited membership. What that Party demands of its members is, in Lenin's phrase, "the whole of their lives."

I feel strongly that there is no possible place for a Communist on a college or university faculty. But, in my opinion, democracy in the State of Washington was not in peril whether three members of the Communist Party were to be retained on the faculty or dropped.

What was in peril, in the Washington case, was the fundamental assumption on which academic freedom rests: the assumption that the teacher is free to pursue truth, and has taken no commitments which disqualify him from membership in the company of scholars. I happen to believe deeply in the responsibilities of the scholar, which are correlative to his rights of freedom. These rights are guaranteed to him because only with freedom can truth be discovered and disseminated. The scholar must be free from the control of the Communist Party and its ideological line as he is free of pressure from any other source.

A real difficulty that confronts American educators today has nothing to do with membership in the Communist party but with the fact that non-Communist teachers at times say things that irritate prevailing sentiment and provoke a barrage of abusive epithets. The history of attempts to smear American liberals with the red brush is long enough to put us on guard.

The current fashion in smearing is to publish a list of faculty members who have joined one or more subversive organizations listed by the Attorney General of the United States as "subversive" and to pad the list by including organizations to which the faculty member under attack had never belonged, and allegations long since refuted in hearings of legislative bodies. The padding may comprise organizations with as distinguished sponsorship as that of the Committee for Boycott Against Japanese Aggression (1937) which was headed by that great American, Henry L. Stimson. I happened to oppose the embargo, but I can see no reason to conclude that those who supported it were reds.

Most Americans are unaware that when the Attorney General lists an organization as "subversive" or as a "communist front," he makes it clear that he is not affirming that all members are communists, but simply that enough communists have bored from within to place that organization on his list.

Freedom of Speech: In Theory

By Charles A. Siepmann

*(An excerpt from the book, "Radio, Television, and Society,"
published by Oxford University Press, copyright 1950.
Used with permission.)*

"*The essence of our political theory in this country is that a
man's conscience shall be a private, not a public affair, and that
only his deeds and words shall be open to survey, to censure
and to punishmnt. The idea is a decent one, and it works . . .
One need only watch totalitarians at work to see that once
men gain power over other men's minds, that power is never
used sparingly and wisely, but lavishly and brutally. . . . If I
shall have to testify that I am not a communist, tomorrow I
shall have to testify that I am not a Unitarian. And the day
after, that I have never belonged to a dahlia club. It is not a
crime to believe anything at all in America.*"

> —E.B. White, in the New York Herald Tribune,
> December 2, 1947

The Danger of Dogma

Freedom, like democracy, is a word so mutilated by reiterated
mouthing that it threatens to become as shapeless and as devoid
of flavor as a piece of chewed gum. This is due partly to the
general debasement of language in our time, and partly to the
vogue of patenting one's own, private concept of freedom and
foisting it on everybody else. We lend ourselves the more
readily to this fashion for its being characteristic of human
kind.

We are so accustomed to freedom that we are inclined to
take it for granted. And therein lies the danger to both our

Charles A. Siepmann is chairman of the department of communications, New
York University.

own clear perception of its worth and to the survival of freedom itself among us. For as intelligent, reflecting human beings we are not, properly speaking, entitled to any freedom the right to which we have not thought through for ourselves. Nor shall we long retain it, for we shall lose the zest for it. No man is whole or free who lives on borrowed judgments that have not passed the censorship of his own critical appraisal. No belief is secure that the believer accepts as a mere dogma.

The more sacred or heartfelt our belief, the more we must subject it to close and constant scrutiny (to be sure we hold to it with understanding and not 'in the manner of a prejudice') and to the test of challenging opinion (lest we have overlooked in it some fault more patent to another eye.) And of all the freedoms we value, none should be more constantly subjected to review, more steadily laid open to general inspection, than liberty of thought and expression. It is the outstanding merit of a true democracy that in it, as compared with other systems of organized society, the liberty of thought and expression permissible to individuals is, in all significant respects, almost identical with the society's needs for its own healthy growth.

Freedom From

The long struggle for the right to individual free speech has been a struggle for the removal of restraints imposed by men or institutions vested with power. Thus Socrates was condemned by an Athenian court as a blasphemer and a corruptor of youth. Christ called men to another way of life and he was crucified. The freedom he sought, the means of individual man's salvation, involved the rendering to God of loyalties Caesar thought were due only to him. Galileo probed the secrets of the universe and was forced to a recantation of his "heresies." The freedom he sought, which was the freedom of pure science, threatened a powerful, vested interest—the temporal authority of the church. Milton, in the broad interests of "truth's" emergence, protested the censorship of books, but the government of England refused to hear his plea.

The two chief agencies of this kind of restraint have, throughout history, been either an established religion, or a governor or government. The struggle for free speech would never have existed if individuals or groups had not arrogated to themselves the power over others. You cannot stop me from thinking. You *can* stop me from saying what I think and from trying to persuade others to think as I do. The measure of your ability to do so is your power over me. The greater your power, the more you will be tempted to exert it, not merely because the exercise of power is tempting in itself but because its possession constitutes a vested interest. Few men having power are eager or even willing to surrender it. Power, like passion, feeds upon itself. On the other hand the measure of your desire to restrain me is your fear of what I have to say. Fear and power provide the ingredients of restraint.

The Occasion of Restraint

Societies in which the power of the rulers has been greatest have (with the exception of a few enlightened tyrannies) been those in which free speech has been most circumscribed. Absolute power (or near approximations to it) having been the rule throughout most of human history, freedom of speech, in a widely operative sense, is a comparatively modern notion and even with us only a partly realized ideal. Any broad concern about it is historically coincident with concern for what we now regard as the democratic way of life.

If we are candid with ourselves, we come to recognize that fear of free speech is in a sense native and natural to us all. Speech is the instrument of thought and thought is dangerous, subversive—and painful. Its danger is to settled ways of outlook and behavior, to dogma of all kinds, to assumptions and traditions readily accepted but rarely scrutinized. We are prone to illusion and are often reluctant to face facts. "We look before and after and pine for what is not." Thought is dangerous, above all, to our peace of mind, challenging us to use our eyes and to take in what we see.

Thought is subversive, challenging the established order,

inviting experiment, championing new rights and claims. It
drives administrators, preoccupied with stability and the maintenance of a "going concern," to exasperation. Caesar, himself
no mean administrator, recognized it.

> Let me have men about me that are fat.
> Yon Cassius hath a lean and hungry look.
> He thinks too much.

And thought is painful—not only in the excercise of muscles
rarely used, but in its pitiless exposure of the limits of our
knowledge ("The further one travels, the less one knows")
and of the surrounding darkness of our ignorance and our
perplexity.

Free Speech in Democracy

It is only in terms of democratic life that we can sensibly
pursue the question of the proper limits of free speech. There
still will be limits, but that the frontiers will be pushed nearer
the edge of the horizon is inherent in the democratic process.
Why is this so?

The case for free speech in a democracy can be stated in
terms both negative and positive. The democratic mind insists
that no man or group of men can either properly or with
assurance be conceded full and unchallangeable power to decide matters of public or private moment on behalf of others.
It insists, secondly, that where the people rule and where
public policy depends upon popular decisions, people's capacity
to develop mature powers of responsible decision will never be
realized without the fullest exercise of free speech. The boundaries or limits of this market place are defined by the public
interest. Within the market place our right to free speech
is inalienable in that it serves the public interest. Outside it
are permissive rights—rights that as private persons we may
enjoy, but which we must be prepared to cede. Thus here
our private right to free speech is provisional—to be enjoyed
as long as it is judged to be compatible with the collective
interests of society. This principle of the "other man's nose"
holds good. Professor Chafee in his book, *Free Speech in the*

United States, gives an example of the limitation here implied. He tells the story of a man arrested for swinging his arm in a public place and hitting another man on the nose. With some indignation, the man asked the judge if he did not have the right to swing his arm in a free country. "Your right to swing your arm," rejoined the judge, "ends just where the other man's nose begins."

Now let us deal with another and more common objection. Is it our inalienable right—and duty—to entertain *all* ideas? What of subversive ideas that challenge our dearest convictions and seek to bring them into contempt? Are these also to be tolerated? Is a man to be permitted to impugn democracy itself, or should not this be regarded as a deliberate incitement to disloyalty and revolution? One of our greatest jurists, the late Justice Holmes, answered this question in no uncertain terms.

"Every idea is an incitement. It offers itself for beliefs and, if believed, it is acted on unless some other belief outweighs it . . . if in the long run the beliefs expressed in proletariat dictatorship are destined to be accepted by the dominant forces of the community, the only meaning of free speech is that they should be given their chance and have their way."

And yet it was Mr. Justice Holmes who, on another occasion, wrote a decision that appears to contradict or at least modify this principle. During World War I certain persons issued circulars strongly condemning provisions of the Conscription Act. They were arrested and condemned for obstructing the draft. The Supreme Court upheld the ruling of the lower court, and Mr. Justice Holmes wrote the decision:

"The question in every case is whether the words used in such circumstances are of such nature as to create a clear and present danger that they will bring about substantive evils that Congress has a right to prevent. It is a question of proximity and degree. When a nation is at war many things that might be said in time of peace are such a hindrance to its effort that their utterance will not be endured."

There are those who question whether, even in time of

war, a democratic people can wisely suspend the operation of a principle embodying so unique and distinctive a characteristic of its way of life. We face here the age-old question whether discretion is not sometimes the better part of valor—whether it is not better to do that which is expedient rather than what we believe to be right. Politicians playing the "art of the possible," are in this sense discreet. On the other hand, the defenders of what in democratic terms seems to them the only right and proper course invoke the Constitution in this issue against Mr. Justice Holmes. To punish men, they say, for the expression of ideas, however unpopular or dangerous is not only to circumscribe their private liberty but to deprive society itself of a healthy and even necessary challenge to the ideas it entertains and of that exercise of tolerance to which in its own best interests a democracy is committed.

Even if we concede that war involves a necessary suspension of the democratic process (an army is by definition an undemocratic institution, and in modern total war, the nation is in a true sense an army), the extension into peacetime of the precedents and practices of war involves the gravest risks. The mischief, as some believe, of Mr. Holmes' decision is that it has created an unhappy precedent for subsequent peacetime decisions in our courts and has lent itself to an ever more elastic interpretation of what constitutes "clear and present danger." The First Amendment is categoric and inflexible in its command. Mr. Holmes it is held, has made it inconveniently plastic.

One of our difficulties today is that the cold war to which we have become committed prolongs indefinitely the period in which we sanction the application of measures of expediency appropriate (if they are ever such) only in times of extreme emergency. The immediate advantages of this plastic interpretation of straight principle are the more seductive in that it provides scapegoats for minds poisoned and crazed by mutual projections of fear and prejudice. The permanent and perhaps irreparable damage done over a long period in which vital

principles are subordinate to expediency can never be anti-
cipated. But the real nature of the danger may be seen if we
consider how tenuous, at the best of times, is our grasp of
the true principles of democratic living and how readily it
is relaxed when fear or passion masters us. One virtue, perhaps,
of a written constitution is that it codifies principles of action
that under stress and strain we shall be tempted to belie.
The greatness of the institution of Law is that it confines us
to that straight and narrow path that we are too often inclined
to desert.

An Exchange of Correspondence

By Herman H. Kahn and Theodore Brameld

(Reprinted from "Letters To The Editors" columns of the Englewood, New Jersey, Press Journal)

To the Editor:

Dr. Theodore Brameld, who spoke in Englewood last week, denied in his talk that he is a Communist. I am advised that there is nothing whatever in his record to the effect that he is or ever was a Communist. I am further advised Dr. Brameld is regarded as a man of honest convictions who speaks fearlessly. Because his speech, which I discuss in this letter to you, seemed to me to be strongly pro-Communist to the degree at least that he made it quite clear he favors no distinction against Communist schoolteachers or other Communist government employees, I feel some comment is appropriate.

Dr. Brameld's recommendation that the Feinberg Law and the Smith Act be repealed, so that Communists be permitted to teach in public schools, and his further recommendation made in the later question period that Communists be permitted to hold Government positions, seem to me to ignore the realities of the times. It seemed to me he overlooked two well enunciated fundamentals of Marxism and Leninism:

1. Socialism cannot be established by peaceful evolution, but only by violent revolution— by smashing the machinery of Government and replacing it with the dictatorship of the proletariat throughout the world.

2. The establishment of this dictatorship of the proletariat can be accomplished only after the violent and forcible seizure of political power by the proletariat under the vanguard leadership of the Communist party.

Herman H. Kahn is a resident of Englewood, N. J. Theodore Brameld is a professor of educational philosophy, New York University, and author of several books on education.

I listened attentively to Dr. Brameld's talk. I have no re-
collection whatever, that in any part of his speech, did Dr.
Brameld's advocacy of communist teachers extend only to those
unjustly accused of being Communist. He would make no
distinction between the avowed communist and the suspect.
Both should be eligible to teach and to work for the government, he claims.

Dr. Brameld did state the reservation that Communists be
discharged from their positions when they have been caught
in the act of doing something wrong—in other words, locking
the stable after the horse is stolen. I believe his advocacy of
Communist teachers and Government workers overlooks these
facts:

1. The American Communist is subserviently obedient to
party line determined by Kremlin leadership.

2. It is a postulate of Communist adherance to the party
line to promote it without question and with the utmost
diligence.

3. The Communist teacher, true to his Soviet allegiance,
will do everything in his power to indoctrinate the young
impressionable minds of his pupils with the idea that Russia
is right and America is wrong, the objective being to establish
cadres for future Communist platoons. In advancing the Communist line, the Communist, working as a teacher or in any
other line of endeavor, is committed to the Leninist formula
of "zig-zag strategy" and that no lie is too great, no act too
mean, no masquerade too deceitful, and no treachery too
base—the end justifying the means.

4. The Government worker of Communist conviction is no
less dedicated to the service of Russia and not America, and
no betrayal of Government secrets, including top atom projects,
is too treasonable. To him "Mother Russia" must be served.

Presumably, Dr. Brameld's approval of Communist Government workers, as well as teachers, would, to be consistent,
extend to their inclusion at the front lines in Korea, the
American truce team at Panmunjom, the atomic energy plants
at Los Alamos, etc., etc.

Brameld referred to George Orwell's book "1984" as a commentary on what is happening in America, warning that Orwell's character, Big Brother, typifies the threat that hangs over "America, England, France, Norway." He did not mention Russia in this respect, a conspicuous omission. He made no mention of George Orwell's having written the book as a disillusioned ex-Communist. He did not point out that Orwell's thesis on "Thought Control" is a warning against Communism itself, and that the character, Big Brother, is the counterpart of dictator Joseph Stalin. This is the very kind of upsidedown talking about which Orwell warned, whereby war is peace, freedom is slavery, ignorance is strength, Communists are liberals, warnings of Russia are warnings of America, etc., and whereby popular words like democracy, peace, freedom, are used by Communists, fellow-travelers and unwitting dupes to confuse and smear those who oppose them.

With reference to the Orwell book, Brameld did not point out that this British novelist, who fought in the Spanish Civil War, saw firsthand what the Communists were up to and had since then devoted all his talents to warning the world of the fate which awaits it if it confuses liberalism with regimentation. In short, Brameld apparently overlooks the fact that this great novel is a frightening satire about the cruel fate of man in a regimented left-wing police state which controls his mind and soul, the very objective of the Communist and of the Communist teacher, who is perfectly willing to rewrite and reorient the perspective of all books—history and otherwise—to make them suit the party line.

Dr. Brameld's statement that we are not at war with Communism "per se," and we are still trying to negotiate a peace through the U.N., made during the question period, was an incredible utterance in the light of the current world situation. If any evidence is needed to the contrary of Dr. Brameld's remark that we are not at war with communism "per se," there are innumerable statements by General MacArthur, General Eisenhower, President Truman, Winston Churchill, and other figures of the great Free World to the effect that Communism expressed in Communist aggression is indeed the enemy faced by the civilized free nations of the globe. Questioned on the point, Dr. Brameld even refused to regard Korea and more than 100,000 American casualties as evidence that a war against Communism "per se" exists.

Dr. Brameld disparaged the crusade against Communism in America, wherein he indicated the Communists are only a small, ineffectual minority, growing weaker every day. This I believe disregards he fact there is a greater number of Communists in America today than in Russia at the time of the Red Revolution, that the Communists in America constitute a hard core of Quislings, poised and willing to commit sabotage in the event of war (a fact eloquently argued and dramatically sustained by the Government in its case against the eleven Communists in the Medina trial), and further ignores that, in the words of Joseph Stalin himself, "A thousand men may be needed to build a bridge; only one to destroy it."

Dr. Brameld spoke with conviction. My letter is written with no less conviction in the belief his views require some comment.

Very truly yours,
Herman H. Kahn.

To the Editor:

May I have the privilege of replying to Mr. Herman H. Kahn's letter in your newspaper, in which he raises some thoughtful questions concerning my addresss at the Community Center on April 23, when I discussed "Academic Freedom in Crisis."

Mr. Kahn considers my views "pro-Communist" because I believe it important to defend the civil liberties of Communists. In precisely the same way, then, I am "pro-Republican" because I equally believe in defending the civil liberties of Republicans. Likewise of Democrats, Dixiecrats, and members of the Englewood Anti-Communist League. The question of whether I agree or disagree with any or all of these people is totally irrelevant to the central thesis I discussed in my address— namely, that a democracy is a society governed by two interdependent principles: the right of the majority to establish policy, and the right of the minority, freely to criticize that policy. As a citizen who takes the First Amendment to the United States Constitution seriously, I would support the right of Mr. Kahn to express disagreement with the policy of the majority, just as I would support the right of the Communist to do so. In this fundamental sense, therefore, I am "pro-Communist" no more and no less than Justices Douglas and Black of the Supreme Court in dissenting from the majority opinion on the Smith Act and the Feinberg Law. I respectfully refer Mr. Kahn to their dissents as an accurate and eloquent expression of my own convictions.

Why do I hold with them that the privilege of criticism and dissent, even by persons or groups whose views may be loathsome to us, must be protected? Because of a faith that Justice Holmes was right when he wrote in another famous dissent that "the ultimate good desired is better reached by free trade in ideas—that the best test of truth is the power of the thought to get itself accepted in the competition of the market." Because of a deep faith, also, in the implied answer to John Milton's famous question: "Who ever knew Truth put to the worse in a free and open encounter?"

The Communist becomes a menace when he is driven underground, when he can argue that the democratic principle of dissent and criticism has become a sham. In a "free and open encounter," he can be exposed—his philosophy and methods can be shown up as false. This is why I want to see Communism, along with every other important issue, studied carefully in the public school. Only when young citizens understand what it is they are against, as well as what they are for, can they hope to grow into responsible rulers of a democratic order.

Mr. Kahn is fearful that Communist teacher or government worker will inevitably promote the cause of the Soviet Union or otherwise take ulterior advantage of his position. I readily admit this possibility. Thousands of persons, however, have been called Communists who are quite as hostile to the Soviet Union as Mr. Kahn himself. The real Communist, moreover, will seldom if ever admit his affiliation. The much safer and wiser course, therefore, is to avoid condemnation on the basis of labels and verbal accusations; rather, the way to determine the fitness of a person for any responsible position whatever is by the test of his strictly professional training and conduct as evaluated on the job by his professional associates. If it should then be proved that he engages in unprofessional behavior—for example, if as a teacher he is found to indoctrinate his students—he should be dimissed for that behavior. By exactly the same public process, so should any other public school teacher be dismissed for unprofessional behavior: a Republican teacher who indoctrinates Republicanism; a Catholic teacher who indoctrinates Catholicism; a Jewish teacher who indoctrinates Judaism. This public process is entirely workable; a good public school should be constantly alert to every phase of its program, and especially to what goes on in every classroom. To increase such continuous alertness, teachers should work more often in co-operative groups rather than in isolation, but this procedure, too, is by no means impracticable for schools willing to try needed new methods of co-operative learning.

Why is this a much safer and wiser course of action? Because, in the first place, it protects the teacher's right to hold any political beliefs that other citizens are entitled to hold—in short, to guarantee him his full citizenship. Because, in the second place, the discovery of the real Communist by the process of ferreting out his beliefs alone becomes almost impossible as well as dangerous. As I sought to show in my address, America is in greater danger of regressing to a state of political primitiveness. In such a state, mythical thinking replaces rational thinking. It produces all sorts of emotional and illogical judgments through such devices as the "loose link" by which we associate two persons together simply because they happen to hold some belief in common. Thus, a teacher may believe in public control of the Missouri River in order to prevent floods; the Communist also believes in such public control; by "loose link" thinking, that teacher may then be called a Communist. One or two more "loose links" of this sort (belief in racial equality, for example) may then lead a school board under pressure to dismiss the teacher, although in fact he is no more a Communist than thousands of other citizens who believe in public control of rivers or in racial equality. We begin by hunting down the Communist; we end by hunting down every teacher with a liberal or controversial thought. Fear of "guilt by association" is already chronic in American education; as it grows it dries up the spring of democracy itself—a society that can thrive only by the free and uncoerced examination of every issue important to our time.

Actually, the few real Communists in education are so infinitesimal in number as to constitute no genuine threat to American schools. It is the mythical thinker that is by far the greater threat. He uses the label "Communist" as a way to frighten teachers, to confuse parents, to censor textbooks. And he does all this by the device of linking beliefs together in a chain of loose associations that encircles and gradually strangles freedom of thought until, finally, conformity alone is left.

And conformity, uncriticized and all-powerful, is another name for totalitarianism, whether it be called "One hundred per cent Americanism" or Stalinism. Mr. Kahn is right in reminding us that George Orwell's famous novel, "1984," paints a dreadful picture of the consequences of a ruthless communist dictatorship at least as much as of a fascist one. If I did not make this point sufficiently explicit in my lecture, it was because the name of that dictatorship, by the time it arrives, is no longer significant. Where Mr. Kahn and I disagree, then, is not in our horror of the grim warning portrayed in "1984." It is in the strategy by which we may avoid that horror. Mr. Kahn would avoid it by yielding to fear, by lack of confidence in the strength of democracy to stand firm before its critics. I would avoid it by scrupulously protecting the democratic process itself. Much as I, too, disapprove of the philosophy and program of the Communist Party, my strategy would be to let Communists or any other legally authorized party speak their piece, and then, with Justice Holmes, to expose their fallacies and weaknesses in "the competition of the market." To do otherwise is to do exactly what the Stalinist dictatorship does when it outlaws and liquidates the dissenter—when therefore it permits only a monotonous and monstrous conformity with its own "infallible" beliefs. As a loyal citizen of a democracy, and a dedicated believer in the power of public education to teach the public how to rule itself, I submit that "the best revenge on your enemy is not to be like him."

Sincerely yours,

Theodore Brameld

III.

THE ATTACKS ON MODERN EDUCATION

"It is important to keep in the back of one's mind the historical and contemporary contexts of the critical blasts and counterblasts; the flowering of the philosophy and practice known as Progressive education; the phenomenal increase of the secondary-school and college enrollments; the encouragement of lay interest in educational affairs; the social economic and political changes in American life, particularly after the two wars; the uncertainty of the international situation; the inborn tendency toward holding down expenses, including tax rates; the distrust and suspicion of the new, strange, and untried; and the weakened state of education as a result of the still unresolved crisis in personnel, materiel, and plant."
   —William W. Brickman in School and Society

The National Commission for the Defense of Democracy Through Education was organized by the National Education Association in 1941. Its purposes: to give the public more understanding of education for all people; to defend the cause of education against unjust attack and investigate charges that involve teachers, schools, educational methods, and procedures; and to work for educational conditions essential for the preservation of democracy.

The Defense Commission was barely nine years old when, on July 3, 1950, its chairman, Harold Benjamin, rose before an assembly of the National Educational Association meeting in St. Louis, Missouri. For most of the delegates—even those who had themselves suffered sporadic school and personal attacks—Dean Benjamin's report was news. His speech made use of military terminology. The dean had spent some years in the army; he had learned to recognize an enemy when he saw one.

Report on the Enemy

By Harold Benjamin

(Reprinted from Defense Bulletin Number 35, published by the National Commission for the Defense of Democracy Through Education.)

In warfare the main job of reconnaissance troop is to get information of the enemy, to tell who he is, to discover where he is, to learn as much about his weapons and his tactics as possible, to find out where he is weak and where he is strong, and to pass that information quickly and accurately to the fighting outfit the troop represents—the combat team—which in turn passes it on to the division, the corps, and the army.

Your Defense Commission is a kind of educational reconnaissance troop, and it has a combat-intelligence report to give you tonight.

It is the estimate of the Commission that a general attack on public education in the United States is now being organized. The enemy is trying our line with a number of local, probing raids, attempting to find out where we are weak or strong, testing his methods of attack, recruiting and training his forces, building up his stock piles, filling his war chest, and organizing his propaganda units.

He has already initiated skirmishes in various places throughout the country. He has elected a school-board member here pledged to return public education to a Spartan regime of confinement to the 3-R's and low taxes. He has whipped up pseudo-popular revolts there against teachers, administrators, and school programs on the grounds that they are indoctrinating the children in communism, socialism, or at least mention-

Harold Benjamin, formerly dean at the University of Maryland, is now associated with the George Peabody College for Teachers, Nashville, Tenn.

ing democracy, and they are helping to increase taxes. He has defeated a school financing project over yonder because it is designed to make children Godless and raise taxes. He is prepared to whip up indignation at a moment's notice on all sorts of topics from the deleterious effects of John Dewey's philosophy on the incidence of juvenile delinquency to the relationship between construction activities in the fifth grade and a lack of respect for the National Colors—but these indignations are largely synthetic and relatively feeble, requiring careful and intensive force-feeding to sustain life—compared with the white-hot indignation about school taxes.

Under the steam of that indignation about spending money for a modern school program, garnished with a variety of pretty, little, cultivated indignations about William H. Kilpatrick's sinister influence and the spread of atheism nurtured by fads and frills, the enemy has lately gone into some full-scale battles, as in Denver, Minneapolis, Upper Arlington, Ohio, and a number of other communities, large and small. In at least one part of the country, the Los Angeles-Pasadena-Glendale area in California, he has apparently started an all-out campaign which he is supporting with every weapon in his arsenal.

Who is this enemy?

He comes under many disguises. He has a lot of aliases, carefully designed to make a layman confuse them with such names as *National Education Association* and *American Council on Education*. Sometimes he dresses in the fancy uniforms of that super-patriotism of which truly patriotic groups have long since learned to beware. I am thinking of the American Legion's great service to our country in the Department of Illinois' report, "Subversive Activities of Hate Groups." Sometimes this enemy drapes himself in the mantle of religious orthodoxy, breathing pious expressions of opposition to sin along with his lies about public education.

This is the same enemy who fought the establishment of common tax-supported, secular, public schools in the country 100 and more years ago. He fought the development of free secondary education. He opposed bitterly and uncompromisingly every real improvement in American public education for three generations.

Who is he?

First of all, he is a taxpayer, but a taxpayer of unusual type in this country, I am proud to say. He is the kind of relatively unusual taxpayer who, when offered a choice between low taxes and an improvement of education for his people's children, will never hesitate. He will step right over on the side of low taxes. Often his motive is not of personal penuriousness. He may be a free spender. He will, without a quiver, plank down more cash for hard liquor in a year than he pays for his share of the elementary education of his community. He may and sometimes does give more money to fight public education in one campaign than support of a vastly improved school system would cost him for five years. He is just operating on principle. He is opposed to spending money for public education. If you left the decision up to him, he would spend no money on public education.

There is something behind that particular principle. It was well expressed a few weeks ago in Washington, D. C., by an official lobbyist of the National Association of Real Estate Boards, an executive vice president of that organization, Herbert V. Nelson.

"I do not believe in democracy," Mr. Nelson wrote in a letter read at a Congressional hearing on April 19, 1950, and quoted by the United Press on that date. "I think it stinks. I believe in a republic operated by the elected representatives who are permitted to do the job, as the board of directors should." In a further statement, he added that only "direct taxpayers" should be allowed to vote. Women, he said, should not be permitted to vote at all. "Ever since they started, our public affairs have been in a worse mess than ever," he said.

Mr. Nelson is to be complimented on speaking his views forthrightly. A number of the people who agree with him lack the guts to speak their minds. They talk instead about how "progressive education" is ruining the country. And so I admire

Mr. Nelson and to show my affection for him I will give him and those in his camp some valuable information.

The teachers of the United States are in a different camp. They believe in democracy. They propose to teach democracy, to help with all their might to make democracy work, and when necessary—as they have done in the past—to draw and fight for democracy. Our fellow Americans in overwhelming force are in the same camp and are pledged to the same missions.

I love Mr. Nelson and people like him, and I say to them earnestly, "Please don't get in the way of this combat team."

The enemy in this campaign against the public schools is also sometimes one, not so admirable as Mr. Nelson, who is often more dangerous because he is a cool and calculating military adenturer. He fishes in troubled waters for the laudable purpose of making a living. He sells his services and his convictions where they will do him the most good.

In the recent Pasadena case, for example, anti-tax groups, heated "patriots," and opponents of Columbia University's "red" pragmatism rallied behind a general, or chief-of-staff, named Allen A. Zoll. Mr. Zoll's preparation for this high post has been impressive. It has been documented in Pasadena *Star-News* for June 20, 1950, by M. M. Morrison. Zoll's service included recruit training with such outfits as the Christian Front of anti-Jewish memory and that fellowship of fascists and subversives (I speak by the Attorney-General's book here), called *American Patriots*. Zoll also had the advantages of early action under such captains as Gerald L. K. Smith, Jew-baiter; Elizabeth Dilling, indicted three times for sedition, and the ineffable Coughlin of Little Flower fame. Then he branched out as a small-unit commander, leading a fight against the appointment of Mr. Justice Frankfurter lest the Supreme Court be polluted by un-Christian opinions. His greatest success to date, however, is his attack on the major Protestant denominations of the United States in his pamphlet, "How Red is the Federal Council of Churches?"

As might be expected, of course, Mr. Zoll ran into a few

difficulties in all these adventures. He was indicted in 1939 on a charge of attempting to extort $7500 from a radio station for calling off a Christian Front picket line, but he was not convicted, so that was not too bad. He was kept out of the Military Training Camps Associated by Army Military Intelligence, perhaps jealous of him. (New York World-Telegram, August 25, 1948).

And then he turned to his present campaign. The schools do not teach the fundamentals. The schools usurp the prerogatives of the Christian home. The schools indoctrinate children in un-American ways of life. Evidence is not bothered with. The Hitler technique of repetition is relied upon. Studies of the achievements of children, facts concerning the results of a modern school program—these are nothing to worry about. The plan to follow is to quote the Constitution, Christian Principles, and say the schools are terrible. It is not even necessary to say that they cost money. The chief-of-staff's followers never forget that. In Pasadena, a few weeks ago, they said they were shocked to learn of Mr. Zoll's past connections but that his pamphlet on "Progressive Education Increases Delinquency" was good stuff, and then they voted overwhelmingly against a badly needed increase in the levy for elementary education.

To the Zolls and their National Councils for American Education, to the tax-haters and the school development councils and school protective leagues which they have set up in many places throughout the country, we need to pay close attention. We need to get more information about them and their tactics, and we need to pass that information back to our great combat team. That team is our professional group only in part. Its heavy weapons, its armored columns are manned by people, by the great civic associations, by the veteran's groups, by the women's organizations, by the trade assemblies, by the congresses of parents and teachers, and by all the other powerful behavior-changing and opinion-directing agencies of this democracy.

What we too often call our school public relations but probably should more often regard as a hard core of our

professional duties—the learning with and for our people—
must be carried to a new level in the American public schools.
We must learn, better than we now commonly know and
practice, the science and art of speaking to our people on their
greatest job and of hearing our people speak to us on the
same topic.

The enemy in this campaign that seems to be impending is
stronger than he looks. If we get our combat team together,
however, get the information it needs for its decisions swiftly
and accurately before it, even a stronger enemy than this one
would make hardly more than a ripple in the smoothness of
our advance.

> *Dean Benjamin mentioned Pasadena and a
> troublesome situation. Even while he spoke, the
> Pasadena affair was coming to a head.*

> *Willard Goslin left Minneapolis in the spring of
> 1948 to become superintendent of schools in Pasa-
> dena, California. Dr. Goslin was cordially received
> by the city. He was nationally known; he had just
> been elected president of the American Association
> of School Administrators; in the words of Time
> Magazine, he was "one of America's ablest educa-
> tors."*

> *Two and a half years later Dr. Goslin was forced
> to resign. The events leading to his resignation had
> national significance and were a cause for national
> alarm. Dr. Goslin alluded to them in his farewell
> speech:*

"Each of us feels that our freedom is in jeopardy. We are threatened from without. I think we are threatened even more from
within. I know of no better way to wreck everything we think is
good in America than to begin to destroy ourselves, one by one,

institution by institution, community by community, throughout the land."

> *What were these alarming events? David Hulburd, a former Time staff writer, was stirred by them to write the book, "This Happened in Pasadena." Reviews of the book by John Hersey and James Conant tell some of the story.*

The Friends of Public Education Rallied – Too Late

By John Hersey

What happened in Pasadena could happen in any community in the United States. People everywhere who consider public school education the cornerstone of our democracy should know this story, so that they can prevent tragedies like Pasadena's from recurring in other places.

What happened in Pasadena, to tell the beginning and ending of the story, was this:

In 1948, the Pasadena Board of Education, looking for a new superintendent of schools who would be able to give the city a substantial, forward-looking community, went right to the top in American public education and selected the president of the American Association of School Administrators, Willard Goslin, then superintendent of schools in Minneapolis. After Goslin paid an exploratory visit to Pasadena, the chairman of the board wrote him a letter officially inviting him to take the superintendency—a letter which showed that the Pasadena board knew how lucky the city would be to make such a catch: "I called a number of people with whom you had talked . . . and several others called me. I asked each one how he or she felt the community would react to paying quite a high salary to the new superintendent of schools. Every one, without a single exception, said that if the offer was to be made to you, he would approve it wholeheartedly. There is no doubt you made a tremendous impression . . . P.S. Both mountain and ocean fishing should be good in California next August."

John Hersey is author of "A Bell For Adano," "The Wall," and other books and is a member of the Westport, Connecticut, Board of Education.

In 1950, the same board, evidently not wishing to confront Willard Goslin face-to-face, took advantage of his absence in the East, where he was attending some educational conferences, to send him a long telegram, which read in part: "We are interested mainly, as you know, in promoting and continuing a fine educational system in Pasadena. We are of the opinion that the school system is suffering and will continue to suffer because of the lack of harmony within the system itself, as well as in the community as a whole. . . . In our opinion, the main controversy in Pasadena settles itself around you as an individual and therefore it becomes our very sad duty to suggest . . . that you resign."

The events which led in two short years from that warm invitation to that curt suggestion are the substance of this book. The events are significant, not because a single educator was cast aside, but because of the way he was ousted. This was a public, not a private, tragedy. The tragedy lay in the fact that the friends of education in Pasadena, who surely could have averted the whole affair, did not organize themselves until it was too late—until after Goslin had been fired. Since the friends of the schools were not organized, a minority group, using half-truthful slogans and catchwords of ignorance, was able to bring about a triumph of educational retrogression and political reaction. The story is a disturbing one, for it reflects an hysteria which has manifested itself in other fields of American life in recent years.

It is good to find a book that ought to be read and easy to read. David Hulburd, who is a professional journalist, not a professional educator, unfolds the Pasadena story with scrupulous attention to its significant details, but also with an eye to its suspense, and to the ever-accelerating onrush of fateful, shadowy, emotional forces that led to its climax. Hulburd has chosen to tell his story mainly in terms of the human beings who were caught in it. As a result, the story seems complex, as what happened in Pasadena must indeed have been; it seems true, and it seems fearfully moving.

The story starts quietly on a note of apparently warranted

optimism. Pasadena had had a fairly placid history in public education. Its last superintendent had held his job for twenty years. The town was uncommonly prosperous: in 1949, "the city's per capita net effective buying power—that is, what each citizen could spend if he wanted to—was fifth highest in the country, a total of $249,745,000 that year for its 39,000 families"; and even the poorest section of the city had a density of population of only 17.2 persons per acre as against 272 per acre in comparable areas of Los Angeles. The Board of Education was solid, sensible, adequately representative, and good-willed: Vernon Brydolf, a substantial lawyer, a civic leader who had headed the local Bar Association and Community Chest and War Chest, father of three grown children; Mrs. Gladys Cummings Rinehart, once a teacher and later, as a mother of school children, chairman of the Pasadena P. T. A. Council; Miss Harriet Sterling, who for twelve years had headed a high-school English department, then had had to retire because of a serious eye operation; Milton Wopschall, a decent young war veteran, secretary-treasurer of his father's prosperous paint-selling business and William L. Blair, associate editor and columnist for one of the city's two newspapers—later replaced by a religious-minded undertaker named Lawrence C. Lamb. These people sincerely wanted the best for Pasadena's schools, and in Willard Goslin they thought they were getting it—and, it appears, they *were* getting it.

Goslin's first year in Pasadena went well. He made a few personnel appointments, saw through a $5,000,000 bond election for new elementary schools, began having stenographic records kept of the board's open meetings, finalized the policy his predecessor had begun of eliminating mid-year promotions, introduced a type of top-to-bottom staff discussions known as "vertical groups," got approval for a series of summer workshops for teachers, and dealt with the never-ending problems of painting classrooms, trying to put cafeterias on an efficient basis, and so on. That first year no one seemed to think, or said if he thought, that Goslin was too progressive or precipitate or willful or anything but what Pasadena wanted.

Then disturbing things began to happen. A group of citizens gathered to discuss Pasadena education; first they met in a private home, then in the American Legion hall. One of its leading members was Mrs. Louis Hawkes Padelford, founder, several years before, of the Pasadena chapter of Pro America. Soon this group was calling itself the School Development Council and was beginning to bombard the school board with letters. One, attacking a proposal of Goslin to bring teachers back a week early in the fall, because it would be too expensive, brought Goslin's first setback from his board. The Council made much of the fact that Goslin had invited to his first summer workshop Dr. William Heard Kilpatrick, of Columbia; Kilpatrick, the Council's reports stated, was a disciple of John Dewey, was a "modern pragmatist" and a radical—and so, therefore, must be Willard Goslin. The School Development Council elected Frank Wells, the owner of a small company manufacturing digging equipment, its president. Wells led a fight against a vital tax election in the town which would have made possible an expansion of the school budget for new construction, for additional teachers, and for increased operating costs—financial pressures universal in the United States then and now. In the tax election Wells and the S.D.C. won; Goslin and Pasadena education lost.

But these things were only a beginning. Now fell across Pasadena the shadow of Allen Zoll and his National Council for American Education, a reactionary propaganda outfit which should not be confused with the excellent National Education Association and the American Council on Education. In the past Zoll had collaborated with the Christian Front, with Gerald L. K. Smith, with Merwin K. Hart. The Attorney General once listed one of his now-dead organizations "Fascist and subversive." Zoll literature now began to appear at meetings of the Pasadena School Development Council, and Zoll phrases began to be echoed by Wells with startling fidelity at public meetings of the school board. On July 11, 1949, the S.D.C. addressed a long letter to the Board of Education demanding "an ideological investigation of curriculum, methods and personnel within the Pasadena school district," and loyalty oaths by school administrators and teachers "stipulating dismissal for those who refused to sign." After the tax defeat, the Board of Education organized a city-wide survey of the schools by a committee, which, when named, proved to be truly representative; it included, along with the presidents of the California Institute of Technology and the Pasadena Realty Board, Mrs. Padelford, of Pro America; yet the S. D. C. was not satisfied and demanded that this survey be "directed" by "such patriotic organizations as the American Legion and the Sons and Daughters of the American Revolution."

Goslin, who was perhaps not as tactful as he might have been, who certainly had an inadequate sense of public relations, who seriously underestimated the nature of his opposition, and who stubbornly pushed straight ahead on the things he believed in, tried to meet these attacks—and many others which Hulburd describes—with quiet reason, and with facts. But these were not enough, and he was alone. The most disturbing element of this whole story is the subtle change which came over the Pasadena school board—climaxed at last, when it sent its curiously craven telegram to Goslin in the East. After that the friends of public education in Pasadena, horrified at what they had let happen, rallied, too late, and the story ends with a heartbreaking anti-climax.

An irony of this story is that when Goslin received his telegram of dismissal, he was in New York for sessions of the National Citizens' Commission for the Public Schools, a substantial, middle-of-the-road, non-profit organization which is dedicated to the founding and nurture in every community in the country of a continuing local body of the supporters of public education—precisely the sort of group which might have staved off Pasadena's distressing story.

The Superintendent Was the Target

By James Conant

(Copyright 1951 by The New York Times Book Review. Excerpted and used with permission of The New York Times and the author.)

The immediate causes for a final rupture between an educational administrator and a lay board can never be adequately assessed. No meticulous historian with access to a mass of documents can satisfactorily portray the growing tensions within an educational system in times of stress nor the reactions of those individuals directly concerned with the decision to drop the pilot.

To one reader at least it seems that Mr. Goslin made an error in underrating the opposition to the tax increase and misjudging the strength of the hostile forces. But even if by some miraculous power Mr. Hulburd could have set down with accuracy all the details of trouble between the half-dozen individuals whose names recur in his story, the author would have added nothing of relevance to his narrative. The importance to all but professional administrators of what happened in Pasadena is the light the events shed not only on the exposed position of public educational systems but on the nature of certain reactionary forces at work in our democracy in these days of uncertainty and fear. For forces hostile to public education seem clearly to have been at work.

Indeed, this book is highly revealing of the reactionary temper of our times. For this reason what happened in Pasadena should be of interest to every thoughtful citizen quite apart from his or her concern with the free schools of the nation. As I finished the final chapter I could not help comparing this narrative of the foolish action of a weak school board under

James Conant is a former president of Harvard University and now serves as United States High Commissioner in Germany.

heavy pressures with the action of the posse in "The Ox-Bow Incident." Not that the firing of a Superintendent of Schools is the equivalent of a lynching, but the forces that generate an irrational mob spirit are as clearly indicated in the one story as in the other.

A better comparison, however, is to be found by turning to the history of England in the Seventeen Nineties. Then, as now, inciters of mob action could inflame public sentiment by the type of misrepresentation we today designate as "smears." A state of near panic could be engendered by pointing to what was happening in another nation, France. As the French Revolution moved into its violent stages and then hardened into an eighteenth-century totalitarian form, the tide of reaction set in across the English Channel. In Birmingham in 1791 "persons unknown" stirred up the inhabitants in the name of "Church and King" to burn the house of Dr. Priestley, a dissenting minister with liberal views and incidentally a chemist of some fame. Such a demonstration of blind fury provoked by a few people bent primarily on doing mischief in the name of conservatism and patriotism, I submit, is not totally dissimilar to what happened in Pasadena.

Among the charges hurled at Mr. Goslin by the Pasadena unit of Pro America and others who led the attack were his association with W. H. Kilpatrick and the "Columbia cult of progressive educators," and his support of a program alleged "to sell our children on the collapse of our way of life."

The superintendent's acknowledged position of leadership among school administrators and his continued advocacy of Federal aid to education were of course, black marks on the books of many of his opponents. In the crucial days of the "tax election" the literature of Allen Zoll's National Council for American Education (not to be confused with the American Council on Education) was distributed. So-called progressive education, it was maintained, had had a very deleterious effect because it is "shot through with the blight of pragmatism." Needless to say, those who were fighting the increased tax levy and attacking the public schools of Pasadena failed to define progressive education or pragmatism and to relate either to the actual conduct of education in this particular California city.

Because of the national significance of the discussion of education, one may note the "smear words" which have become the weapons of those who are hostile to our free public schools. None seems to me more widely used than "pragmatism" unless it be the name of John Dewey. Indeed, a highly respectable dignitary of one of the Protestant churches has gone so far as to write, "the Communist would only substitute the logical secularism of Karl Marx for the pragmatic secularism of John Dewey."

Perhaps for all who regard with horror any form of education other than church schools the word "only" in this quotation may be well chosen. But it is interesting to note that a recent article by a leading Soviet educator has this to say on the same subject: "Pragmatism, as a form of subjective idealism, is an ideology of imperialism and absorbs everything reactionary from the past. Thus pragmatism not only fails to repudiate religion but views it as part of philosophy."

Thus, in the Nineteen Fifties the "party line" in Russia is that pragmatism is the label of a reactionary bourgeois educational philosophy which fails to repudiate religion. The "party line" in some quarters in the United States is that the same word denotes the doctrines of those who are dangerously liberal in their political views and bent on driving all moral and spiritual values from the public schools.

The one thing both parties have in common is an identical technique—the arousing of emotions by words which are repeatedly so twisted as to have only evil connotations in the minds of certain types of readers. We have become accustomed to the use of this and similar techniques by the Nazis and the Communists; it is still something of a shock to find them increasingly used by individuals and groups who, in more than one city and state, are ready to spring to the attack of our public schools.

But we must face the realities of the Nineteen Fifties: the

tide of reaction is flowing strong; there are sincere opponents of all forms of non-denominational schools and colleges; there are others far from sincere who, as in every age, like to exert power by causing trouble, by urging the posse to lynch the victim, the mob to burn the dissenter's house, or the school board to fire the "progressive" administrator. All this is made clear in the story of what happened in Pasadena; the more who read it the better, for these are days when those who believe in tolerance and rational discussion of public matters must realize the consequences of passivity and inaction on their part.

A debate on school issues is a healthy sign and informed criticism is to be welcomed even by the most devoted friends of the public schools. But venomous attacks are another story. Against government by intimidation all believers in democracy must be ready to stand, whatever may be their personal views about education.

The NEA's Defense Commission, in the Fall of 1950, undertook a study of "unjustified attacks" on school systems in the United States. 15,239 questionnaires had been sent to superintendents, advisory members, local association presidents requesting information on these attacks and to determine their characteristics as they occurred in various communities. By "unjustified attacks," the Commission made clear, it meant attacks which appeared to be aimed at "nothing less than the emasculation of the American system of free public education."

The survey disclosed that these attacks had greatly accelerated in the past two years; there were at least twice as many attacks since 1948 as in the same period before 1948. It also confirmed the fact that the leading attacks centered about these charges:

—*The schools do not teach the Three R's properly.*

—*The schools cost too much money.*

—*There are "too many frills and fads" in the schools.*

Other charges frequently heard were that the schools fail to teach moral and spiritual values; that there is insufficient emphasis on the teaching of U. S. history; that there is need for more rigid discipline in the schools; that "progressive education" is being used and is, per se, bad; that the school is usurping the functions of the home. Other attacks, generally worded, declared that the schools are subversive, communistic, "teaching the welfare state," collectivist.

The questionnaire showed that the largest number of criticisms were local in origin. But it was evident—and a substantiation of Harold Benjamin's "Report on the Enemy" charges—that many unjustified attacks, if not directed by national organizations, were at least inspired by them.

The Defense Commission attempted to analyze some of these organizations in a series of articles appearing early in 1951.

They Sow Distrust

By Robert A. Skaife

(Condensed from The Nation's Schools, January, 1951)

While we hate communism and everything that it represents, we should not blind ourselves to some of the other forces that are endangering the rights of citizens in this country. There are a number of right-wing "front" organizations that could become just as dangerous as the Communist groups. With the searchlight of public attention focused on communism, these pseudo-patriotic groups escape attention. They operate largely by coming forward with "noble programs." They want to restore our Constitution rights; they want to drive "Reds" out of our public schools; they want to eliminate "collectivism" from our government, which is attempting to dominate the lives of all people; they want Supreme Court justices free from the taint of socialism. By waving the American flag vigorously they deceive many honest people who, either misinformed or uninformed, subscribe to malicious propaganda, actually thinking they are contributing to the noble cause of "saving America."

The public cannot be deceived for long. There comes a time when the subscribers to these "fronts" groups become enlightened and withdraw their financial support. This in no way stops the activities of the fearmongers, who, when one campaign is exhausted, immediately promote another one. Furthermore, they have a kind of professional fraternity. One promoter circulates the propaganda pamphlets of another, and the favor is later returned.

The following questions arise:

Who are these groups that have attacked or are now attacking the public schools?

Robert A. Skaife is field secretary, National Commission for the Defense of Democracy Through Education.

What are some of the specific statements and types of propaganda they have used?

How are they financed?

The National Commission for the Defense of Democracy Through Education has been observing closely the operation of a number of these organizations now active or which have been in existence during the last 10 years. In general, these organizations have openly suggested or stated that the public schools, teachers or textbooks have been infected with communism, statism, collectivism or socialism. For the most part, the materials they put out contain generalizations for which no proof is offered. Their aims and purposes are sometimes clothed in respectable slogans.

Although many damaging statements have been made in the propaganda put out by some of the organizations listed, the illustrations in some of their pamphlets do even more to create false impressions. One pamphlet entitled "How Red Is the Little Red Schoolhouse" pictures on the front cover a Russian soldier injecting a needle labeled "Organized Communist Propaganda" into the little red schoolhouse. Below this picture is the statement, "It's *high time* American parents knew the facts!" On the second pages is pictured, among other things, a classroom teacher craftily winking his eye at children who are looking at a blackboard with the words "decency," "honor" and "sincerity" written on it. Above the teacher's head is the comment he is supposed to be thinking: "Corny stuff." Headings, some of them in red ink, state, "The Treason Ring is out to make Reds of your Children" and "Textbooks can be Red propaganda."

Under the words, "What is the sensible way to deal with these problems?" is a picture of a man and woman turning the wheel of a press in which are placed three textbooks. Red drippings, signifying Communist propaganda, are being squeezed from the pages.

This brochure is probably no longer in circulation, but there are other pamphlets of a similar nature being sent out. One, for example, pictures a woman of the cranky schoolmarm variety, obviously a teacher, swinging an axe at the trunk of a tree. On the trunk appear the words, "The American Way of Life." The branches are labeled "Truth," "Honor," "Justice," "Loyalty" and "Order."

Here are a few statements taken from publications put out by these organizations:

"It is in order to propagandize for their favorite ideologies that many zealots become teachers. In our schools, over and over again, academic freedom has been grossly abused. It is high time to bring this shameful situation to a halt. It is never honorable nor honest to foist upon young people extracurricular opinions based upon no more than teachers' personal prejudices, which, in turn, are based largely upon their own weaknesses or confusion or upon their own frustrated ambitions to profess bamboozlement.

"Those thousands of Reds among the educators of our land —how many of them write the textbooks your children study?

"So-called 'Progressive Education' and Communism are one. The fundamental base of the 'Activity Program' is the same base upon which communism rests, a materialistic, antireligious base. Let us recognize the menace before it is too late.

"For more than three decades, a deadly fifth column of un-Amercan propagandists has been vigorously at work in the schools and colleges of the nation—infiltrating, undermining, boring in like termites.

"These subversive forces have made such inroads that, if allowed to continue, they soon will have the entire school system completely under their control. Unless effective steps are taken promptly to stop the present trend, the situation will be beyond repair.

"For a generation your tax money has helped pay the salaries of poisonous propagandists who have been endeavoring to make radicals out of the youth of our land; trying to corrupt them and lower their moral standards; destroying their faith in God and country; attempting to rob them of their self-reliance and substituting dependence on the government, on doles, on subsidies; seeking to ensnare them with the false doctrine that it is better to have statism than liberty; undermining the Christian principles and ethics on which this nation was founded; scoffing at everythng American and exalting everything Communist."

By making it appear true that the schools of this country are filled with Communist teachers or with teachers whose views range from a deep red to a light pink, these pamphlets encourage efforts on the part of community groups to compel teachers to use straitjacket methods of instruction. The enriched curriculum of a permissive school program is labeled "frills and fads," the schools are accused of failure to teach the three R's adequately, and juvenile delinquency is traced directly to the alleged lack of training in moral and spiritual values.

The available evidence indicates that many of these organizations are financed through donations to their "noble" causes by donors with particular interests in mind, by membership subscriptions, and through the sale of pamphlets and booklets. Membership lists are exchanged, and one promoter frequently inserts advertising circulars for another organization in the same envelope in which he includes one or more of his own circulars and booklets.

Sometimes a wealthy donor purchases hundreds of copies of a book that supports his "interest" and circulates copies free of charge to schools, colleges, legislators and influential citizens.

The public schools belong to all the people, not to one particular segment of the population that desires its own limited interpretation of the American way of life to prevail. To condemn freedom of inquiry per se as un-American or to link it with socialism, collectivism, statism or communism is tantamount to saying that no progress shall be made through a pooling of individual judgments—in other words, through group action. Is group action in a democratic society operating within the framework of our Constitution to be condemned? Are we to say that no change whatsoever may take place in our social institutions? To do so would certainly stultify progress of all types.

Whatever motives, obvious or hidden, lie embedded in the

propaganda put forth by these organizations attacking public education, the end product apparently desired by them is a system of instruction in which thinking is channeled through narrow passageways.

> *Among the groups listed by the Defense Commission as "front" organizations and enemies of public education were these:*

AMERICAN EDUCATION ASSOCIATION, New York
  Slogan: "Keep Our American Schools American."
  Publishes: Signposts
  Milo F. McDonald, *Executive Director*

CHURCH LEAGUE OF AMERICA, Chicago
  Publishes: News and Views (Periodical), Can We Preserve our American System in the Postwar World? (Book).
  George Washington Robnett, *Executive Secretary*

CONFERENCE OF AMERICAN SMALL BUSINESS ORGANIZATIONS COMMITTEE ON EDUCATION, New York
  Publishes: Educational Reviewer
  Lucille Cardin Crain, *Secretary and Editor*
  George D. Hawkins, *Chairman*

EMPLOYERS ASSOCIATION OF CHICAGO, Chicago
  Publishes: "How Red is the Little Red Schoolhouse"? and "So They Hog-tied Zeke the Zebra." (Brochures)
  John T. Beatty, *President*
  Gordon L. Hostetter, *Executive Vice-President*

FRIENDS OF THE PUBLIC SCHOOLS OF AMERICA, Washington, D. C.
  Publishes: Friends of the Public Schools
  Major General Amos Fries, *Editor*
  Mrs. Claud I. Palmer, *President*

NATIONAL COUNCIL FOR AMERICAN EDUCATION, New York

Publishes: Educational Guardian

Kern Dodge, *President*

Allen A. Zoll, *Executive Vice-President*

> *A number of educational agencies analyzed the attacks and found that a fairly consistent pattern was evident.*

The Pattern of Attacks

(from "Danger! They're After Our Schools!")

"First, a few citizens who are especially eager to keep taxes low are corralled into a self-styled and self-appointed 'citizens' council, or 'school development council.' These misguided individuals are then featured in press releases denouncing school leaders, demanding 'action' from school boards and rehashing the 'dangers' of present-day education.

After showering the community with demagogic pamphlets and leaflets, an invitation is issued to all who are dissatisfied with the schools for any reason whatsoever to join a local 'council' or one of the national groups.

Then comes the heavy pressure campaign!

Demands that the schools return to the '3 R's.'

Attacks on textbooks that encourage inquisitive thinking and individual reasoning.

Attempts to malign leading modern educators and any teachers, principals or members of the local board who dare to defend modern education.

A hue and cry about the need for greater 'discipline' in the schools.

Calls for a legislative investigation of teachers, textbooks and school administrators.

Mounting pressure to eliminate the 'frills and fads'—by which are meant such vital services as nurseries, classes for the handicapped, testing and guidance, programs to help youngsters understand and appreciate their neighbors of different backgrounds, and all other activities which make the school a nerve center of an intelligent modern community.

Danger! They're After Our Schools! Sponsored by American Association of Colleges for Teacher Education, Committee on Tenure and Academic Freedom, N.E.A.; Department of Classroom Teachers of the N.E.A.; Department of Higher Education, N.E.A.; American Jewish Committee. John Dewey Society; National Association of Secondary School Principals; Commission for the Defense of Democracy Through Education, N.E.A.

The entire school issue becomes confused and charged with emotion. Epithets such as 'communist,' 'socialist,' 'collectivist,' 'secularist,' and 'un-American' are thrown around freely to exploit the sentiments of genuinely patriotic, anti-communist citizens. Teachers are intimidated, school boards coerced."

The book by David Hulburd, the series by Robert Skaife in The Nation's Schools, the publications and convention reports of the N. E. A. and other educational agencies—all these helped school administrators and teachers throughout the land gain some inkling of the nature of the forces operating against them.

But generally, when school systems were under attack, the people who were the victims felt terribly isolated. In most communities—whether it was Ferndale, Michigan, or Eugene, Oregon; Atlanta or Scarsdale—school people and concerned citizens often felt that the problem was peculiar to themselves and their town. Even when they knew about school attacks in other places, they usually knew nothing at all about the methods others had used to meet them. Many persons connected with school systems knew about the ouster of Willard Goslin; the knowledge was not very comforting. If an acknowledged leader of American education could have been victimized so easily, how could they— lesser known administrators, teachers, parents— fight back?

One attempt to answer this question was the series of workshops and conferences held throughout the country in 1951 and 1952. The New York University School of Education conducted three "Conferences on Attacks on the Public Schools" in order to analyze the nature of attacks and to discuss ways "by which the schools and the community can work together in strengthening educational programs."

Each of these conferences was preceded by two week workshops calling for an exchange of ideas about various school problems. One of the problems, workshop participants agreed, was occasional poor, inaccurate, and sometimes just-plain-biased press treatment of school matters—a great hazard to good school-community relations.

The students at the first conference were treated to a rare example—almost a laboratory dissection— of this problem. Frank Hughes, a staff writer for the Chicago Tribune, had covered the conference and filed stories which appeared in the Tribune on July 13, 14, and 15, 1951. The stories were brought to the attention of the conference coordinator who distributed them to the men and women who had been present at the meetings discussed.

Of 147 graduate students in the workshop—almost all of them active administrators or teachers—54 found that the Tribune stories contained major "omission and distortion of facts." Of the 147 students, 47 said that the stories contained "misinterpretation of the purpose of the entire workshop." Eight students considered the articles "an attack on education in themselves."

Another example of unfriendly press treatment of educational affairs appeared in the Saturday Evening Post of July 14, 1951. A guest editorial, written by Frank Chodorov, was headed: EDUCATORS SHOULD BE WARNED BY THE PASADENA REVOLT. The editorial repeated all the charges — including socialism — hurled at the modern public school. It suggested, hopefully, that the Pasadena affair portended the downfall of "progressive" educators in cities everywhere.

Mr. Chodorov's position as friend and counsel for better public education was considerably weakened by another one of his editorial products float-

ing around the country at the time. His pamphlet, titled "Private Schools: The Solution to America's Educational Problems," had become a best-seller for its publisher—the National Council for American Education, the Allen A. Zoll group. In it, Mr. Chodorov had some interesting thoughts about public education:

"The public school has been pictured as the guarantee of an informed citizenry . . . This plausibility has obscured the fact that the public school is a political institution, and as such can be used for ends quite the opposite of freedom. For example, Hitler, Mussolini, and Stalin did not abolish the public school, but rather favored it as a necessary integral of their regimes; and the word "freedom" was not erased from their textbooks. Does the word carry the same weight in present usage that it had before the first World War? At that time, as an instance, freedom and conscription were opposite ideas; are they now? Freedom in those days implied an obligation of the citizen to his government, while today it has acquired quite the opposite connotation; one is free only in proportion to the amount of social security, unemployment doles, subsidies and parity supports the tax-fund can furnish him. The public school has not been the entire cause of this perversion, but it has helped greatly."

Press treatment of a completely different order came to the help of embattled educators just a few months later. It came from an unexpected source; an old conservative magazine for women, McCall's, which featured the following article as its cover story:

Who's Trying To Ruin Our Schools

By Arthur D. Morse

Public education in America is under the heaviest attack in its history. This attack is not aimed at the improvement of free education. It is aimed at its destruction. So far it has struck at school systems from Port Washington, New York, to Pasadena, California.

"We place the greatest importance upon this attack," Dr. Willard E. Givens, executive secretary of the National Education Association, whose membership consists of 850,000 teachers, said recently. "In recent months campaigns against our schools have been intensified in number and effectiveness. Since they strike at the very roots of our system of free public education, they are a very real menace to democracy."

The most notorious success yet achieved by the forces that are undermining our schools was made at Pasadena. The shoddy developments that led to Willard Goslin's ousting had nothing to do with his talents as an educator. His removal—as David Hulburd makes clear in his book *This Happened in Pasadena*—was the result of shadowy fears generated in the community with the aid of individuals and organizations as far away as New York City.

The shame of Pasadena cannot be undone. Nobody knows what community will be next.

"You say this hasn't happened to my school, to me," Dr. Richard B. Kennan, a well-known educator, told the 1951 convention of the American Association of School Administrators. "Maybe not. But it has happened in California, in New Jersey, in Louisiana, in Massachusetts—and your school may be next,

---

Arthur D. Morse is a free-lance writer whose articles have appeared in many national publications.

particularly if you are in a large school system where new buildings and increased school tax support are needed."

To see how these attacks begin, who is behind them and how the assault is waged, let us look at the case of Englewood, New Jersey—an attractive, prosperous community of approximately 25,000, situated across the Hudson River from New York City.

Englewood has long been properly proud of its school system, brought to a new peak of achievement under its present superintendent, Dr. Harry L. Stearns. Dr. Stearns, who admits to being politically somewhat conservative, has made many sound improvements in the Englewood school system. One of the most successful was the installation of a Child Study Department, staffed by two psychologists and a nurse. He is firm in the belief that "if public education fails it will spell the end of a free society in America." Until October 7, 1950, Dr. Stearns had no reason to believe that this opinion was not shared by every citizen of Englewood.

Then came the bombshell.

The Englewood branch of all the American Association for the United Nations was celebrating official U.N. Week with an open meeting at the Roosevelt School. As the principal speaker was being introduced, an Englewood resident named Frederick G. Cartwright rose in the audience and demanded to be heard with regard to the speaker who originally had been scheduled to deliver the principal address—*not* the man being introduced. Cartwright claimed the originally scheduled speaker was a "suspected Russian agent" who had been denied re-entry into the United States.

The next 20 minutes were chaotic. While the chairman, together with a minister and a rabbi who were on the speaker's platform, attempted to restore order, Cartwright walked to the stage and began reading a prepared speech, cheered on by followers in the audience who had been alerted for this demonstration.

Eventually Cartwright sat down again. Meanwhile the police had been called. Cartwright was arrested and charged with disorderly conduct. As he was being removed from the auditorium a firecracker exploded in the corridor. A young girl in the audience became hysterical.

So U.N. was thoroughly spoiled, although the speaker went on to trace the North Korean aggression and to discuss the guilt of Soviet Russia in the current situation.

Shortly after the meeting, but before his trial, Cartwright publicly demanded an investigation "into the activities and possible Communistic ties of some of the teachers in the Englewood public schools." At the same time, the commander and the past commander of the local post of the Catholic War Veterans announced that their organization had decided to support Cartwright (who is an Episcopalian) in this proposal.

The attack was under way.

At Cartwright's trial for disorderly conduct the pattern of the attack began to emerge. It was a pattern familiar to anyone acquainted with the attacks in Pasadena and in other cities, where the anti-public-school elements have, almost without exception, been aligned with an organization that is imposingly and misleadingly called the National Council for American Education (not to be confused with the highly reputable National Education Association or the American Council on Education).

The so-called National Council for American Education is run by Allen A. Zoll, who bears the title of executive vice-president. Because Zoll and his organization have figured so prominently in the nationwide campaign against the public schools, we will examine them more closely later on. It was to be expected that they would show up in Englewood.

Cartwright said at his trial that he had donated $200 to the National Council for American Education. In addition Cartwright, who is in the investment business in Wall Street, said that he was acquainted with Zoll and that his information about the original speaker had come from Zoll.

The judge found Cartwright not guilty of disorderly conduct, though deploring and disapproving of his actions. But the trouble in Englewood did not end there. By that time Cartwright had founded an organization which he called the Englewood Anti-Communist League, and tremendous tension began building in the community.

As the poison of recrimination began to spread through Englewood, Cartwright and two of his Anti-Communist League associates went before the Board of Education and recited instances in which (they alleged) teachers had displayed pro-Communist sympathies. The Board ordered superintendent Stearns to make a full investigation.

In March of this year Stearns opened an inquiry into "subversive activities" in his schools. Under his questioning the "evidence" presented by Cartwright and the two other complainants turned out to be an assortment of hearsay, gossip and rumor.

For example, Frederick H. Grein, the past commander of the Catholic War Veterans, said several students had complained of objectionable remarks made by teachers at the Dwight Morrow School. But he admitted that he had got this information second-hand and that one of his informants was not even a pupil at the school.

A mother, who happened to be Cartwright's secretary, charged that her daughter had been reprimanded by a teacher for making an anti-Communist classroom report. But it developed that the teacher, surprised by the peculiar material in the child's report, had merely asked the source of the information. It turned out to be a book titled *Communism Unmasked,* by Major General Amos A. Fries, Retired, whom we shall meet later. It fit the pattern that his name should also turn up in Englewood.

As a witness Cartwright was not impressive. He rambled on disjointedly about a variety of matters not connected with the suspected subversion in the schools, and it required all of Dr. Stearn's patience to keep him on the subject. Eventually Cartwright did attack the textbook *American Democracy Today and Tomorrow,* though he admitted that he had not read it.

After Cartwright had attacked another textbook that he had not read the following exchange took place, according to the official transcript:

Mr. Cartwright: . . . it is possible, I mean very highly probable, in a majority of cases that the teachers can be teaching subversively without being aware of the fact that they are teaching subversion.

Dr. Stearns: In other words, you are saying that without the teacher knowing it she is teaching subversive activity?

Mr. Cartwright: I would say in the majority of cases.

Dr. Stearns: In this particular case? You have not read the book, and you don't know what the teacher is actually teaching in the course?

Mr. Cartwright: No, I do not.

At the conclusion of the hearing the Board of Education announced that the charges had been found to be based on hearsay, and it exonerated the teachers of "any implications of subversive activity."

Though Cartwright's charges against the schools and his subsequent veiled accusations had not been substantiated, a subtle and distressing change was creeping over Englewood. The teachers were jittery. They were afraid the healthy open discussion that had previously characterized their classes would somehow be misconstrued. Several teachers told Dr. Stearns they were sure that some students, under instructions from their parents, were trying to trap them into making incriminating statements.

This atmosphere of uneasiness was not confined to the schools.

"There is a community menace that is growing here like a cancer," the Englewood *Press-Journal* said in an editorial, and went on to observe: ". . . it is arousing religious hatreds . . . Catholic against Protestant against Jewish. His (Cartwright's) methods are similar to those of Allen Zoll, to whose campaigns against our schools Mr. Cartwright has contributed funds . . . when he sets group against group, he is endangering our community life and our Americanism itself . . ."

The attack on the Englewood schools is still being waged. The Anti-Communist League is holding frequent meetings and distributing literature attacking the schools. Allen Zoll has made several appearances in Englewood. "He is advising us, and we think he is a swell fellow," a leading member of the Anti-Communist League recently remarked.

Frederick Cartwright and Frederick Grein have appeared on a television program emanating from Newark, New Jersey, during which they repeated substantially the same accusations made during the Board of Education inquiry. Cartwright has become more and more blatant. He now claims to be in contact with the FBI. Innocent Englewood citizens who do not share the Cartwright-Zoll viewpoint are increasingly familiar with rumored threats to report them to the government for subversive activity.

To counteract the activities of the Anti-Communist League, a number of prominent Englewood residents have recently formed an organization which they named the Englewood Citizens Union. A representative group composed of both the conservative and liberal elements in the community, it is coming to the rescue of Englewood's beleaguered school system. In Pasadena some citizens finally organized to fight the attack on their school, but only after it was too late. Everyone who is for good education and against government by intimidation must hope that the Englewood Citizens Union will get the widest community support and that its work has been started in time.

Though the nature of the attack on the schools varies somewhat from place to place, the general pattern is identical. The attackers use the same techniques, the same literature and the same sweeping charges. They accuse teachers and textbooks of being subversive; they link modern educational practices with Communism; and they attempt to stampede parents into believing that our public schools are the breeding grounds of totalitarianism.

Chief among the groups that are exploiting the widespread misunderstanding of modern education and the consuming fear of Communism is Allen Zoll's National Council for American Education.

Many well-intentioned people, lured by the dual prospect of

fighting Communism and reducing school taxes, have joined local groups which, like the Englewood Anti-Communist League, are linked to Zoll's organization. Anyone who is a member of, or has been invited to join, one of these groups should be interested in learning something about Zoll, whose career is not without interest.

Educators are usually cooperative in arranging interviews with reporters, but I found that in this respect, as well as in others, Zoll is not in the tradition. When I phoned his office, which is in New York, he was reluctant to grant an interview, until I pretended that I was in sympathy with his aims and wanted to gather material to further the cause. Then he agreed to see me.

"This will be the first interview I've granted since I've been in this thing," Zoll remarked and concluded by saying, "If you smear me I'll cut your throat." (This is not, of course, the kind of remark that one often hears in educational circles.)

Before seeing Zoll I looked into his background and found, among other things, that he was the founder and national commander of an organization called American Patriots, Inc., which appears on the Attorney General's list as a Fascist organization. The Patriots (now defunct) had their biggest fling during the years immediately preceding World War II, when Zoll, who cannot be accused of lacking a talent for opportunism, exploited the division of sentiment in this country toward the war.

At meetings of American Patriots, Inc., national commander Zoll presented such speakers as Elizabeth Dilling, who was indicted for sedition three times during the war and was a defendant in the mass sedition trial of 1944 (which was declared a mistrial when the presiding judge died). Other Patriots who addressed the group included John Eoghan Kelly, later convicted as an unregistered agent of France; Joseph McWilliams, also a defendant in the sedition trial, who once boasted, "I'm one hundred per cent for Hitler"; and the notoriously anti-Semitic Gerald L. K. Smith. Zoll introduced Smith as "without doubt the most dynamic and inspiring speaker on Americanism today."

Zoll had a pretty good year in 1939. In January he appeared at a Senate hearing to oppose the nomination of Felix Frankfurter as a Justice of the Supreme Court. Zoll said he didn't like Frankfurter's record or his religion. Senator Borah was moved to remark, "So far I as am concerned, I do not propose to listen to an argument against a man because of his religion . . . you are raising the same question that is drenching Europe in blood."

A while later Zoll was in the news again. For months the New York radio station WMCA had been picketed by Christian Front followers of Father Coughlin in protest against the refusal of the station to broadcast the priest's inflammatory speeches. In July, Zoll, who was one of Coughlin's most vocal supporters and one of the originators of the picket line, was arrested on an indictment charging that he had attempted to extort $7500 from WMCA's president, Donald Flamm. In return Zoll had allegedly offered to call off the pickets. Zoll was never brought to trial, and the indictment was dismissed.

The publicity that Zoll received as a result of this untidy affair was not flattering. He accordingly drifted off into shadows, where he worked for a few years as a salesman (he sometimes refers to himself in print as an "Internationally Known Sales Consultant") for such professional anti-Semites as Merwin K. Hart and Joseph P. Kamp.

In 1948 the internationally known sales consultant, sensing a new market for a somewhat different brand of goods, organized his National Council for American Education. Ex-National Commander Allen Alderson Zoll now appeared as Allen A. Zoll, Ph.D.

The office of the National Council for American Education occupies a large room on the tenth floor of a shabby building at 1 Maiden Lane, in downtown New York. It has a staff of three: a receptionist, a typist and Zoll's secretary. The room is cheerless, sparsely furnished and undecorated except for numerous pictures depicting scenes in the life of George Washington. In the rear, partially blocked off by storage cabinets and stacks of old newspapers, is the small cubicle occupied by Zoll, from which he emerged to greet me.

At the age of 55 Zoll is a man of average height, weighs about 200 pounds and is growing bald. His eyes, which are his most distinctive featue, are narrow and glinting. His manner is restless.

At the outset I told Zoll that I was familiar with his main arguments against the schools: that "progressive education" is a menace, that most teachers and textbooks are subversive and that children are not learning the three Rs, which should be taught to the exclusion of virtually everything else.

"That's about it," Zoll said. "Most teaching and textbooks are Socialistic, and the teachers colleges are implanted with Socialism. These Socialist plotters are deliberate saboteurs, and we're in serious danger from them—just as much as from the Communists. There are plenty of bad people who haven't joined the Communist party, and we're out for them too." Zoll leaned back in his chair. "You're either for individualism or collectivism. The middle is a barbed-wire fence. I tell kids that in my talks to them."

I asked just how he was attempting to improve this situation.

"Well," he began, "neither the FBI nor the Un-American Activities Committee knows what's being taught or what's in the heart of a teacher. The only person who knows that is the person right on the ground. I help these local outfits. Like in Punxsutawney it might be called the School Development Council [in Pasadena the antischool faction *was* called the School Development Council]. I've also formed a pro-American underground of teachers."

After Zoll had exhausted himself on the subject of disloyal teachers I asked what he was doing about subversive textbooks. "We have an office in Wisconsin," he replied. "Their job is to review about sixty books a year. It's under the direction of our vice-president in charge of research Verne Kaub."

I had run across Kaub before and knew that he, like Zoll, is a Johnny-come-lately to education. Until recently Kaub was working the religious side of the street, writing articles for the anti-Jewish publication *The Individualist,* as well as distributing a pamphlet titled "How Red Is the Federal Council of Churches?"

Zoll said that Kaub's job of ferreting out un-American propaganda in the children's books is sometimes pretty difficult. "Once," he said with a straight face, "we had to have a book reviewed eight times before we got a good analysis."

I asked Zoll what he believed the proper aims of education should be.

"That's a good question," he said. "I just sent a memo to our Board asking them to give me their ideas on that matter."

That didn't seem like a very good answer, but Zoll was indicating that he wished to wind up the interview.

"Any other questions?" he asked.

"Well," I said, "can you tell me what's right with the schools?"

He did not dignify that query with an answer.

I remarked that nearly all educational authorities agree that approximately 500,000 new classrooms need to be built within the next ten years, and asked Zoll if he also considered this a vital problem.

"That's a lot of fuddydud, about new buildings, when the old ones are just as good," he replied. "The factor of age has nothing to do with the efficacy of school buildings."

There seemed time for only one more question. Since Zoll now signs his writings "Allen A. Zoll, Ph.D.," and prefers to be addressed as "Doctor Zoll," I asked him about the degree.

"I got that from Temple Hall," he said quickly, and then seemed embarrassed by his hasty remark. He rose, and the interview was over.

After leaving "Doctor" Zoll I learned that Temple Hall College and Seminary (now defunct) was a one-man diploma mill operated by a man named D. Scott Swain. Swain's qualifications as an educator included the serving of a six-year prison term on six charges, including running a confidence game, obtaining property under false pretenses and passing bad checks. While running his "college" Swain conferred upon himself the title "Archbishop Primate." Probably the high point of his career was reached at a meeting in New York City, when the "Bishop" got roaring drunk and in a burst of expansiveness passed out Temple Hall Ph.D.s to his entire audience. The exact moment when Zoll was awarded his doctorate is unknown.

Zoll would be funny, if his aims were not so deadly. He cannot be dismissed as a harmless crackpot, for, though his statement to me that his organization has 10,000 members and is linked to some 400 local groups is an obvious exaggeration, it is nevertheless true that he has been a potent influence in every city whose schools have come under attack.

Zoll's influence is widely exerted through the pamphlets that he publishes and distributes. At the height of the school controversy in Pasadena, citizens picking up their morning newspapers found copies of Zoll's pamphlet "Progressive Education *Increases* Delinquency" on their doorsteps.

"So-called progressive education," the pamphlet said, "shot through as it is with the blight of Pragmatism, has had a very deleterious effect upon the original character of American education . . . The public school system in hundreds of cities and towns throughout the land . . . is fatally committed to these subversive principles of 'progressive' education." Zoll goes on to explain that modern education does not permit absolute truth, hence those who believe in it cannot be true Christians. And he makes the further observation that "currently it is popular to plug hard for the democratic equality of all men."

This pamphlet made such a vivid impression on the president of the School Development Council in Pasadena that he recited passages from it almost verbatim in his speeches attacking the school administration.

In Denver the forces attempting to oust superintendent Kenneth Oberholtzer (who is also president of the American

Association of School Administrators—the highest honor his profession accords) presented copies of "Progressive Education *Increases* Delinquency'" to each member of the Board of Education and to members of many other civic groups.

Other Zoll literature includes pamphlets bearing such titles as "They *Want* Your Child" (the Communists, that is) "Private Schools: The Solution to America's Educational Problem" and "How Red Are the Schools?"

The philosophy in these pamphlets is being advocated by the Parents Council for Education in Eugene, Oregon; the Citizen's School Committee in Los Angeles; the Parents' Council in Minneapolis; the Three R Parents Committee in Columbus, Ohio; and by similar groups in many other communities.

Zoll's satisfaction in the wide distribution of his literature is not altogether spiritual. His most popular item, "Progressive Education *Increases* Delinquency," sells for 20 cents a single copy; 6 copies for $1; 1,000 copies for $60; and customers are offered a "special price on larger quantities." In all of his pamphlets Zoll makes a strong pitch for contributions. People who join his Council are rewarded with various titles, the rank conferred depending on the amount of cash they send in. They can become an Associate for $5, a Patron for $150, or a Benafactor for $1,000.

By the end of 1949, when Zoll was just swinging into action, his pamphlet sales and contributions had netted him an estimated $45,000. With the way his business is booming at present, there is no reason to believe that his efforts are not now being even more respectably rewarded.

Though Zoll's organization is the most important rallying point and serves as general headquarters for the enemies of education, other operators are busy turning out weapons for waging the attack.

One of the most destructive of these—a kind of secret weapon—is a quarterly publication called the *Educational Reviewer*. Edited by Lucille Cardin Crain, and financed by a lobbying organization with headquarters in Washington, D. C., the *Reviewer* has been used effectively in Englewood and in other widely scattered cities across the country. Its sole function is to try to discover subversive material in textbooks.

The methods used by the *Educational Reviewer* can be illustrated by its treatment of Dr. Frank Magruder's textbook, *American Government*. This text, which in on the recommended list of all 48 states, has been a classic in its field for a quarter of a century. It was appropriately selected for review in the first issue of the *Reviewer,* which appeared in July, 1949. The writer of the review was a woman named Edna Lonigan. How she made her point that the textbook is subversive can perhaps best be shown by comparing excerpts with which she purported to express Magruder's views with actual passages from his text:

Magruder, According To Lonigan:

Italy and Germany were dictatorships but not the Soviet Union.

The United States and the Soviet Union are equals fighting for "world leadership."

By democracy we mean that form of government in which the sovereign power is in the hands of the people collectively.

Magruder's Actual Text:

Russia is leader of the dictatorial nations, most of which are Communistic.

The United States and the Soviet Union, the most powerful of the allies in the Second World War, now find themselves as the two only powerful contenders for world leadership.

By democracy we mean that form of government in which the sovereign power is in the hands of the people collectively, and is expressed by them either directly or indirectly through elected representatives.

In the last instance above, by deleting half of the sentence, Miss Lonigan was able to prove to her satisfaction that Magruder was an advocate of the collectivist state.

Unfortunately she proved it to a number of others, including

radio commentator Fulton Lewis, Jr., who, a few minutes after
the review appeared, read considerable portions of it on one of
his broadcasts.

The response was big and prompt. The State Textbook Commission of Georgia immediately banned the book, as did the
Houston, Texas, school board. Parents in Portland, Oregon, demanded that similar action be taken there. A newspaper in
southern California quoted Lewis, attacked Magruder and concluded that the "public schools are bound to destroy this
country." In places like Council Bluffs, Iowa, and Trumball
County, Ohio, where the broadcasts also caused a stir, some
people took the trouble to read the textbook—and so avoided
taking precipitate and foolish steps.

Referring to the *Educational Reviewer,* a report recently issued by a committee of the House of Representatives observed
that "the review of textbooks by self-appointed experts smacks
too much of the book-burning orgies of Nuremberg to be accepted by thoughtful Americans without foreboding and
alarm."

That kind of talk infuriates the editor of the *Educational Reviewer,* Lucille Cardin Crain, who is convinced that any critic
of her publication is a Communist.

Allen Zoll described Mrs. Crain to me as "a charming woman,
very lovely"; and I found upon meeting her in her office, which
is in a brownstone house on East 36th Street in New York
City, that she does possess the most attractive figure in the antischool movement. She is 50, has cool blue eyes, a cameo face and
a fondness for using rather fancy words. To indicate her personal interest in children Mrs. Crain sometimes says exuber-
antly: "I'm a grandmother seven times." This reference is to
the children of her husband (who is 71) by his first wife. Mrs.
Crain is childless.

Like Allen Zoll, Mrs. Crain joined the educational ranks
recently. Her scholastic background consists of the equivalent
of a high-school education, which she received at a convent in
Minnesota. She is suspicious of most recognized educators who
hold degrees, and she has expressed strong disapproval of what

she calls our "compulsory state-operated educational system."
What she is in favor of is a mystery.

When I asked Mrs. Crain what she thought the proper aims
of education should be, she seemed to be pushed as far out to
sea as Allen Zoll had been when I asked the question of him.
After remaining silent for a spell Mrs. Crain, moved by a sud-
den inspiration, said brightly, "I like our little slogan on the
Educational Reviewer." (This reads: "In the light of truth,
objectivity and established American ideals, to examine the
publications used in instructing American youth.") There
seemed little point in pressing that subject further.

In other respects my interview with Mrs. Crain was not unusually rewarding, partly because she consumed most of it by
delivering a diatribe against the National Education Association, which she thinks is subversive. Her reasons are not monu-
ments of persuasion. Reading from an N.E.A. pamphlet, she
remarked, "They say here they're 'committed to the democratic
ideal,' " adding, as she tossed the pamphlet aside, "whatever
that is."

The *Educational Reviewer* has been specific in explaining
what it thinks democracy is. "Democracy," the *Reviewer* said
in the October 15, 1949, issue, "is a government by demagogues
leading to the tyranny of the majority over the minority."

A few steps behind Mrs. Crain is another foe of modern
education—78-year-old Major General Amos A. Fries, Retired.
The aged general is editor of a widely distributed monthly publication ironically titled *Friends of the Public Schools*. "Anyone who calls our government a democracy," this publication
pointed out, "is either completely un-American or a moron."

The general stands four-square against nurseries and kinder-
gartens, health, welfare and recreational activties, services for
handicapped pupils and vocational guidance, among other
things. "Where one child is overworked," he says, "a thousand
aren't worked enough."

The general's educational program, if such it can be called,
stems from his apparent belief that things were better in the
good old days when fewer children went to school.

These three—Allen Zoll, Lucille Crain, General Fries—by themselves would, of course, be ineffective. What enables them to carry on their programs is the support of well-meaning but misinformed people in communities across the country, who are frequently prompted to join a local, innocent-sounding school group because its main interest seems to be controlling school taxes or carrying out some other aim that appeals to the pocketbook or the emotions.

This article provoked fast and lively response from hundreds of sources. To anyone concerned with the use and effectiveness of a single magazine piece in a particular situation, some of the history of "Who's Trying To Ruin Our Schools?" will be interesting.

The editors of McCall's had first tried to evaluate the significance and worth of the article through discussion with various educators. Convinced that the piece was honest and important, they made it a cover story and gave it top promotion.

Releases were sent to hundreds of newspapers summarizing the article. The story was carried by major wire services. It was inserted in the Congressional Record by Senator Murray of Montana. Many radio and television programs—from the disc jockey program of Barry Gray to the broadcast sessions of the New York Herald Tribune Forum— made use of its facts. Scores of newspapers, particularly in towns with school tension situations, editorialized on it.

McCall's had to hire a staff for the express purpose of handling reprint orders for the article— more than a quarter of a million copies have already been distributed. In its February, 1952, issue, McCall's carried four columns of letters-to-the-editors on the article. "Some readers strongly denounced the piece," wrote the editors, "but the over-all ratio of favorable letters over unfavorable was more than 8 to 1." How sensitive a spot the article had touched became even more evident when McCall's discovered that many of its leading advertisers had been approached by persons in widely-scattered cities; persons who suggested. that advertising be withdrawn in reprisal for the Morse article. McCall's easily weathered the storm of attempted intimidation; its subsequent issues were among the best in its history—in advertising and circulation.

And, in 1952, the article was given three of the most coveted awards in magazine journalism—the Sigma Delta Chi, the Education Writers Association and the Sidney Hillman Foundation Awards. McCall's had found that its courage was wise—and immediately made plans for additional coverage of the subject of attacks on modern education.

The article inspired local action too. In Georgia, writing in the Atlanta Constitution, Ralph McGill discussed the article and its local significance in an editorial titled, "McCarthyism in the Classroom." Due in part to this exposure of reasons why the Magruder textbook, "American Government," had been banned in Georgia, the ban was "temporarily suspended" by the Georgia Board of Education just two months after the McCall's article appeared.

In Englewood, New Jersey, Frederick Cartwright was fairly well discredited as an impartial, rational friend of the public schools and lost much of his bite, if not his bark. But he still stumps the Bergen County area with several allies in quest of "subversion" in the public schools.

Allen Zoll, named in the article as a leader of the attacks, had his defense. He tried to explain away the reasons why his organization, "American Pa-

*triots, Inc." had been termed fascistic by the At-
torney General of the United States in 1940. Franklin D. Roosevelt wanted to get rid of the Dies
Committee, Zoll explained. Congressman Martin
Dies and his research director, J. B. Matthews, had
addressed several metings of "American Patriots."
Therefore, Zoll concluded, Roosevelt had his Attorney General, Francis Biddle, call "American Patriots" a fascist group "for political purposes."*

*Several persons came to the support of Mrs. Lu-
cille Crain although none of them presented her
qualifications to serve as an educational authority.
One of her supporters was John T. Flynn, a noted
author and lecturer who in recent years has been
charging the New Deal with "betrayal"; a few years
earlier he was a chairman of the America First
Committee; a few years before then, astonishingly,
a frequent contributor to the New Republic, a
weekly magazine with strong New Deal sympathies.*

*Flynn complained that the McCall's article at-
tempted to put Zoll on one side, General Fries on
another, and "then Mrs. Crain is put in between
these two in a kind of squeeze play to smear her
with the odium which the writer attaches to
(them)."*

*Flynn's charges of "smear-by-association" would
have been more convincing if he had not lapsed
into that technique himself in the preceding para-
graph of his article. There he said that the author
of the McCall's article, Arthur Morse, "was at one
time a commentator on the air for the extreme
left-wing organ, The Nation." Extreme left-wing
or not, The Nation has never employed Morse as
"a commentator on the air." Morse has written for
The Nation just as Flynn has written for the New
Republic. Unlike Flynn's articles, however, Morse's
were not political; his series concerned the radio*

stations and Federal Communications Commission requirements. The fact that Morse wrote about radio at all must have led to Flynn's confusion.

Flynn's discussion of the McCall's article was presented in a broadcast and copies were released by an agency known as America's Future, Inc., a group affiliated with the Committee for Constitutional Government. It appeared in the Colorado Springs Gazette Telegraph, a newspaper owned by R. C. Hoiles, a publisher of several dailies, a man whose strong convictions were recently expressed when he made a public appearance to take the affirmative position in a debate entitled, "Resolved: Shall the Public Schools Be Abolished?"

Another debate, which received far more national attention, took place in New York City on November 13, 1951. The platform: America's Town Meeting of the Air, broadcast by 277 stations of the ABC network. George Denny, Jr., was moderator. The participants were Willard Goslin and Lewis Haney. Dr. Haney's invitation stemmed from the fact that, in addition to teaching economics at New York University and writing a column for the Hearst newspapers, he is a member of the advisory committee for Lucille Crain and her Educational Reviewer.

The Crisis in American Education

Moderator Denny:

Good evening neighbors. If you don't think there is a crisis in American education today, it's very likely your opinion will be changed after you hear our distinguished speakers this evening. Both of them answer tonight's question in the affirmative, but for sharply different reasons.

Since this is the Town Meeting being held in the midst of American Education Week, we should be true to our American traditions and hear both sides and ask our speakers to answer questions from a representative American audience. Both Dr. Haney and Dr. Goslin are professional educators. Dr. Haney is Professor of Economics at the Graduate School of Business Administration at New York University, and Dr. Goslin is Director of School Administration and Community Development at George Peabody College in Nashville, Tennessee. Dr. Haney is also a syndicated columnist, author of *The History of Economic Thought* and many other books on economic and financial subjects, including one on "How To Understand Money." We'll hear first from Dr. Lewis H. Haney.

Dr. Haney:

I think Dr. Goslin and I can agree on three facts. First, nobody is attacking our public schools or seeking to destroy them. That is a red herring charge. Second, nobody wants the little red schoolhouse again, or teaching only the three R's. That is a straw man. Third progressive education, while improving teaching methods, has gone to some extremes considered undesirable by many educators and parents.

Why do even the National Education Association leaders shift to the meaningless term "modern education?" The crisis in American education is exactly the same as in our athletics, tax collections, morals, politics and money. In all these we find the same lack of standards—standards of truth, honesty and stable values. We used to believe in the sanctity of marriage, in local self-government, and in pay according to product. Now there is a lack of such bases for general agreement so we call each other names.

I think we are like a boy brought up in a country home where he honored his folks and George Washington and had to go to school and church. He then goes to the big city and falls in with progressive youth who show him what they call the good society, advising him to do only what he wants to and to take things easy.

At the bottom lies the attempt by some to shift the responsibility for our lives from us individuals to the nations. The American system is built on belief in the importance of the individual, on faith in free initiative and thought, and it is built on education that develops the individual child, equips him with knowledge, the means of exhanging ideas, and with faith in certain enduring values.

But along come those who see in the child only something to be socialized and adjusted to the government which is to care for him. Like all collectivists, they would subordinate the individual, you and me, to some group over and above the family, and would begin when we are very young, before we can develop independent thought. So the crisis centers in the question, "What form of society is good?"

Two main practical fronts are : (1) Statism. Are we to go in for the welfare state socialists or fascists? (2) Progressive or modern pedagogy. Are our children to be socialized by conditioning them for what the organized educators call the good society? Are the teachers and their superintendents to replace the parents and to mold the whole child to their pattern of collectivist group behavior?

What to do about it? First, let us quit calling names and smearing and be reasonable. What does the United States stand for? Are the politicians to run the economy? Is the federal government more and more to supersede the state and local governments? Finally, is the nation to surrender its sovereignty to a world government

What do our public schools stand for, Dr. Goslin? Are they to train our children to be citizens of the United States as we know it through history, dedicated to the greatest possible freedom of thought and choice? Or are the schools to take from the family and the church the responsibility for personal adjustments and to condition the whole child for the organized educators' notion of a good collectivist society?

Relatively few teachers and textbooks, I think, have been slanted towards communism, but many teachers and many texts are encouraging socialistic thinking that tends toward communism. Now many of us oppose this. Isn't it our duty to fight against it?

I am sure the N.E.A. leaders are mistaken in charging that the hundreds of spontaneous outbursts of criticism of what goes on in the schools from Port Washington to Pasadena are a plot or anything else than the honest indignation of local citizens. The organized educators have been active in attacking and smearing all persons who criticize the spreading of socialistic doctrines in our public schools. Do they then favor such doctrines?

I don't believe that the National Education Association under the leadership of such men as Benjamin, Givens and Skaife, or the schools of education that work with them are representative of the mass of patriotic American teachers and superintendents. They, these latter should be reorganized and themselves be conditioned for the good society that is our true America.

Moderator Denny:

Thank you, Dr. Lewis Haney. Our next speaker, Dr. Willard E. Goslin, is a native of Missouri. A graduate of the University of Missouri who served as superintendent of schools in Missouri cities until 1944, he went to Minneapolis as superintendent of schools there, and in 1948 went to Pasadena, California. Dr. Goslin is a past president of the American Association of School Administrators and is currently a member of the Advisory Panel of the National Citizens Commission for the Public Schools. Dr. Willard E. Goslin, welcome to Town Meeting.

Dr. Goslin:

There is a crisis—a deep and alarming crisis—in American education, Dr. Haney, but I don't think it's the one you describe. It has been building up during twenty years of depression and war. The crisis is born mainly out of the distraction of the American people about the mounting complexities and tensions of our times. The American public school system is staffed by a million loyal, hardworking citizens of this nation, doing a great job under terrific handicaps.

The handicaps fall into three groups. First, the public school system of America is being starved financially. The public schools are caught squarely between our tradition of local support and the brutal fact that we now collect most of our tax dollars at the federal level. We have fifty billion dollars a year and more for defense, nine billions a year for alcohol, but only a little more than five billion for our public education—not enough to build a classroom or hire a well-prepared teacher for tens and hundreds of thousands of American children.

I would like to ask Professor Haney as an economist for a positive suggestion about how to solve this part of the real crisis in American education.

We lost over four hundred thousand teachers for reasons other than death and retirement between 1940 and 1950. That proportion of loss would produce a crisis in any institution.

This is a nation of free enterprise, a country of free choice as to one's life work, a land where you have to pay the going price for services and commodities or do without them. I would like to keep it that way. However, the blunt truth is that we are not willing to pay the going price for school teachers, either in salary or working conditions, and as a consequence we are running out of school teachers.

A free people must dedicate enough of the best of its youth as teachers if it expects to maintain its freedom. We're not doing it. One of the greatest obstacles to good teaching and to an adequate program of education in this country lies in the number of children assigned to each teacher. No teacher can do a good job with forty or fifty children in her room.

We have fallen behind in supplying classrooms, adequate teaching materials, and teachers at the same time that our enrollments are increasing at the rate of about a million children a year. A million children require thirty thousand new classrooms, and they deserve thirty thousand bright-eyed, red blooded young Americans as teachers.

These deficiencies, Dr. Haney, are part of the crisis in education.

My second concern has to do with how we decide educational matters. In some nations, programs and politics in education would be handed down by the church or passed along by the central government, but in America, as long as we are free people, program and policy in education must be hammered out by citizens working with their teachers in community after community across the land. It's in this area that most of the discussions and debates about education are centered.

No institution in the United States needs or deserves more of the benefits of our traditions of public analysis and evaluation through public discussion and criticism than the public school system. However, the American people and their school teachers have a right to expect that the criticism be analytical in nature and constructive in intent. They are frequently otherwise.

The crisis in American education, Dr. Haney, is further deepened by the fact that the public school system is caught in the cross-fire of nearly every top internal issue of struggle in the United States. For example, the problem of the relationship of religion to the organized phases of American life is mounting in this country, and the discussions and struggles are centered almost exclusively on the public schools. In the interest of the religious and educational rights and privileges of every citizen of this nation, this question needs to be brought squarely into the open while all of us search for the right answer.

Another example. This nation is in the midst of a period of evolution and adjustment in many of the relationships between citizens of different racial backgrounds. Many areas of our society can dodge the problem. Churches with their present organization and stratification would rather face the question. The public utility is not interested in the color of its subscribers, but a public school system has to live with this issue and all of its manifestations.

Your presentation, Dr. Haney, shows clearly that the schools are caught squarely in the middle of our conflicts about economic and political policies. I think the shortage of teachers, buildings and equipment, the problems of reaching a decision on program, and the struggles over such issues as I have mentioned constitute the real crisis in American education.

I think we need to do four things about this crisis. One, work out an understanding of the area of responsibility of the schools. They are not everything to all men and never should try to be.

Second, find the largest areas of common agreement on which to stand while we debate our differences.

Third, keep the public channels of communication and discussion about education open to all the people.

Fourth, take every promising step to bring more and more of the American people into direct working contact with their school system. The broad base of the American people will retrieve their public schools from a crisis situation and defend them against all comers at the point at which they understand the problems and needs of their schools.

Moderator Denny:

Thank you, Dr. Goslin. Dr. Haney, you sat there quietly while Dr. Goslin presented his views and he threw a few challenges to you. Would you like to comment at this time?

Dr. Haney:

Well, it seems, Dr. Goslin, that we are surrounded by crises on all sides—here a crises, there a crisis.

First, I'll try to help you solve the one you like, then I'll ask you to come out and play with me and my crises. You are worried about finances. Well, you can't avoid taxes by passing the buck to the federal government. The way to pay for our schools,

I think, is to reduce our cost of federal government—say, foreign aid and farm subsidies, to start with—and then increase our local taxes for our local schools. And if you want to keep your teachers, it seems to me that you will have to let them teach our children and not baby-sit them. In teaching them respect for their American history and Constitution and government, and so forth, I think you will give them a basis for self-respect that will make them happier. (Applause)

Mr. Denny:

Thank you. Is that intended as a question, Dr. Haney, for Mr. Goslin, or do you want to ask him a question in addition to those comments?

Dr. Haney:

I think that that will give Dr. Goslin something to think about while I prepare another question.

Dr. Goslin:

Well, I'd like to see Dr. Haney do a little more thinking, too. For instance, in the early part of your statement, Dr. Haney, you say that the crisis in American education is exactly the same as in our athletics, tax collections, morals, politics, and money and in these we find the same lack of standards, standards of truth, honesty, and stable value. Now I want to ask you this. Are you saying that the tens and hundreds of thousands of citizens in America who are members of boards of education, a million people who are teachers in the schools of this country, several million Americans who are working directly as lay citizens in connection with their school system—are you saying that they are lacking in standards of truth and honesty and value in relation to education or the American scene?

Dr. Haney:

It is hardly necessary to reply to that question. Of course, no one does that. My question as to the crisis that I want Dr. Goslin to play with is put forth in the words of Carey McWilliams, a well-known communist-fronter,* who states the problem to be this: "The opposition was commanded by Willard E. Goslin. The victory which the enemy has just won in Pasadena, therefore, demands careful study as a model in miniature of the big battle for control of public education which is now shaping up in the United States." It is that big battle in which this communist-fronter sides with you, Dr. Goslin, in the battle of Pasadena, that I want to play with tonight.

Dr. Goslin:

Well, I wasn't aware that we were to refight the battle of Pasadena. I thought we were here to discuss the crisis in American education, and that covers a lot of territory beyond Pasadena.

Dr. Haney:

Well, let us take the question, then, of the smear article published in *McCall's* Magazine recently, which you recently favored in *Herald Tribune* talk, and which was later supported also in similar terms by the communist paper, the *Daily Worker*. What do you have to say to that, Dr. Goslin?

Dr. Goslin:

I say that it is perfectly clear that Mr. Haney does not wish to deal with the crisis in American education. (Applause) Now if we wish to carry on this discussion without bringing any enlightenment to the American people, all we have to do is go back and forth between articles of this sort; and I would like to

---

* The published transcript of this broadcast carried an editor's note:

The following is a statement by Mr. Carey McWilliams in reference to Dr. Haney's remarks.

"Having enjoyed the free speech permitted on America's Town Meeting of the Air many times, I am glad that Dr. Lewis Haney was permitted to say what he had to say on this program, including his reference to me as 'a well known communist fronter,' but I am grateful to Town Meeting and George V. Denny, Jr., for this chance to state that the reference to me was not only a feeble substitute for an argument but a smear and a wholly inaccurate statement, Speech only remains free where an opportunity is given those maligned a chance to refute their maligners. I look forward to appearing on the same platform with Dr. Haney one of these days."

say I can name some, Mr. Haney. I've been reading your column rather consistently for some time now.

Mr. Denny:

I want to take this occasion to say, Dr. Haney, that the views expressed by yourself and Dr. Goslin are solely your own and not necessarily the opinion of the American Broadcasting Company or the Town Hall. I say that advisedly, sir, because of the appellations you've attached to certain individuals. We believe in free and open discussions, but I just want to point out that these are entirely your observations and not ours.

Dr. Haney:

Well, they are the observations made by the California Senate Committee, their quotations.

Now I want to state something I know about a crisis, which is not unrelated to the one that I have thus far emphasized, in my experience with students in my classes—aside from bad writing and spelling, which of course we all suffer from or with. Too many of them don't know any history; too many of them don't expect to do any work; too many of them have poor command of the English language, no vocabulary; too many of them feel about things, they feel, feel, feel, and don't think or know anything; and they accept the idea that the government will provide. That is the fruit I think, of the kind of progressive education or modern education which perhaps you can better explain than I, Dr. Goslin.

Dr. Goslin:

Professor Haney, you seem to have had a change of pace. Your number two sentence in your presentation was, "Nobody wants the little red schoolhouse or teaching only the three R's. That is a straw man." I'd just like to point out that teaching the R's is not a straw man to a million school teachers in this country. They think it's a tough rugged business trying to do a competent job in that field for thirty million American children where they are frequently overcrowded and working with the handicaps of insufficient materials along the line.

Dr. Haney:

Well, Dr. Goslin, you say the main source of the school problem as you observe it consists or results from religious differences, racial issues, labor versus capital, party politics and so forth. Now I think that in that you are wrong, because in my town I find no religious issues, no labor capital issues, no racial issues, no party issues in the school question, or in the election of the school board. There is only one line of cleavage there, only one issue, and that is the issue of progressive education closely connected with the idea of a socialist slant.

Dr. Goslin:

In the first place, I didn't say that the major issue had to do with these conflicts, but I did identify it as one of the areas contributing to the crisis in American education. But then when you raised the matter of socialism in relation to education, if that isn't saying that politics are impinging upon the schools, then I don't know how to say it.

Mr. Denny:

All right, gentlemen, I think that seems to dispose of your major issues at this time. The aisles are full of people ready with questions.

Man: Professor Haney, what do you mean by collectivism?

Dr. Haney: By collectivism I mean a system of thought and social organization in which the individual is subordinated to the state. It may be either socialism or communism.

Man: Mr. Goslin, "progressive education" is a much abused phrase. Will you please bring some light to a phrase now beclouded by confusion?

Dr. Goslin: I'll be glad to try. In the first place, I'd like to point out that the phrase "progressive education" means whatever the individual wants it to mean who happens to be using it at the moment. It's a very much kicked-around phrase in this country at the present time. However, if by progressive education or progressive school you mean one where citizens and teachers and parents are sitting down to talk through and think out the problems of their community and their children and then to try to set up a school system that will teach children in the light of those problems, I think that's in line with good education.

If you mean by progressive education one where teachers and parents are trying to come to an understanding as to how much each child can learn in relation to the important areas of subject-matter and skill that we have found in American life and help him to learn it in the light of the best knowledge that we have about child growth and development, if that's what you mean by a progressive school, then I'm for it, and I think that's the kind that the American people are for.

If you mean by progressive education a school that recognizes that when a child comes, that what happens to him in school is going to have something to do with his physical stamina and his emotional stability and so forth, and that you are going to try to plan and develop the school so that it contributes to this child's total citizenship development, if that's what you mean by progressive education. I'm for it and I believe the American people are for it when they understand it (Applause)

Mr. Denny: Thank you. Since both of our speakers used this phrase, I think Dr. Haney ought to have a right to give his definition of progressive education.

Dr. Haney: Well, I don't know what the people of Pasadena think about this progressive education, but I do know that there is connected with it the idea of a collectivist philosophy essentially and necessarily connected with the education that comes down through Karl Marx, to John Dewey, Kilpatrick and the others, which is essentially the idea of taking the whole child out of the influence of the family and the church and subjecting him to a conditioning process, subordinating him to the group. And in the so-called common learning scheme which Dr. Goslin left at Minneapolis, I have seen that program and it calls for subjecting the child first to learn what he can do for his school; second, to learn what he can do for his community, and third, finally, to find out what he has to do to adjust to his family.

I think that is typical of the bad side of this progressive education.

Dr. Goslin: I know, after working in the schools of this country for a long time and being pretty well a part of this controversy for the last few years in American education, that what Dr. Haney has said is exactly what he and some others are trying to attach to good development in education in this country in order to stampede the American people and their teachers back to some kind of a skeleton of education that will set this country up for the kind of controls that it seems some folks would like to exercise in America. (Applause)

Mr. Denny: Thank you, Dr. Goslin and Dr. Haney. Next question from the gentleman over on the left.

Man: Dr. Haney, you spoke copiously against smearing those you disagree with in educational politics. What, in this welfare state, that in your own words tends to communism would you want social studies teachers or history teachers to denounce— public housing, social security, or a free public school system?

Dr. Haney: I wouldn't ask the teachers to denounce anything. I would ask them merely to tell the truth about things without slanting or bias. (Applause)

Man: Well, let's not smear and let's not say the New Deal, the Fair Deal, or the Welfare State or the Republican Party tends towards communism. What in the welfare state that you denounce would you want us to denounce?

Dr. Haney: I'm not talking about the political parties and I refuse to consider this a political issue. It's an ideological issue. It's the fundamental difference between the individual and his rights and the subordinating of him to the group, the state, and so forth, welfare or not.

Mr. Denny: Let's not ask Mr. Haney to repeat his initial speech. I think the things he wants to denounce are implicit in the statements that he made at the opening of the program. The lady over here.

Lady: Dr. Goslin, I'm a parent and I'd like to do something about this. How important is a selection or the election of a school board who will insure sound democratic methods in curriculum in our public schools?

Dr. Goslin: I consider that the United States has had its best experience with representative government in terms of lay membership on boards of education in this country, and therefore I consider that it is the foundation of the welfare of a school system for a community to select an adequate cross-section of its people for membership on its board of education.

Man: Dr. Haney, is there justification for a demand for a uniform national set of requirements for high school teachers? If not, why not?

Dr. Haney: Well, I think that depends upon how intensive the demands are. If you demand that the high school teacher be honest and intelligent and clean and a good American citizen, I think you have the rudiments for getting a good teacher to start with.

Man: That's rather evident. I'm speaking of courses that the teachers are required to have on their transcripts.

Dr. Haney: Well, I think it would be very fortunate to encourage, as I am afraid there is a tendency now, a sort of monopoly on the part of certain schools of education for advancement to the higher positions, at least. As I understand it, you have to take certain courses which are given by people who are pretty heavily weighted in these directions that I refer to as collectivism.

Mr. Denny: All right, thank you. The lady over on the right.

Lady: Dr. Goslin, what methods would you suggest might be used to work towards solving this question of religion in the public schools

Dr. Goslin: I think that the matter of public discussion and the complete ventilation of this issue, both as it relates to education and as it relates to every other phase of American life, is fundamental to our health and happiness as a nation in this country.

Man:Dr. Haney, can we continue as a republic with democratic ideals and at the same time deny students a look at competitors?

Dr. Haney: I think I know what you're driving at, although it's pretty hard to get it from your words. I think that certainly education requires looking at and understanding the nature of all the pertinent facts of life. All I object to as an educator is attempting to teach people things which they can't understand and which constitute a process of molding or conditioning.

Man: Dr. Goslin, since all schools are not perfect, how specifically would you have parents work toward better schools and text-books?

Dr. Goslin: I would have teachers and parents and other citizens work together in terms of developing policies, in hammering out programs and making the important decisions about education that have to do with the public welfare of this country, as well as the educational welfare of this country. I would have them on committees that have to do with determining financial policy and all of the basic items that relate to the welfare of the educational program in a community.

Lady: Dr. Haney, what, if any, would you say is the salient difference between progressive education of the past ten years and that of, say, 25 year ago?

Dr. Haney: The progressive education of the earlier decades to which you refer was largely focused on the problem of the child and his development—the discovery of the best periods at which to introduce various subjects—and matters of that sort, the appeal to interest, the technique of pedagogy. As time has gone by, as I observe the thing, those educators who are centered more on the social problem and the collectivization of the child have gone on. John Dewey has changed somewhat, modified his ideas from '30 on. I rely partly on the judgment of Professor Ulich, of Harvard for that.

Now, then, we come to this more difficult problem of the tendency not only to take the child, but to take him for the purpose of molding for what they think is the good society.

Dr. Goslin: I want to say a word about that. I think I know about as many of the practicing school teachers in this country as anyone around this nation, and if there's a group in America who is trying to develop the individual capacities and the strength of each individual child so that he can go out and stand on his own two feet in American life and face the tough problems that are before us, it's the school teachers of this country.

Dr. Haney: I want to say "Amen" to that, and it is the millions of school teachers who belong only nominally to this National Education Association bunch with their monopoly or trust of education to which I am appealing. It is these leaders who are seeking to lobby. They even have their goon squads out in different towns. If anybody ventures to make any criticism of the teaching in the schools it wants, Brother Skaife is on the job publishing material in the papers, and so forth, and it's taken up by their amplifiers, and you have a regular pressure group brought to bear on it. I know. (Applause)

Dr. Goslin : Dr. Haney, who has just spoken, is the same gentleman who read his initial statement in which he said we ought to stop calling names. (Applause)

Mr. Denny: All right. Next question.

Lady: Dr. Haney, is part of the crisis in education due to the fact that parents are expecting schools to teach what they themselves neglect to do?

Dr. Haney: I'm afraid that that is true. I'm afraid that is true.

Man: Dr. Goslin, do teachers and superintendents of schools welcome or resent criticisms of the schools?

Dr. Goslin: I believe we are moving into a period now where criticism is more completely invited—criticism and discussion and debate—on the part of teachers and leaders in American education than at any time in the whole history of this country. I tried to say in my statement that there is no institution in American life more in need of the benefits of public discussion and debate about its policies and objectives and responsibilities than the American school system, and I find that that point of view is supported on the part of school people all over this country.

Mr. Denny: Well, we ought to have some Town Meetings in schools, Dr. Goslin. Next question.

Man: Dr. Haney, if you believe textbooks are slanted, what method of censorship do you propose?

Dr. Haney: I don't propose any method of censorship. Censorship is a bad thing, and I have nothing to say in favor of it. Why should you put the question in that way?

Man: Well, Dr. Haney, what method of judgment do you bring to bear as to what textbooks are used?

Dr. Haney: Why, by the fair and full discussion of them, which is so resented, so bitterly resented, by all the people whom I come in contact with in the schools in my town.

Man: Dr. Goslin, to what extent can child delinquency be caused by such progressive education which does not recognize moral values?

Dr. Goslin: Well, I don't know any education, progressive or otherwise, that doesn't recognize moral values. And I do not know any education, excepting places where education is so weak by neglect and lack of support, that can possibly be said to be contributing to delinquency in this country.

Lady: This probably bears on the same question. Dr. Goslin, do you think religious education on release time should be encouraged in order to rebuild higher standards of public morals?

Dr. Goslin: I don't think I know. But I do think that the American people, and I'm repeating now, of all shades of religious points of view and of all interests in education need to get this whole problem of the relationship of religion to education and the other phases of organized American life out into the open, talk it back and forth, and try to find the largest area of common agreement on which we can all stand in America to keep us from going along and threatening our very unity by division over this particular subject in American life.

Dr. Haney: I just want to say "Amen" to what Dr. Goslin has just said.

Mr. Denny: All right, Dr. Haney, thank you very much. We find agreement at the end. I want to thank you both for a very lively contribution to a very important subject.

> *Dr. Haney's casual dismissal of attacks on teachers and textbooks, his implications that N.E.A. "goon squads out in different towns" were magni-*

fying the crisis, come in sharp conflict with facts
reported in The New York Times of May 25, 1952.
Benjamin Fine, Times education editor, reported
that a nationwide book survey disclosed:

1. A concerted campaign is under way over the country to censor school and college textbooks, reading materials and other visual aids.
2. Voluntary groups are being formed in nearly every state to screen books for "subversive" or un-American statements. These organizations, not accountable to any legal body, are sometimes doing great harm in their communities.
3. Librarians are intimidated by outside pressures in their choice of books and other materials. Unwilling to risk a public controversy, they meekly accept the requests of the self-appointed censorship groups.
4. Several textbooks and other materials have already been removed from school or college libraries and are effectively on "the blacklist."
5. The attacks on the "subversive" school texts appear to be part of a general campaign against public schools and other educational institutions.

The Battle for the Schools

By Dorothy Dunbar Bromley

(Condensed from the summary program of a five-part tape-recorded series prepared for broadcast by WMCA, New York, in April, 1952. Used with permission of WMCA.)

Announcer: Throughout the country today, there is genuine concern for the welfare of the public education system. From Maine to California, in many communities where free public schools are guaranteed as a basic freedom of American democracy, attacks on the schools have been made. They have not always been successful, but in all instances the same disturbing pattern is evident. What are the sources? What do they stand for? Only by knowing the answers can public support be rallied to defend the schools.

Mrs. Bromley: Dr. Richard B. Kennan of the National Education Association has read off a list of towns and cities where attacks against the schools have already been made or have been threatened.

Dr. Kennan: In the Far West; Los Angeles, Antelope Valley, California, Eugene, Oregon, Kennewick, Washington. Moving Eastward, in Denver, Colorado Springs, Minneapolis, Chicago, Indianapolis, Columbus, Detroit. In the Southwest, you have Little Rock, Arkansas, and Houston. In the South, Atlanta, Birmingham, Bulford, South Carolina, Washington, D. C., Arlington, Virginia. In the East, New Haven, Hartford, Springfield, Vermont, Washington, New Jersey, and in your own area, Englewood, Port Washington and Scarsdale.

Mrs. Bromley: How the offensive against the schools shaped up in these last three towns and how it was met should be an instructive lesson to good citizens everywhere, for these things could happen in your town, too.

Dorothy Dunbar Bromley is a former staff member of the New York Herald Tribune and a contributor to national magazines.

In Port Washington, the battle for the schools started two years ago over a $375,000 school bond issue. This fast-growing Long Island community badly needed three new neighborhood schools and a new senior high school. Opponents sprang up who claimed the whole package wasn't necessary. They touched the pocketbook nerve of taxpayers, particularly the well-to-do. The following analysis of the situation was given us by Stephen Cox, Port Washington Republican, a member until last June of the Board of Education, and a man who fought for the new schools.

Mr. Cox: There are two groups of people, those who patronize the public schools and those who don't. In the second group there are many people, usually large holders of real estate, who no longer have children in the schools and resent an increase in the amount of school taxes that they are required to pay.

Mrs. Bromley: To insure the bond issue, a pro-school group rapidly organized. They won the election by a narrow margin of 62 votes. We took you not long ago through our tape-recorder, to a dedication of one of the new schools. Having lost the bond issue fight, the opposition turned its guns on the textbooks used in the Port Washington schools. Leading the attack as before is the vociferous Fred H. Johnson. An insurance broker, a resident of the affluent Sands Point section, Mr. Johnson is on the board of governors of Allen Zoll's organization. Mr. Johnson told me when I interviewed him, that New Dealism is the same as Communism and that all New Deal laws should be condemned in all textbooks that are now in use in Port Washington.

Mr. Johnson: Well, see, I wouldn't trust any of them, in any school, for this reason—

Mrs. Bromley: (Interrupting) Well, would you write our text books yourself, then?

Mr. Johnson: No.

Mrs. Bromley: What would we do for textbooks?

Mr. Johnson: You might have to throw them all out and start new.

Mrs. Bromley (narrating):

It happened that the two books against which the loudest hue and cry was raised in Port Washington were standard texts on American government and history in use all over the country. But they had been condemned by a sheet called the *Educational Reviewer* edited by Mrs. Lucille Cardin Crain. Any board of education member or local citizen who's sent a copy of the *Educational Reviewer* should know that it is subsidized by the Conference of American Small Business Organizations. The reviews it prints have been characterized by the House Select Committee on Lobbying as smacking of the "book-burning orgies of Nurenberg." Last year Mrs. Crain appeared in person in Port Washington, talked there on pink-tinged textbooks. Her views were hotly disputed by the very active pro-school group and a lot of people wrote letters to the editor. Make a note of that—if there is an attack on the schools in your town, use the local newspaper as a forum of public opinion. In Port Washington the two books under attack are still in use as textbooks.

In Englewood where new school buildings weren't an issue, there was a kamikaze attack on three teachers alleged to be teaching un-American doctrines. The attack was made by Fred G. Cartwright and his newly formed Anti-Communist League. An investment broker, Mr. Cartwright came to this country when he was 16 years old and he had no subsequent schooling. He calls himself Communism's greatest enemy. When Cartwright and his crowd singled out three teachers last spring, the Englewood Board of Education called on him in a public hearing to present his evidence. This is part of what he had to say about the affair of the teachers, in our tape-recorded interview.

Mr. Cartwright: I made no allegations that three teachers were using slanted teachings. None whatsoever. Well, I hadn't made . . . as a matter of fact there was one parent whose daughter attended the Dwight Morrow High School who made one of the allegations . . . charges.

Mrs. Bromley: The parent made the charge?

Mr. Cartwright: Yes.

Mrs. Bromley: And what was the charge?

Mr. Cartwright: The charge was that this girl in an oral English class had given a two-minute talk against Communism and at the termination of her talk a teacher had reprimanded her for speaking against Communism and asked the girl if she knew where did she get her information from and she had said that she got it from the Un-American Activities records and the teacher was alleged to have said, "Well, you don't believe what you read about the government, do you?"

Mrs. Bromley: Now that testimony was given at the hearing.

Mr. Cartwright: Yes.

Mrs. Bromley: And what was the upshot of the hearing?

Mr. Cartwright: The upshot was this, that the whole purpose, as far as I could see, in my opinion, was to get Mrs. Smith who was the mother of the girl, Frederick Grein, who had also alleged that there was possible Communistic influences in the Englewood schools, and myself, to get us to allege that the teachers were either subversive or Communists.

Mrs. Bromley: Oh you had not before named those teachers to anyone? Why were they there then?

Mr. Cartwright: Why were they there? The question you asked me is regarding red-slanted textbooks, is that correct?

Mrs. Bromley: No, I was asking you about the three teachers. You had named them at some time, hadn't you?

Mr. Cartwright: I had named two of the teachers, yes.

Mrs. Bromley (narrating): For a report on how a group of civic-minded people got together to defend the schools, I talked with Mrs. Abert C. Lord, old Englewood resident, and asked just what the newly formed group, the Citizens' Union, had done for the teachers.

Mrs. Lord: We asked up some of them to come and talk to us and when we had convinced ourselves that there was nothing in these charges, we engaged a lawyer, Judge Abram Lebsen, to appear at the hearing and defend them. They were very much concerned when the charges were first brought, but when they realized that a group of citizens in the community who were interested in helping them, they felt very much relieved and as it turned out at the hearings, there was really nothing in the charges.

Mrs. Bromley (narrating) : These days Cartwright is busy denouncing textbooks. When I asked him if he got his tips on textbooks from Allen Zoll's organization, Cartwright entered a vehement denial, but he did admit, after a long, embarrassed pause, that he had given $200 to Zoll's organization. For his tie-up with Zoll, Cartwright has been denounced in Englewood by the former state commander of the American Legion, Conrad Schneider, an attorney. His methods also have been condemned by the Protestant Ministers Association. The Catholic War Veterans are no longer working with him as a group and membership in his Anti-Communist League is dwindling, the newspaper editor reported. Yet Cartwright stirred up enough of a rumpus about textbooks to get a reaction from the Board of Education. Last December the Board issued a surprising directive. Every teacher was to be required to sign a paper about each textbook saying there was nothing subversive in it, nothing inimicable to free enterprise. Textbooks that were considered to have objectionable passages were to be kept under lock and key. But the Board had to back down and suspend the order. Some of the teachers took the matter to their state federation. The ever-vigilant Citizens Union entered a protest, proving how important it is for friends of the public schools to stay on the alert. Now the Englewood Board of Education is showing backbone. At a recent board meeting, when Cartwright demanded a complete list of textbooks and collateral readings, the president told him to see the board's lawyer.

In Scarsdale, the Board of Education has shown backbone from the first. There the battle for the schools began in 1949 as the battle of the books. The Board took a firm stand against censorship and for freedom of inquiry. It was backed by an impressive list of prominent citizens. Two weeks ago the book-purgers erupted again. They're lead as before by Mr. Otto Dohrenwend, an investment broker and the Reverend Mr. William C. Kernan, assistant to the rector of the Protestant Episcopal Church, St. James the Less. On March 27th, these gentlemen repeated their old complaints about Communist-tainted school books. They declaimed against certain persons heard in public school building, all but two of whom addressed adult audiences. They claimed that a communist conspiracy is at work in Scarsdale and they call the Bord of Education irresponsible and apathetic. The Scarsdale Superintendent of Schools said the charge were totally unfounded and despicable. The PTA's and the boards of the women's organization in town issued strong statements defending the schools. Coming up in the news later this week will be a statement from the Board of Education itself. Everyone in Scarsdale knows that it will be along the same lines as the report the Board issued in the fall of 1949. That report was digested for the radio audience in this series by Mr. G. Stanley McAllister, president of the Board until last December. He said in brief.

Mr. McAllister: In November of 1949, the educational policies and teaching staff committee submitted a report to the Board which was adopted by the Board. In essence the main part quoted something like this: "That protection against subversive influences can best be achieved by the positive approach of vigorous teaching rather than by negative methods of repressive censorship. The latter ensures undue attention to the censored items and substitutes fear of ideas for freedom of inquiry."

Mrs. Bromley (*narrating*) : Right now there is being circulated in Scarsdale from house to house an open letter expressing confidence in the Board of Education and in the school's quote "excellent and thoroughly American teaching program," unqote. It is sponsored by the Parent-Teacher Associations and other civic groups and many hundreds, if not thousands of people are expected to sign it. The real test will come in Scarsdale on May 6th at the Board of Education election. It is not known whether the Dohrenwend-Kernan group will put up their own candidates. Other years they have not dared to to test their strength. *

How this tradition can and should be inculcated in students

---

* On Scardale's Election day for its school board, 1,392 citizens turned out to give the incumbent administration a resounding vote of confidence.

was set forth in a speech made before a PTA by Dr. Courtney C. Brown, assistant to the chairman of the board of the Standard Oil Company of New Jersey.

Dr. Brown: Young people must be given the power of discernment and the courage to accept change as an inevitable part of life. The schools themselves know best how to do these things. But they must do these things as their primary interest. They must teach people how to think, not what to think. By the provision of accumulated knowledge they can attack prejudice; by the inculcation of self-confidence in all their pupils they can free them from hate and from fear.

Mrs. Bromley: In Scarsdale, Englewood and Port Washington, good citizens have been more alert than were the people of Pasadena when they let Dr. Goslin go. But Pasadena will be in the news again soon with the story of a vast survey of its schools made by teams of citizens and professional workers. Dr. Clyde M. Hill, head of the Yale University Graduate School of Education was co-director of the survey. His associate was Dr. Lloyd Morrissett, Professor of Educational Administration at the University of California in Los Angeles.

Sitting here in the studio in New York, Dr. Hill is smiling a bit like the cat that swallowed the mouse. For the year-long Pasadena school survey that runs over 1200 pages at last has all the i's dotted and the t's crossed. But there's no use, Dr. Hill warns me, in asking what conclusions were reached on a variety of contentious subjects. The Pasadena Board of Education is having a first look at the survey it commissioned. But there's one aspect of the subject Dr. Hill is bursting to talk about. He says it's the biggest story of all.

Dr. Hill: Now hold on to your hat, here Mrs. Bromley. We had over a thousand volunteers, working hard—working on steering committees and on subcommittees. They worked days and evenings for months on end. The women, of course, pitched in like Trojans. Some of them, for the first time in years, hired maids so that they could get their housework done by other people, thus releasing full time for them to work on the study.

Mrs. Bromley: But how about the men?

Dr. Hill: We had almost as many men as women. For instance, on the committee that was studying the schools' personnel problems, we had leading personnel experts and managers of leading industries, companies and department stores. At least a score of professional people gave their services. Not least among them was the President of the California Institute of Technology.

Mrs. Bromley: But did they dig into the questions over which there'd been heated debate—the selection of textbooks, for instance?

Dr. Hill: Oh yes. These were covered too in their own areas of the elementary, secondary and junior college levels, just as were the questions of whether sound principles of Americanism were being inculcated in the younger generation, and so forth.

Mrs. Bromley: I suppose the proof of what Pasadena has learned as a city will come when a survey, now still in your secret files, is presented to the Board and eventually passed on by the citizens?

Dr. Hill: You might say, yes. But Dr. Morrisett and I believe that no matter what action is taken immediately, the results of the survey, which will run into two fat books, will be only a by-product of the study itself. By working on the survey, a thousand citizens in Pasadena have developed new faith and new interest in their schools. Where there were weaknesses they looked for ways to make going to school a rich experience for the children. This is a far cry from the highly emotional criticism which is so often associated with school studies and with people's interest in their school.

Mrs. Bromley: It was a good story you had to tell, Dr. Hill, about what 1000 citizens did for their schools, and I thank you.

Mrs. Bromley (narrating): If Pasadena had made its school survey a year or two earlier the story of what happened there might have been very different.

There's a democratic formula for preventing such crises, the National Citizens Commission for the Public Schools declares.

This Commission was organized back in 1949 at the suggestion of President James B. Conant of Harvard and other leading educators. Money flowed in from the Carnegie, Rockefeller and other foundations, and the Commission got off to a flying start. Roy E. Larsen, President of Time, Inc., one of the organizers, serves as its chairmen. The Commission's other 32 members are nationally-known figures—newspaper and magazine publishers, editors and writers, labor and welfare leaders, industrialists and businessmen. The executive director is Henry Toy, Jr.

As chairman, Mr. Larsen gives about as much time to the schools as he does to the enterprises of Time, Inc. At the Commission's office, 2 West 45th Street, he was good enough to record the following interview.

Mrs. Bromley: Mr. Larsen, would you tell us, please, what your Commission's magic formula is?

Mr. Larsen: It's really a very simple one, Mrs. Bromley, a grass roots formula. We try to inspire every local community we can reach to form a large, over-all citizens' school committee. We urge that the committee be a true cross section of the town—a geographic, economic, social, political and racial cross section.

Mrs. Bromley: I know we're great at forming committees in this country but too often they don't move either heaven or earth. What do you outline for these committees as an action program?

Mr. Larsen: We're telling the Committee members that it's their job to evaluate their own school systems. But note that word "evaluate." This means a real survey job that will keep any number of sub-committees busy.

Mrs. Bromley: Have you any guide that lists a mode of organization and questions that committees should take up and look into?

Mrs. Larsen: Yes, our Commission has recently published a little pamphlet called, "How Can We Help Get Better Schools?" It is the result of our observation of the way many successful school committees have gone about this job.

Mrs. Bromley: You should have a great demand for that little booklet but does the Commission do other things than distribute literature, Mr. Larsen?

Mr. Larsen: Yes, we try to be helpful when our advice is asked in specific cases. Two years ago, for example, a tax payer in Haddon Township, New Jersey, wrote us an irate letter charging us with exaggerating the need for new school buildings. He said he had defeated one bond issue for a new Junior High School in his town and would do it again. Mr. Toy answered his letter, urged him and his group to make a study of the rising school population, gave him information on other building programs. The material we sent him seemed to make good sense to him for he proceeded to form a real citizens' committee.

Mrs. Bromley: And what happened then?

Mr. Larsen: Well his group ended up by asking their fellow citizens for a bigger bond issue than had first been proposed.

Mrs. Bromley: How many citizens' school committees have been formed, Mr. Larsen?

Mr. Larsen: About 1600, and I should point out that the most effective are the ones whose members work closely with the Superintendent of Schools and the board of education even while they think for themselves.

Mrs. Bromley: Thank you, Mr. Larsen.

Mrs. Bromley (narrating): Now in the great city of New York, fortunately, there's been no concerted move made by uninformed, self-appointed groups to undermine public confidence in the schools' leaders, teachers or textbooks. But for years there has been sniping at the activities program by which elementary school children learn by doing. There has been sniping, too, at modern methods of teaching reading. Just the other day I heard of a school in Queens that for some unexplained reason reverted to the old-fashioned, A B C method. We have crowded classrooms, children going to school in double shifts; certainly our school building program needs constant attention.

A watch-dog organization that has worked for 57 years to

protect and improve the New York City schools, is the Public Education Association. It has over 3500 informed members. It is also a clearinghouse for the large civic organizations concerned with the welfare of the public schools. The great United Parents Associations is, of course, one of these.

Because the PEA has some new plans afoot, I asked its board chairman, Mrs. Samuel A. Lewisohn, to speak to the radio audience.

Mrs. Bromley: Would you tell us, please, Mrs. Lewisohn, about the PEA's plans for the near future?

Mrs. Lewisohn: There are actually in New York City now, 6000 new groups that want to do something about our public school problems. Some are very small, in settlement houses and in public housing projects.

Mrs. Bromley: Well do you hope by any chance to get them all working together in a vast, over-all survey of the New York schools such as Dr. Hill directed in Pasadena—the same kind of thing that your National Citizens Commission recommends?

Mrs. Lewisohn: But first PEA hopes to get money from foundations to start a pilot project. We want to take a given area and get in touch with all the big and little groups concerned with school problems. PEA could supply them with literature to guide them, with speakers, and we could give them "know-how." We could tell them how to approach the Board of Education on specific matters, how and when to speak up over the school budget, how to make themselves heard at City Hall, how to make themselves felt in Albany.

Mrs. Bromley: That would be a big order. I hope you can get it started. Thank you, Mrs. Lewisohn.

Mrs. Bromley (*narrating*): All who seek to defend and improve the public schools of America walk in the footsteps of Thomas Jefferson who clearly foresaw that only free public schools could preserve our representative form of government and safeguard the guarantees of freedom spelled out in the Bill of Rights. "We must have free public schools," he said, "for the more general diffusion of knowledge to educate and inform the whole mass of the people." Now, a century and a

half after Jefferson lived, our vast, modern public schools are
the envy of every other country.

.But well-established as they are, they face a crisis today.
The struggle is on at home as well as in Asia and Europe
between the authoritarians and the lovers of freedom. Public
school teachers and professors in the colleges are the natural
targets for the enemies of freedom. For if they can be silenced,
the rest of society can be kept in ignorance. To be discerned
from coast to coast is a clear and present danger to our schools,
a danger far more threatening than the danger of Communist
infiltration. It is a danger of an infiltration of fear and hysteria
which will, if not checked, destroy our schools as the foundation for a free democratic society. But once the danger is
clearly recognized, alert citizens can mobilize community support for the schools as they did and are doing in Englewood,
Port Washington and Scarsdale. There has never been any
doubt that our public schools have the confidence, the trust
and the love of the great majority of our people. But too often
we neglect our schools—take them for granted. The simple
lesson to be learned from this series of broadcasts is that every
civic group in every town should study its own schools—keep
in touch with them. Then divisive tactics will not work and
crises will not arise.

> In many places throughout the country, there
> seems to have been a stiffening of resistance in the
> face of unwarranted attacks on public schools and
> educators. The cases of Port Washington, Engle-
> wood, and Scarsdale are not unique. But the threat
> to modern education seems as grave as ever. A
> recent blow came from a source that has actively
> cooperated with the National Education Associa-
> tion for many years—the American Legion. It came
> in the form of an article in the American Legion
> Magazine called 'Your Child is Their Target," by
> Irene Corbally Kuhn. The national commander of
> the American Legion, on receiving protests from

various educators, declared that he had seen the article before publication and it expressed his opinions, too. The authors of the following letter, Mark Smith, Superintendent of Bibb County Schools, Macon, Georgia, and Joy Elmer Morgan of the NEA, fear that this development presages a new type of attack.

Second Round

(*From Horace Mann League Letter* 266, *based on an article in The Nation, May 31, 1952.*)

With the publication in the June issue of the *American Legion Magazine* of an article attacking the National Education Association, the "battle for the schools," has entered a new phase.

In itself the article—Your Child Is Their Target, by Irene Corbally Kuhn—is unimportant. It simply repeats and elaborates charges used in all recent attacks on the public schools: failure to emphasize the three R's; the use of Communist-influenced textbooks by "subversive" teachers; and the evils of progressive education. The importance of the article stems from two facts: it appears in the official publication of the American Legion and it directly assails the National Education Association.

While Miss Kuhn's article attempts to drive a wedge between the membership of the NEA and the top echelon of its leadership, and concentrates its fire on the NEA's National Commission for the Defense of Democracy Thru Education, it can only be read as a direct attack on the NEA as a whole. "One of the strongest forces today in propagandizing for a socialistic America," she writes, "is the hierarchy of the National Education Assosciation." And in a reference to the organization itself she says: "Some of its performances have been more typical of the tactics of a captured labor union, complete with goon squads, than of a respectable national organization." To appreciate the significance of the appearance of an article using such language in the *Legion Magazine,* it should be recalled that the Legion and the NEA have been active allies since the establishment of a joint committee on educational problems some twenty years ago. What exactly has happened, then, to prompt this aggressive and provocative attack by the most influential veteran organization in the United States on the largest educational organization in the country?

There is more to the developing feud between the Legion and the NEA than meets the eye. The key is probably to be found in the success of the NEA's counter-offensive against the enemies of public education. Drawing a sharp distinction between honest criticism of the schools, however drastic, and organized attacks on public education, the National Commission for the Defense of Democracy has effectively alerted communities from coast to coast to the dangers, and has exposed the activities, of such groups as Allen Zoll's National Council for American Education, the American Education Association, Lucille Cardin Crain's Committee on Education of the Conference of American Small Business Orangizations, and other groups which, under the pretext of opposing progressive education and other symbolic targets, are out to capture control of the public-school system. The NEA's counter-offensive, which Miss Kuhn denounces as "an all-encompassing-umbrella smear campaign," has been so effective, in fact, that in not a single test engagement have the enemies of public education been able to win a clear-cut victory. In Pasadena they did succeed in forcing the resignation of Superintendent of Schools Willard E. Gosling, but only at the cost of alerting the community and the nation to the dangers of their campaign. In Scarsdale, New York; Englewood, New Jersey; and in Denver, Minneapolis, and Palo Alto the "enemy" has been forced to retreat if not to capitulate.

At the same time, there has been a tremendous growth of citizen interest in the public schools; Benjamin Fine, writing in the New York *Times*, estimates, for example, that some 5000 citizens' organizations concerned with education have been formed in the last five years. Now that the first assaults have been thrown back and this formidable body of public opinion has been organized, the "enemy" cannot resume the battle to capture control of the schools without first bringing into play new forces powerful enough to impose "coordination" upon the NEA. If this can be done, then the next objective will be to capture control of the grassroots committees and organizations that have come into being since 1947. Miss Kuhn hints for example, that these groups will be "linked together at the appropriate moment." One can readily surmise that the appropriate moment will be when the NEA has been forced to repudiate or disband its National Commission for the Defense of Democracy. As a matter of fact, the Legion attack on the NEA was foreshadowed by a report which the Sons of the American Revolution issued last summer, blasting the NEA as "the chief culprit" in a conspiracy "to force socialism and communism on the United States." A copy of the report was submitted to the House Committee on Un-American Activities.

The forces that launched the "battle for the schools," of which Pasadena was the first major skirmish, have not been able to break thru the defenses which were so quickly and effectively thrown up by the NEA and other bodies. These forces are now being regrouped for another assault. The strategy, however, is already clear. It will aim, first, at removing the roadblock which is the NEA's National Commission, and second, at capturing control of the various citizen's grassroots committees and fusing them into a mass movement under Legion auspices and control. The new congressional committee that was recently established to investigate the foundations will doubtless inquire into the various grants that the NEA has received—a matter which is touched upon, incidentally, in Miss Kuhn's article. It would be difficult, therefore, to exaggerate the importance of the second offensive in "the battle for the schools" of which the Legion article is the first major fusillade.

IV.

EDUCATION AND ITS CRITICS

*It is good to have criticism of educational prac-
tice. When it is sincere and well-founded it contributes to improvement of our education. But
criticism based on dishonesty, misinformation, and
misunderstanding serves only to confuse the public,
to interfere with the effective discharge of duty by
our teachers.*

*The educational profession, in many ways, has
tried to distinguish between the honest type and
the dishonest or attack type of criticism. The following analysis of the two general types of groups
offering criticism was presented at a recent meeting
of the National Education Association.*

Honest vs. Dishonest Criticism

By Virgil Rogers

Honest Group Type

1. Meets under auspices of regular organization, e.g., PTA or school advisory council.

2. Has sanction of school authorities and cooperates with local teachers and officials.

3. Makes criticisms that are constructive and specific.

4. Welcomes teachers and administrators in meetings, usually jointly held with them.

5. Gives evidence of sincerity by seeking the truth based upon facts.

6. Avoids use of propaganda literature, shuns sensationalism.

7. Rejects the inflammatory orator, radio commentator, or newspaper letter-writing addict.

8. Uses American way of getting at the truth—let all be heard, listen to both sides, and make up your own mind.

9. Keeps on issues and avoids bringing in personalities.

10. Makes decisions based upon all available evidence and only after exhaustive study.

11. Makes open and objective reports without attempting to embarrass officials, such reports having been previously submitted to the whole group for study and consideration.

Subversive or Dishonest Group Type

1. Meets initially under authorized group, perhaps; may then begin holding secret or off-record sessions.

2. Tends to work under cover and to use devious means of evading school officials and faculty.

Dr. Virgil Rogers is Superintendent of Schools, Battle Creek, Michigan, and president of the American Association of School Administrators.

3. Attracts emotionally unstable people to it and often these are given command of the group.

4. May break away from an honest, firmly established group and set up its own splinter organization with a high-sounding title, indicating patriotic motives or unselfish concern for public education, e.g., The National Council for American Education.

5. Uses smear literature, poison pamphlets, usually imported from the outside, or lifts phrases, slogans, and titles from them.

6. Introduces extraneous issues, rather than concentrating on the agreed-upon area of discussion.

7. Accepts rabble-rousing techniques, "dust throwing," "name calling."

8. Permits only one side of the issue to be presented fully.

9. Frequently passes resolutions without thoughtful deliberation and regardless of all the evidence. Persons making such resolutions are frequently fanatically critical of the schools.

10. Attacks personalities—the superintendent or principal becomes the "whipping boy."

11. Makes a pretense at getting the facts, then issues ultimatums to be answered in a limited amount of time. Sometimes these attacks take the form of a list of questions to the school official or to the board, often given to the press simultaneously.

12. Frequently uses press in the campaign.

13. Secures funds through collections and gifts solicited, not through regular constituted membership.

Complaints that Need Our Attention

By New York University Graduate Students

*New York University graduate students—meeting
in "Workshops and Conferences on Attacks on the
Public Schools" in the summer of 1951—attempted
to define the various kinds of honest criticism
which require remedial action. Their findings were
compiled by Gertrude Noar, formerly with the
Philadelphia public school system, and Herbert
Bruner, conference coordinator and formerly superintendent of schools in Minneapolis.*

Who Makes Them	What They Say	Why They Say It	What You Can Do
1. *Dissatisfied parents*	Children are "short changed."	Classes are on half-time.	Get the facts about lack of facilities and teachers to the people.
	Children do not like school.	Children complain, want to stay home, refuse to do their home assignments.	Begin to study and to change the curriculum you offer in the light of the children's needs. Make sure that teachers and pupils and community participate.
	Discipline is poor.	Some "teachers" cannot control their classes. Inadequate substitute service. Lack of understanding as to why the modern classroom is not silent.	Help the teacher who is having trouble. Tell the community the facts about teacher supply, especially in relation to pay. Make it possible at once for parents to see children at work in classrooms.
	My children can't read, write, spell, or do arithmetic.	Many children have not acquired these skills as fast or as well as parents wish.	Study the performance levels in relation to ability in your school. Institute in-service education work in teaching technics. Set up guidance services. Have parents study your findings with you and plan with you to better the situation.
	My child is not treated fairly because he is a Jew (or a Negro or a member of another minority group).	Prejudice and discrimination exist in our schools.	Call in consultants to help teachers and parents to study together: —the structure of American society —the causes of prejudice and technics for changing behavior —human relations.

Who Makes Them	What They Say	Why They Say It	What You Can Do
2. *People who are not in agreement re the function of education.*	School should teach only the 3 R's and facts from a text book. Other things belong to the home, church and other agencies.	They either do not know or they misunderstand the purposes of education in a democracy and the facts and conditions of modern life.	Cooperative planning for the study of modern education is called for; observation and demonstration helps.
3. *Dissatisfied teachers*	Children can't read but we "have to promote them just the same."	In every classroom the reading range goes over at least 4 grade levels. Some teachers will not accept their own responsibility for teaching the child whatever he needs to know — that includes reading. Some teachers do not understand why children should remain with their age mates.	Begin school wide staff study of the nature of learning and the technics of teaching reading. Employ an extra teacher or more, for "remedial reading," instruction. Begin staff study of: 1. Human growth and development 2. Mental health. Organize inter-visitation programs for teachers so that elementary, Jr. Sr. H. teachers become informed about the problems and technics of teaching at all grade levels.
	We are subject specialists and must not be asked to teach "Common learnings," "General Education."	Too many are in an "educational rut." They do not want to do the work involved in changing the plans and technics which they have used for many years.	Although background training is important, the vast scope in every area makes it essential for every teacher to continue to learn what his pupils need to know. In those areas where unit teaching is done, the idea that the teacher must be an encyclopedia

Who Makes Them Dissatisfied	What They Say	Why They Say It	What You Can Do
teachers Continued:		They have had no experiences in their own educational backgrounds other than the "lecture-text-assignment-tests" technics. They are fearful and insecure because sufficient help is not provided during transition periods.	is not valid. Teachers can learn along with their pupils. Set up in-service learning experiences, utilizing the technics of modern education. Subject matter specialists are needed and can be recognized in the specialized courses open as electives in the upper secondary school years.
	My pupils misbehave because the teacher they come from allows too much freedom.	This teacher doesn't know that the pupils react badly in his class room because of what *he does* and because of their attitudes toward *his program.*	Set up opportunities for teachers to observe each other, to confer with each other about children, to work together to meet pupil needs.
	My classes are too large and (in secondary schools) I must meet too many students to really know them.	In some cases classes are too large. Also modern methods cannot be used in departmental organizations where the pupil load is 200.	Reduce class size. This is often a matter of organization. Organize the day so that a larger block of time is spent with one teacher.
4. *Administrators*	School plants are lacking or are in serious need of repair and modernization.	Building programs have been at a standstill because money has not been made available. Building pro-	Create citizen-professional survey committees to get the facts to take them to the people and to make plans for the kinds of buildings the people

Who Makes Them	What They Say	Why They Say It	What You Can Do
Continued: Administrators	Qualified teachers are not to be had.	grams have not been able to keep up with population increases. Many small children are on half time. Many class rooms are manned by substitutes who have little background and no training. Young people are not willing to go into teaching as a career. Pay is inadequate.	want and for raising the money to build them. Take the facts to the people. Organize "Future Teachers" clubs in senior high schools. Make plans with the help of citizens, to raise enough money to provide tenure, adequate salary schedules, welfare, and retirement plans.
5. *Some Parents and Teachers*	We do not like the methods used in modern schools.	Parents do not understand the methods. These teachers do not know the facts about how learning takes place, are unwilling to learn them and to change their own methods, do not want to do what they believe will be harder work.	Set up study groups of teachers and parents to discuss the nature of the learning process. Give parents opportunity to take part in all the experiences in the modern classroom. Gather facts which will show the relative merits of methods used.

Who Makes Them	What They Say	Why They Say It	What You Can Do
6. *Frontier Thinkers*	Schools are not meeting the needs of children and are not preparing them for life in today's world.	In a large number of schools content and method have not changed in accordance with new knowledge about the nature of learning. In these schools, no account is taken of the changes in life due to modern inventions and war. Facilities, equipment, materials, supplies are lacking.	Provide professional leadership. Create an in-service education program planned cooperatively with the teachers. Provide for participation of teachers, citizens and pupils in policy making, administration and control.

A workshop group in secondary education at Ohio State University outlined another type of criticism—the "attack" type—and found that it fell in ten major areas:

1. Schools are not effectively teaching children the fundamental skills.

2. Schools are not developing obedience, respect for authority, a sense of responsibility or a sense of the importance of hard work.

3. Schools fail to stimulate competition among students and to reveal to parents the comparative standing of their children.

4. Schools are trying to educate many young people who cannot profit sufficiently from such education.

5. Schools have not been effective in interpreting their programs to the public.

6. Schools fail to develop a wholehearted allegiance to the American way of life.

7. Schools are taking over the functions and responsibilities of the home and other institutions.

8. Schools are not teaching boys and girls to make a living.

9. Schools have not kept pace with social change.

10. School personnel are incompetent to deal with the complex problems the modern school faces.

Five of these criticisms are examined in the following extracts from the group's report.

Let's Look at the Attacks on the Schools

By Harold Alberty and Others

(Published by the College of Education, Ohio State University, Columbus, Ohio, 1951. Used with permission)

I. THE CRITICISM. *Schools are not effectively teaching children the fundamental skills.*

Some laymen today charge that schools are not effectively teaching children the fundamental skills, that is, reading writing, and arithmetic. It is their belief that the conventional curriculum of the elementary and secondary schools of the past, in which the three R's were narrowly defined, did a more effective job. Parents are complaining that boys and girls cannot multiply, spell simple words, write decent paragraphs, or recite the alphabet.

II. THE EVIDENCE

Research workers in the field of education have been trying for many years to determine whether or not there is any improvement in the development of basic skills in the modern school as compared with the traditional school. Studies have been carried on by colleges and universities as well as by local schools systems, and a summary of their findings should help school people, parents, and other interested citizens to judge achievement in this respect. These studies provide evidence about the relative effectiveness of instruction of basic skills in the present-day curriculum as compared with the older and more traditional practices.

In Houston, Texas E. E. Oberholtzer evaluated the teaching of skills in a modern elementary school curriculum as contrasted with teaching by means of more traditional exercises and methods. A group of pupils following modern methods and a comparable conventional group were tested by means of the *Thorndike-McCall Reading Scale*. The results reveal that children in the newer curriculum achieved a grade score of 6.4 in reading comprehension compared with a grade score of 6.3 for matched children under conventional practices. Furthermore, the newer type group of pupils spent less time than the conventional type, and on this account devoted more time to other skills and to other activities.

In the Roslyn, Long Island elementary schools, where modern practices have been instituted, *The Metropolitan Achievement Test in Reading* was administered. Pupils under conventional practices received a grade score of 5.9 as compared with 5.8 for newer practices. In this instance the traditional school scored slightly higher.

At the Lincoln School of Teachers College, the pupils were given the *New Stanford Achievement Test* and although there was a tendency for children in the lower grades to be a little below the test averages in reading, by the end of the elementary grades the children had learned as much about reading skills as other equally bright children in the larger population. Pupils under the newer methods received a grade score of 6.6 and those under the older 6.5.

In New York City, Jersild and his associates administered the *Modern School Achievement Reading Test* to comparable groups of activity and non-activity pupils. The test results for the groups reveal that the activity, or newer-curriculum group, excelled slightly the achievement of the non-activity, or conventional curriculum group. The scores were 5.8 to 5.7.

In Los Angeles, California, the *New Stanford* tests in reading have been administered over a period of years. From the records in the central office, a comparative study was made of achievement in thirty-three elementary schools for which data were available for the school years 1923-24 and 1933-34. Between 1923 and 1933 a modern curriculum was introduced into the Los Angeles elementary schools. In comparing the achievement in reading it was found that the 1933-34 sixth grade group had a gain of six months over the earlier group. The grade score for the conventional group was 6.0 as against 6.6 for the newer group.

At the secondary school level, Boatley discovered that pupils in certain junior high-schools that enriched the curriculum content through a reduction of time devoted to the so-called fundamental skills did not have their growth in reading hampered by the change. Washburne and Raths found that the achievement of pupils from the Winnetka elementary schools was on a comparable level with that of pupils from more traditional schools in high-school English, including reading. Evidence from the study by the Evaluation Staff of the Commission on the Relation of School and College of the Progressive Education Association indicates that students from the experimental high-schools read as well or better than comparable students from conventional high-schools.

The simple concept of arithmetic and other branches of mathematics as comprised largely of computational skills has been revised by leaders in the field of mathematics during recent years. These leaders propose that in the modern curriculum, mathematics should include not only the function of teaching skills in computation, but other related skills which have a direct application to present-day living.

The newer and conventional curriculum groups studying arithmetic in Houston achieved practically equivalent grade scores of 6.8. At Roslyn, Long Island, there was no difference in the level of achievement made by pupils under the two curriculums.

The Pistor study, the Lincoln School study, and the Wrightstone study reveal superior achievement on the *New Stanford* test by pupils in the newer curriculum practices compared with pupils in the conventional curriculum. The achievement was about 0.2 higher in each study.

In Los Angeles, California, the New Stanford tests in arithmetic administered to pupils in seventeen schools. It was found that the attainments of the older and the newer groups were practically equivalent.

Hizor and Harap demonstrated that activities may be so

arranged as to give the pupils practice in all the computations in decimals. The authors concluded that at least under conditions of good teaching, an arithmetic activity program based on real life situations incorporating the basic arithmetic steps may be undertaken with considerable assurance that these steps will be mastered.

At the junior-high-school level Boatley found that pupils were devoting less time to formal learning experiences in arithmetic but were progressing as well as comparable pupils in more conventional school organization. Washburne, Raths, and Wrigtstone found that the achievement of pupils in high-school mathematics was as high as that of pupils who were taught through more traditional practices.

Fawcett has demonstrated that pupils can be taught to apply some of the logic in mathematical relationship in the analysis and discussion of problems in other subject matter fields and at the same time master the essential mathematical concepts.

The old idea that language was largely a study of grammar, composition, spelling, and penmanship has for some time been replaced in the modern curriculum by a new definition of language, learning to do better those language activities that pupils will practice in their every-day living. This change, practiced in present-day core curriculums, has placed an emphasis upon the good usage aspects of language. The exercises are no longer isolated from other activities but are developed through meaningful social situations in the classroom.

In language usage, the Roslyn study shows that the newer curriculum had stimulated growth definitely above the comparative averages of the test; those averages are based mainly on the performance of pupils in conventional schools. The New York City study shows an advantage of one month in grade-score achievement in favor of the newer over the traditional methods. In a like manner, the Lincoln School study shows a one-month advantage on the language-usage test in favor of the newer practices.

In spelling achievement, the Houston study reveals a difference of two months in favor of the conventional-school pupils, but the Pistor study and New York City study reveal differences in favor of the newer-school pupils.

Spelling test data in Los Angeles showed that the newer curriculum had contributed a gain of four months over the earlier achievement.

The achievement of Winnetka high-school students in English was found to be slightly superior to that of students from more conventional schools. In the Progressive Education Association study of the success of experimental high-school students in college, a superiority with respect to grade points in English and the humanities was evident.

In a series of interviews taken in Columbus, Ohio, it is interesting to note that 132 adult persons considered the teaching of fundamental skills as "very important," 27 as "fairly important," and one "don't know." These same people rated the job being done in the teaching of them in the following manner: 71 "good," 66 "mediocre," 12 "poor," and 10 "don't know."

III. THE INTERPRETATION

The evidence of growth in basic skills, both at the elementary and the secondary levels, reveals clearly that in the modern curriculum these skills are achieved as well or better than in the conventional curriculum. This is true for the basic skills discussed here, namely, skills in reading, arithmetic, and language. The evidence of growth cited here has been drawn from the major experiments and research studies that have been conducted and reported in recent years. Although many smaller and less comprehensive studies might have been cited, such evidence tends to support the findings already indicated.

Studies in many communities, both large and small, show that pupils in the newer curriculum master reading skills as well as or better than comparable pupils in the conventional curriculum. A variety of reading tests were employed in the studies; hence the consistent trend of evidence seems well established.

Achievement on a variety of arithmetic tests in a variety of communities provides evidence that pupils in the newer schools are obtaining standards equal or superior to comparable pupils in conventional schools. Evidence is presented for the achievement of mathematical skills at the elementary and at the secondary levels.

For the elementary school evidence in language skills is presented for language usage and for spelling achievement. In general, the newer type of curriculum produces pupils who surpass the pupils of the conventional type of curriculum in language usage. In spelling achievement, however, there is no difference. Studies of achievement in English at the high-school level are favorable to the newer practices.

I. THE CRITICISM. *Schools are not developing obedience, respect for authority, a sense of responsibility, or a sense of the importance of hard work.*

It is charged in some quarters that schools have adopted a new type of pedagogy which regards the child and his wishes and desires as sacred. The business of the teacher is to find out what the child wants to do. To *force* him to do anything against his will is likely to warp his personality. This attitude on the part of the teacher fails to develop, so the charge runs, sound habits of discipline and a wholesome respect for hard work, even though it may be distasteful.

The attitude expressed in the criticism is perhaps typical of a group of people who look back on the rigors of their education with satisfaction. They tend to think that many of the evils of modern day living could be eradicated if the schools were to return to the system of coercion and regimentation of the "good old days."

This criticism is voiced not only by laymen, but also by certain groups of educators who are advocates of classical education and rigorous mastery of subject matter as the only road to improvement of society.

II. THE EVIDENCE. What evidence is there to support these charges? The lack of "respect for authority," "a sense of responsibility," and "a sense of the importance of hard work" is difficult to prove. Even though we might admit that there is much juvenile delinquency today, we have no way of demonstrating that it is due even in part to the failure of the school. The fact that we have suffered two devastating world wars within a generation would be a more likely explanation for, as Quincy Wright states:

> Wars of large magnitude have been followed by anti-intellectual movements in art, literature, and philosophy, by waves of crime, sexual licence, suicide, venereal disease, delinquent youth; by class, racial and religious intolerance, persecution, refugees, social and political revolution, by abandonment of orderly processes for settling dispute and changing law; and by a decline in repect for international law and treaties.

Obviously, it is impossible to prove objectively whether or not the schools of today are less effective in cultivating a sense of responsibility, self-discipline, etc., than was the case a generation ago. These behaviors are intangibles which cannot be measured with calipers or a yardstick. They would need to be studied by means of careful observation of hundreds of students both in and out of school, as well as in communities having traditional and "progressive" school systems. Even then there would be no way of determining how the results compared with the effectiveness of schools a generation ago. The best that we can do, therefore, is to look critically at the situation in terms of current trends and practices in our culture and in the schools and draw whatever inferences are warranted.

III. INTERPRETATION. Many of those who make these charges against schools of today rely upon memories of their youthful experiences in schools to make their point. These charges usually are prefaced by: "Now when *I* went to school. . . . ."

The setting of the modern school has changed vastly. Urbanization has brought with it tremendous problems of housing. Science has multiplied many-fold the productive capacity of workers not only in the factory but on the farm as well. Science has made possible an economy of abundance, but we have not yet learned how to utilize fully the fruits of science for promoting human welfare.

The modern high school, unlike its predecessor, is called upon to deal with youth of all degrees of intelligence and abilities. It now enrolls approximately seven out of ten American youth and the percentage is advancing rapidly. These youth, with their enormous diversity of abilities and interests must be prepared to face a complex and confused world in which old standards and values are passing, and in which new ones have not yet been fully developed. The youth who attend these high schools, by and large, have been robbed of the opportunities for developing self-discipline, social responsibilities, and a sense of the importance of hard work because of the changed character of the home and the community. In other words, the school can no longer regard itself as a supplementary agency. It must become the principal institution of the community for developing, interpreting, and extending the democratic way of life.

The concepts of obedience and respect for authority have to be interpreted in terms of the kinds of behavior which characterize them. The traditional school sought to develop unquestioned obedience and respect for authority. It was for the schoolmaster to decide what was to be thought and done, and for the students to obey. It is not difficult to see that such interpretations are well suited to a totalitarian society in which the leaders tell the people what to think and what to do. The new school, however, recognizes that democracy requires a reinterpretation of those concepts. If citizens are to play their part in the preservation of our freedoms, they must be taught that authorities are to be evaluated, and that only those that promise most for improving democratic living are to be trusted and followed. How else are students to learn to distinguish between the stateman and the demagogue, between truth and propaganda?

Teacher-student planning is not a surrender of the teacher to the whims of the students. It is a genuine attempt to teach the values of democracy by living them in the classroom, the

shops, the studios, and on the playing fields. Externally imposed discipline gives way to increasing power on the part of
students to assume responsibility for their own conduct.

The critics seem to make a virtue out of work that is especially hard and distasteful. Forcing the student to perform
inherently disagreeable tasks is supposed to train him for the
rigors of life outside the school. Furthermore, such tasks are
supposed somehow to "train the mind." What the critics fail
to recognize is that much has been discovered in recent years
concerning the nature of learning and the conditions under
which it takes place most effectively. It is now a commonly
recognized principle that learning is most effective when the
task is accepted by the learner as being worthwhile and when
its accomplishment is accompanied by a feeling of genuine
achievement. In other words, students work hard at tasks which
have significance in their lives. The modern school, therefore,
organizes its program in terms of the problems and functions
of present-day living, instead of in terms of the dead past.

Good schools everywhere are struggling to relate their programs to the realities of living in a complex and confused
world. The critics are obligated to use their criticism to further
the task, rather than to destroy the gains which have been
made.

1. THE CRITICISM. *Schools fail to stimulate competition
   among students and to reveal to parents the comparative
   standing of their children.*

In many schools throughout the country, scholastic achievement is regarded as only one aspect of the growth of children.
These schools are concerned with the total development of each
individual as he works and plays in various school situations.
Thus, social, physical, and academic growth are all watched
with interest and carefully evaluated. This evaluation takes
the form of a detailed letter discussing such subjects as the
child's health, his ability to get along with his classmates, his
character, his desires and needs, his dislikes, his skills (reading,
writing and arithmetic), his interests, his strong points and

where he needs to improve.

Some parents have attacked this system on the grounds that it does not show clearly and precisely where their children stand in relation to the other children in the class. They believe that "competition is the spice of life" and that only by giving the marks, A, B, C, or 90, 80, 70 can a child be induced to work. These parents feel that there are so many values in competition and in the comparison of scholastic achievement, that the schools should include number or letter grading at all levels.

II. THE EVIDENCE. On June 14, 1950 a group of seventy citizens from Upper Arlington, Ohio, signed a petition in which they requested changes in their schools. One of these things they wanted was to include some grading in both high-school and the elementary school. This group of parents called "The Education Improvement Association of Upper Arlington," urged other Arlington parents to join and received some support from citizens of Columbus, Ohio, as well as from people in other states. The Arlington movement began to spread. Their executive committee had contact with groups in the following cities: East Lansing, Michigan; Denver, Colorado; Pasadena and Glendale, California; Minneapolis, Minnesota; Franklin, Indiana; Eugene, Oregon; and Scarsdale, New York. The Denver parents and the Arlington parents had recommendations that were alike. The text of their recommendations as printed in the Columbus Dispatch was as follows: "Both groups ask for reintroduction of grading systems as the basis for encouraging individual initiative and supplying progress information to parents."

In many public high schools throughout the country, teachers are required to promote pupils from one grade to the next; they are permitted to fail only a very small number. In New York City, pupils in the General Course do not take the Regents Examinations. Also, there are no failures; everyone is promoted. This situation disturbs some people.

In a poll of 165 people in Columbus, Ohio, the following question was asked, "Do you think grades are a good, very good, or bad way of letting parents know how their children are progressing?" Out of 165 people, 101 said that grades were good or very good.

What are the evils of our grading system? First of all, the teacher has the power to say who shall pass and who shall fail. This can result in great unhappiness for large numbers of children. The most striking example is what happened in New York City last year at the close of school. The *New York Times* stated, "900,000 students quit school happy. Less joyous, perhaps, were 32,000 students who will attend summer high-schools to make up courses that were failed during the regular academic year."

Children feel very strongly about this question of marks. Professor Ruth Strang says in the article "What Did You Get On Your Report Card?" in the National Parent-Teacher Magazine:

> "They worry, and they worry, and they worry! At the end of every six weeks,' one child says, 'you feel you would like to be up north in a lonely part of the world.' Remembering punishments for previous failures, some children feel positively sick when they see low marks in their report cards. They entertain thoughts of running away, signing their parents' names—even, in some cases, committing suicide. Some children *pray* for good marks.

The competition which stems from our grading system can cause children either to become very nervous and high strung or to feel inferior and defeated. Those who learn slowly will soon say "What's the difference. I'll never catch up with the others." They usually hate the children who manage to get the high marks. The bright students often become cocky and spend their time ridiculing the dull pupils. One seventeen-year old said, "There ought to be a law against so much competition in the schools; it doesn't do anybody any good; it does lots of kids a lot of harm." Unfortunately you cannot convince many mothers and fathers. They still say, "Competition is the spice of life," or "To set up a classroom where no competition exists is to create an unreal situation." Two out-standing professors claim that our system of competition in schools can put a great strain on most children and can seriously damage their personalities. They believe that a child is better able to meet the problems of life if he is not tormented from early childhood by competition.

In Pasadena, California, workshops in several schools discussed what bad effects grades had on children. Their conclusion stressed "the importance of working for something other than grades."

One teacher reminds us that the qualities which really matter to our friends are in the following order of importance: "honesty, generosity, thoughtfulness; and last of all, intelligence; good marks are afterthoughts." How important are marks in our life today? Ida C. McGuire replies:

> With the whole world crying for peace among all its people, how can educators, teachers, or parents stand around crying for marks or awards in academic skills? If marks and awards it must be, let's place them on citizenship, on fair play, on the recognition of the rights of others, on personal honesty and trustworthiness, on good will and respect for every other individual regardless of race, creed, or economic status.

"The National Council for American Education," has published a booklet by Allen A. Zoll called, *Progressive Education Increases Delinquency*. In his chapter, "Competition Is the Staff of Life," Zoll declares that progressive schools are doing irreparable harm to children by neglecting to teach them how to compete with one another. He believes that the schools are creating a dream world in which boys and girls are not being prepared to face a ruthless, cold, unsentimental society. He states that competition is as much a part of our physical make-up as the function of breathing.

The modern school is entirely aware of the "dog eat dog" philosophy which is sometimes rampant in our society today. But, unlike Zoll, our modern schools are willing to fight this deplorable situation. They are teaching the children to respect each others opinions and to share and exchange ideas as they work together for the good of the group. Thus, they are striving to replace competition by cooperation. Zoll offers no evidence in support of his assertions. He has obviously not made a follow-up study of the graduates of modern schools. In the follow-up study made of the graduates of the University School, The Ohio State University, it was found that these alumni did very well in college and were making successful places for themselves in society.

In another chapter, "Automatic Promotion," Zoll claims that all pupils in progressive schools are graduates provided they "hang around" a certain number of years. Again he does not present any proof that this is true. At the University School, The Ohio State University, children who do not work up to their mental capacity and who do not show evidence of social and emotional growth do not advance with their group. Promotion depends on the satisfactory completion of requirements set up by the group and the teacher. On the other hand, children whose mental ability is low are not expected to do the same caliber of work as the very bright children. It is not reasonable to require pupils of low ability to produce work which is impossible for them to do.

Another organization, "The American Education Association," has published a booklet by Milo F. McDonald called: *"Progressive" Poison in Public Education*. In his chapter, "One Hundred Per Cent Promotions," McDonald attacks the practice of awarding high-school diplomas to children of retarded mental development. He believes that these children are not entitled to high-school diplomas. Our modern high school believes that high-school diplomas should be given to all students who have developed socially, academically, morally, and emotionally to the best of their ability. A grave social injustice is committed when diplomas are denied to children of low ability if these children are making an effort to develop all their capacities. The modern high-school recognizes individual differences and realizes that maturation is slower in some children than in others. Since this is a biological fact, the modern school does not penalize under-developed children by withholding diplomas.

III. THE INTERPRETATION. Grades can be an unjust, unhealthy practice. The marks, A, B, C, or 90, 80, 70 really have no meaning since they do not tell anything about the many sides of the personality of the child. Competition can lead to cheating, flattery, defeatism and envy. Examinations really ask for a parrot-like reproduction of facts. Students are passed from one grade to another, whether or not they show they have learned anything. The child is not asked to take part in judging his own work.

The modern school realizes the importance of the teacher and the child and the parent working together as a team in order to collect all possible information about a child before making a report on his progress. Van Miller, a professor at the University of Illinois, says:

> A report more helpful to the development of the child could be a report *from the home to the school*. What is important is not the English the child uses in English class, but the English the child uses around the home; not the class marks in social studies but the extent to which the child plays with the children of the neighborhood and fits into the situation or improves upon it; not how the child reads in reading class but what the child reads and how much he reads out of school time.

The child's opinion of his progress is necessary. Some people believe he should have the opportunity to write his own report and then read it to the teacher. A meeting between the teacher and pupil should follow in order to see where the teacher and child agree or disagree. The goals had been set up long before by the pupils and the teacher. It is up to the pupil and teacher to see whether the child reached these goals satisfactorily or not.

The modern school knows that competition is a part of life in America today. It does not say that competition, if handled wisely is bad. The important question is what the attitude of the child is toward competition. Edith G. Neisser writing in Parents Magazine says:

It is the attitude toward competition which he or she "caught" in early childhood from the atmosphere of home, that largely determines whether rivalry is a destructive force or whether it can be turned to good account. Whether or not his early experiences give him a sort of immunization that helps him take competition easily, makes him overvalue it or fear it, depends on the dosage, the timing, and the handling of these early experiences.

I. THE CRITICISM. *Schools fail to develop a wholehearted allegiance to the American way of life.*

The charge that schools fail to develop a wholehearted allegiance to the American way of life is frequently heard. The attacks range all the way from claims that there is too much textbook teaching and not enough practice of democratic principles to the accusation that our schools are subtly teaching socialism or communism. It is further claimed that our schools are neither preparing youth for adult life nor for effective citizenship.

II. THE EVIDENCE.

A small group of 70 Upper Arlington parents, representing 35 or 40 families out of 940, wrote a letter to the Board of Education, in which it was charged that there was a lack of instruction in history, civics, and geography.

The Church League of America claims that the "discernible swing to the left" in our political orientation has its source in the school system, and that there are forces which are trying to bring about radical changes in the "American way" and which use education as an instrument for this purpose. Similar charges are made by the National Council for Education and its Executive Vice-President Allen A. Zoll. The Conference of American Small Business Organizations' Committee on Education brings forth this charge in the form of reviews of textbooks which they feel endanger our American way of life. Their publication, the *Educational Reviewer* also publishes attacks on the schools in other forms such as a testimonial of a student called Roger MacBride (April, 1950 issue). MacBride claims in his editorial entitled, "What They Are Teaching Us" that "very few young people finish school today without having a tinge of collectivism ingrained in them."

The School Development Council of Pasadena claims that it is part of the modern educational program "to sell our children on the collapse of our way of life and to substitute collectivism for it. One enemy of this type of education claims his daughter came home "interested in nothing but happiness and security." In his booklet entitled *"Progressive" Poison in Public Education,* Milo MacDonald condemns textbooks because of "communistic leanings." He claims the activity program was introduced in Russian schools for the sole purpose of creating anarchy. This in turn justified the rigid indoctrination which was desirable from the communist point of view.

Other organizations that are making charges similar to that made by Allen Zoll in a pamphlet *Progressive Education Increases Delinquency* and who claim that "progressive education promotes socialism, wrecks the individual, opposes individualism and produces social delinquency," are: The Employers Association of Chicago, the National Association of Pro-America, and small local organizations in Minneapolis, Minnesota; Denver, Colorado; Pasadena, California; Scarsdale, New York; New York City; Upper Arlington, Ohio; Englewood, New Jersey; and Antelope Valley, California. Most of the attacks range from the charge that subtle indoctrination for socialistic attitudes is being effected, to charges which are similar to those in the pamphlet issued by the National Council for Education entitled, *They Want Your Child,* in which the following statement appears: "The infiltration and control of American education became communism's number one objective in America. They want the children of America. They want your child."

Representing the second direction to which we have referred are the participlants in a Youth Forum which was held in Yonkers, New York. This group protested that academic schooling failed to prepare them for life; that too little attention was given to American history, current events, and to the use of newspapers and periodicals.

III. THE INTERPRETATION. These are samplings of cri-

ticisms of the teaching of the American way of life in high-
schools in the United States.

The cause of the criticism that our schools subtly teach
communism and socialism probably evolves from 1) a misunderstanding of the practice of discussing different ideologies
in the classroom, 2) some much publicized attacks on the
Rugg books, and 3) the attack on the newer methods of education by certain "front" organizations.

Socialist and communist idelogies are included in units of
work in civics and other subjects that are concerned with the
various forms of government that may be found in the world
today. The reasoning behind the inclusion of these ideologies
is that we must know as much as possible about other forms of
government in order to know the dangers and difficulties into
which we may fall unsuspectingly.

These critics fail to remember that modern principles of
education provide for the use of the method of intelligence
and this method *does not* condone indoctrination.

In order to assure parents that teachers are not communists,
teachers are required to subscribe to an oath to support the
Constitution of the United States. This oath is supplemented
by another oath to not try to overthrow the government of
the United States by force. The writer made a limited survey
of the education laws of many states and found that such laws
were frequently included in the school codes and that many
teacher contracts contained provisions for the oath of allegiance.
The oaths are intended to protect the schools against subversive teaching.

Critics of modern education assume that students who learn
the pledge of allegiance to the flag, the Preamble to the Constitution, and the Declaration of Independence are automatically loyal to their country. This is wrong. Learning facts and
rules does not inevitably result in appropriate action. In the
conventional school the students recite the pledge of allegiance,
memorize the Preamble to the Constitution, and discuss American ideals. No effort is made to interpret and to relate them
to their daily living. After a short period these lessons are

forgotten. The modern high-school students not only learn the material mentioned above but they participate in programs and face problems that make the material under discussion alive and meaningful. They relate the material to their daily living and thus it becomes a part of them. Lessons thus learned are more realistic and not so easily forgotten.

The modern high-school student knows the dangers of totalitarian government and has had practice in recognizing and evaluating propaganda for what it is. He is not likely to become a victim of this and other vicious schemes that are utilized by all totalitarian governments. Loyalty to the American way of life goes deeper than a pledge of allegiance, beautiful words, and flag waving. One must experience democratic practices and living if these values are to be protected, retained and extended.

The habit of good citizenship can and should be developed in our schools through the use of modern methods of education. This would inevitably lead to thoughtful participation in local and national affairs.

Students should be able to learn about many different careers while in school so that they may intelligently choose their future work in order that society as well as they themselves will receive the greatest benefit.

The school should help the student to learn to live happily and cooperatively with others, thus building a better citizen and a stronger nation.

None of the important elements of the American way of life can be learned efficiently from textbooks alone. It is the duty of the modern high-school to teach our way of life by leading the pupils actually to experience it in every way possible. Democratic living must be practiced, not looked at.

Our schools should be organized so as to exemplify democratic living at its best. They must be so organized and administered that the children will have an opportunity to live democratically by the actual process of living, working, and planning together.

I. THE CRITICISM. *Schools are taking over the functions and responsibilities of the home and other institutions.* Many persons have recently declared an "open season" on certain educational practices of the modern school. They express the belief that the schools are going too far in their expanded programs; that schools are meddling with the affairs of the home and other institutions which contribute to the total education of the child.

This issue needs thorough study because of the widespread criticisms of parents and because of the frequent attacks which are being made by certain pressure groups which wield strong influences in shaping community opinions and supplying "right" answers for our schools.

II. THE EVIDENCE. In the June 14, 1950, issue of the *Columbus Evening Dispatch,* an article appeared which stated that a parents' group in Upper Arlington, Ohio, was dissatisfied with the teachings of societal understandings in their schools. They stated that such social values should be left to the home.

It is understandable that certain parents would object to most any phase of the school program. Much of this comes about because they are uninformed of the function of the modern school. Many parents believe that the sole function of the school is to teach the fundamental skills. They fail to realize that the schools have had to change in order to meet the needs of a world which has changed. Today it is not sufficient to be competent in the three R's. Our present-day society is extremely complex. It demands a social development and a preparation for living in an atomic age. The modern school must, therefore, be interested in the all-round development of its children. It must look upon each child as a total being whose psychological drives, problems to be solved, and ideals to be developed are every bit as important as his achievements in spelling.

In today's schools are found children who represents a cross-section of every ethnic, social, economic, and religious group in America. The homogeneity which characterized the school of earlier days is not found in the schools of today. The modern school must, therefore, devise ways of meeting the needs, not of a few, but of all. This the modern school is attempting through providing learning activities which are of benefit to everyone. That some parents are able to do better some of the things which the school sets out to do cannot be refuted, however, there is the danger of the child's being taught in isolation from the society of which he is a part. In too many cases both parents must work in order to produce an income sufficient to satisfy the demands for material goods, in the face of the ever mounting cost of living. With such families, there is not adequate time to devote to meetings all the needs of the children as once might have been the case. In other instances, many children come from broken homes which, of course, present a difficulty not unlike the one mentioned above. In some homes there is an adequate library; parents can afford broadening travel experiences and other activities which aid the educative process. In others, the merest semblance to a book is, perhaps, a comic book or some pulp magazines. The schools of today have been forced to widen ther programs and to base them on the development of desirable attitudes, appreciations, and understandings needed in a democratic society. Failure to do so leaves to change the strengthening of the very foundation upon which our society rests.

III. THE INTERPRETATION. In a view of the lack of uniformity of the criticisms of the school, it is difficult for the modern school to determine just what it can do. That is, the school program functions in some areas which can be thought of as "home" areas with apparent parental agreement; yet, in others, it is thought to be meddling. Through the aid of the federal government, our schools may provide hot lunches for a small fee, special provisions being made for those who cannot afford to pay. Certainly it is not felt that it is the special duty of the school to provide nourishment for its students; there are, of course, parents who object to the practice.

Through various work experiences programs in the areas of business education, trades and industries, home economics and agriculture, the schools provide on-the-job training for students who elect these programs. Some parents criticize the schools for this, while at the same time, others accuse the schools of making no effort to teach boys and girls how to make a living.

The schools provide health services—giving examinations, extracting and cleaning teeth, administering vaccinations, and in many cases, short-term hopsitalization for purposes of observation. Few parents object to this but frequently such programs are under fire from certain professional groups who regard such practices as "socialistic."

It goes without saying that name-calling and harsh criticism never end in providing workable solutions; they almost inevitably widen the breach. Those who criticize the schools owe it to themselves to find out what the schools are doing. Through the cooperation of parents, teachers, and administrators, there can be developed the kind of understanding which will make our schools go forward and thus obviate the endless hours of bickering about a thing which is indubitably of mutual concern.

This proposal for a solution begins with a consideration of the child. John Dewey states the matter succinctly as follows, "What the best and wisest parent wants for his own child, that must the community want for all its children. Any other ideal for our schools is unlovely; acted upon, it destroys our democracy." The child is a member of society and all learning activities should be so planned that they will make him better able to participate in that society.

These are definitions of some of the criticisms levelled against the modern school and answers to the major ones. It is clear that some of the harshest critics—even the ones who repeatedly make the most frequently-refuted charges—are often persons of good intention, who believe strongly in public education but fear that it is sometimes remiss. In the following article, an attempt is made to analyze some of these statements as expressed by spokesmen for this type of criticism.

Patches for the Tattered Cloak

By Archibald W. Anderson

(Excerpted from the article, "The Cloak of Responsibility: The Attackers and Their Methods," and published in Progressive Education, the journal of the American Education Fellowship, January, 1952. Used with permission.)

In the baldest form, the new development in the attacks consists of a claim that the educational profession is attempting to smear by implication all critics of education. Individuals in reputable positions come forward and say, in effect, "These organizations you talk about are minor affairs. Most of us never heard of them and wouldn't have anything to do with them. We may make similar criticisms but we are respectable people and, therefore, our charges are respectable and should be accepted as valid." This is a curious inversion of the *argumentum ad hominem* technique. Instead of impugning the criticism by attacking the critic, it seeks to validate the criticism by honoring the character of the critic; honest men make honest criticism. It is certainly true that educators cannot *disprove* a criticism by showing that some of the people who make it have bad motives. But, on the other hand, critics cannot *prove* their criticism by demonstrating the purity of their motives.

This new contention of the critics is fallacious on two counts. In the first place, it is not true that the educational profession is attempting to smear all critics and thus stifle criticism. Actually, one of the most productive, although not the most dramatic, phases of the profession's counter-attack has been the stepping up of its already proceeding efforts to establish school-community advisory councils or other avenues of communication through which criticism can be channelled, dispassionately evaluated and acted upon if valid. The profession is receiving material assistance along this line from the National Citizens Commission for the Public Schools which is financed by the Rockefeller Foundation and the Carnegie Foundation. This Commission assists in the formation of local committees representing a cross-section of the community and furnishes such committees with free materials explaining how to organize, what to look for in evaluating schools, how to work with local educators, etc.

In the second place, the contention is in error because it confuses three things: (1) the question of the validity of a particular criticism (which in most cases is a question of fact and not of opinion); (2) the question of the motives of those making the criticism; and (3) the question of what the educational effects of acting on the criticism will be. Although not without interrelationship, these are independent questions in the sense that answering any one of them does not necessarily provide an answer for the others. Perhaps this point can be made clearer by examining a specific illustration.

The October 27, 1951, number of *School and Society* contained an article, "In Defense of the Critics of American Public Education," by Hugh Russell Fraser, Education Editor, *Pathfinder News Magazine*. In this article Mr. Fraser scolds the educators for "impeaching the motives of the critics" and urges them "to cease terming all critics as 'the enemy.'" He states that if a layman or a parent suggests that there are basic problems to be examined in the schools of today, "the educationist will not only refuse flatly to study the problem sympathetically, but he will regard even the raising of the question as an impertinence."

Having indicated that educators reject any and all criticism from any source, Mr. Fraser assures his readers that in discussing the activities of Zoll and others the educators are "setting up 'straw men' and knocking them down." He not only gives the general assurance that there is "nothing to fear from the crackpots" because "they are few in number and essentially ineffective," but he specifically says that "Zoll had no more to do with what happened in Pasadena than the flowers that bloom in May." Just how realistic this interpretation is, each individual must judge for himself. However, the evidence contained in the investigations reviewed earlier in this paper is not likely to induce many friends of the public school to join Mr. Fraser in his carefree view of the innocuousness of the groups who are encouraging unjustified attacks on education.

With the "crackpots" dismissed as negligible, Mr. Fraser demands that the "educational hierarchy" face "the most perceptive criticism," explore its validity, and either disprove or act upon it. He then says that he has "yet to see any of the high priests in the teachers colleges do this." Mr. Fraser regards Bernard Iddings Bell as "probably the most perceptive critic of education today" (his use of the word "perceptive" has a significance which will be apparent later) and refers to the statements by Bell about the school's failure in the "disciplines of word, number, and form." Fraser later says that the greatest defect of the schools is lack of training in character, and he agains quotes Bell in support of this statement. Perhaps a more detailed clue to Mr. Fraser's ideas concerning perceptive criticism and perceptive critics may be found in an article in the education section of *Pathfinder* for October 3, 1951. This article is unsigned and there is no evidence that Mr. Fraser wrote it. However, the fact that he is editor of the education section of the magazine, and the further fact that the views expressed in the *Pathfinder* article coincide with those in his *School and Society* article, give reason to suppose that he may have had something to do with the remarks made in the *Pathfinder* article. According to that article, the burden of all the attacks is that the three R's are inadequately taught, that some subjects are too lightly touched, that discipline is lax, and that teachers colleges are turning out teachers trained in methods of teaching, but lacking in knowledge of what they are supposed to teach. The article also says that educators have ignored such "real and effective critics of U. S. public school education" as Dr. Bell, Dr. Robert M. Hutchins, and Albert Lynd, a businessman whose article, "Quackery in the Public Schools," appeared in the *Atlantic Monthly*. The article states that "the central theme of the major critics is that the schools are not doing as good a job as they could do," and later says that although educators have denied the neglect of the 3 R's and the failure of discipline, the "charges of emphasis in teachers colleges on teaching methods at the expense of subject matter have not thus far been refuted." There is not sufficient space to reply in detail to the various items in this bill of indictment. Our concern here is with the way in which these particular criticisms relate to the previous charge that educators are intolerant of criticism and ignore it.

So far as Dr. Bell's charge of the failure of the discplines of word, number, and form, is concerned, there is ample evidence to show that educators have devoted a great deal of time and attention to these disciplines, and have not failed in teaching them. Similarly, educators have been devoting a great deal of attention to character education, as a glance at the articles on "character education" and "personality" in the revised edition of the *Encyclopedia of Educational Research* will show. Actually, Bell seems less concerned with character education of a generalized type than he is with securing public funds for church-controlled schools. Far from ignoring this point of view, educators have been debating it at great length. One full dress discussion is contained in a series of articles in Progressive Education for February, 1949. Numerous other discussions have appeared within the last few years, notably *The Attack Upon the American Tradition in Religion and Education,* by R. Freeman Butts. One proposal of Dr. Bell's which is not mentioned by Mr. Fraser is that at about the age of 16 common men should be shunted into special schools providing manual training and "simplified study" of certain academic subjects, while the intellectual elite, "a chosen group," will continue in an education which will prepare them to be "the interpreters and directors of a sane, common life" and to be the "leaders" of "their less perceptive brethren." The reasoning on which this proposal is based is an integral part of Bell's whole educational and social theory. To accept Bell's "perceptive criticism," as Mr. Fraser seems to be urging educators to do, would be to use the schools to develop a governing intellectual aristocracy. A crucial issue is at stake here. As Wheeler has said in his article, "Education and the *Aristoi*":

> "It is fashionable these days to attack our American experiment in universal education. . . . Considering the prevailing fashion, it is all too easy to dismiss more sophisticated criticism of American public education as apart of a trend which will soon pass. To do so, however, would be to fail to recognize the significance of a more fundamental movement of which the above mentioned fashion may be only a superficial manifestation. The deeper movement is an attempt to discredit our democratic and pluralistic society in which the elite govern the common people. Education, then, would fit the requirements of the elite while the common people would simply be trained to perform those tasks necessary to support the plans of the favored few. Bell's *The Crisis in Education* is without apology a plea for a government by gentlemen."

Such an aristocratic critique of education as that embodied in Bell's book has not only been considered by educators—*Pathfinder* to the contrary nothwithstanding—but it has been rejected by them, and by the American public as well.

Hutchins is another critic whom the *Pathfinder* article says educators have ignored. In view of the vast amount of discussion of Hutchins' ideas in educational journals, meetings, and books since the appearance of his *Higher Learning in America*, in 1936, it seems strange that anyone would make so absurd a statement. It is true that much of the discussion among educators has been critically and it is true that relatively few of his educational proposals have been adopted even, it might be added, by those who approve his views; but whatever else may be said about Hutchins, it is simply not true that he has been ignored. Rather, he has won the profoundest respect of the teaching profession, including those who differ with him on educational theory, for his prompt and courageous defense of the essential element of a democratic education: freedom in teaching. He has been among the first to oppose the kinds of restriction and prescription upon education which are primary aims of the attacks encouraged by the pressure groups Mr. Fraser tells educators blithely to disregard. At the convocation of the University of Chicago in July, 1949, Dr. Hutchins said:

"The heart of Americanism is independent thought. . . . To persecute people into conformity by the non-legal methods popular today is little better than doing it by purges and progroms. The dreadful unanimity of tribal self-adoration was characteristic of the Nazi state. It is sedulously fostered in Russia. It is to the last degree un-American.

American education has not been constructed on such un-American principles. In general, the practice has been to give the student the facts, to try to help him learn to think, and to urge him to reach his own conclusions. It is not surprising that the heart of American education is the same as that of Americanism: it is independent thought. American education has not tried to produce indoctrinated automatons, but individuals who can think, and who will think always for themselves."

It is in defense of these principles of American education that the educational profession has taken up, and should take up, cudgels against *all* who would deny them.

Still another critic who is ignored by educators, according to the *Pathfinder* article, is Albert Lynd. His article, "Quackery in the Public Schools," is essentially an attack upon teacher training institutions which he accuses of superficiality and of exercising a dictatorial control over public schools, a control which the "educational bureaucracy," he alleges, has usurped from local parents and school boards. He also accuses professors of education in colleges and universities of putting over a revolution in the public schools and of filling the school with hocus-pocus to the detriment of good education. *Pathfinder* is not alone in mentioning Lynd's article. It was mentioned, and a portion of it was quoted, in a newspaper column by George E. Sokolsky, another of whose columns was published in the *Educational Reviewer*. It was also mentioned in *News and Views,* a publication of the Church League of America, where it was called "one of the finest and latest critical appraisals of 'progressive' pedagogues and their handling of the public schools." In view of the *Pathfinder's* statements that educators were ignoring Lynd's article, and that the charges of emphasizing teaching methods instead of subject matter had not been refuted, it is interesting to note that in none of the three places just indicated was there any mention of the excellent reply to Lynd's article written by Dr. Gilbert E. Case of Brown University and also published in the *Atlantic Monthly.* Nor did they mention that the *Atlantic Monthly* reported that it had received "upwards of a hundred" other replies to Lynd. Could it be that those responsible for these omissions were "ignoring" Case's and the other replies because they did not want to call attention to the fact that Lynd's charges could be, and had been, refuted?

The discussion so far has served to illustrate certain points about the independence of the three questions, noted earlier, which tend to be confused in the line of argument exemplified by the *Pathfinder* article and Fraser's article in *School and Society.* The judgment expressed in rejecting Bell's proposal is based on what the educational effect of acting on his criticism would be; and the judgment on that question is not affected either by his standing as a churchman or the invalidity of his charges that there has been a failure in the discipline of word, number, and form. The same point is illustrated in the case of Hutchins. The fact that many educators disagree vigorously with him on some points of educational theory does not alter the fact that they support him on other points with equal vigor. The plain fact is that educators, and particularly those in colleges and departments of education, are continually engaged in examining a great variety of issues in terms of what the educational effects of adopting one or another position with respect to any issue will be. They do this both apart from and in reference to expression of that position by any one person. Any important expression of a particular position by a particular person usually receives, sooner or later, specific examination. However, the fact that that particular person is not mentioned in a discussion of an issue does not mean that the position he represents is not being considered; and the fact that his position is eventually rejected does not mean it has been "ignored."

> *Certainly there are weaknesses in modern education which make it susceptible to the unfair or "attack" kind of criticism. In these three articles, Gordon McCloskey, John Eklund, and Herold Hunt point out some of these weaknesses—the deficits in modern education—and suggest methods of wiping them out.*

Meeting Attacks on Public Education

By Gordon McCloskey

(*Excerpted from Progressive Education, January,* 1952.
Used with permission.)

The attacks on education are serious. Unless they are met
with vigor and skill they can become more serious. For that
reason, as a teacher who has had six years of public relations
experience outside of education, I am going to speak plainly.
I am as guilty as any of the mistakes and omissions I am going
to mention. I accept my share of responsibility for the results.
The statements which follow are not intended as criticism. I
hope they will help all of us in the teaching profession develop
and protect educational programs that provide for the fullest
possible development of human capacities.

The effects of recent attacks on education are partly our
fault. We all know that public education depends on public
support. Public support depends on public understanding. In
a democracy people are entitled to an understanding of the
public enterprises they support. Most of the attacks now being
made on education are possible only because many people are
poorly informed about the objectives and values of modern
school programs. That is our fault. We have been negligent
and careless in at least four respects.

1. *We have failed to devote sufficient effort to the creation
of public understanding.* Whether we like it or not, whether
it should or should not be so, education is in competition with
many other products and services for financial support and
public interest. Public school patrons—parents—taxpayers—are
constantly subjected to hundreds of purposefully and skillfully
designed advertising and propaganda campaigns. Each school

Gordon McCloskey is a professor of education at the State College of Washington.

patron encounters many appeals for his dollars and for his interests.

During decades in which commercial organizations, government and many professional groups have been developing high powered sales and information programs, we have, too generally, assumed that the value of education was so obvious that it would automatically command public interest and support. In general we have neglected or refused, to use the time and energy needed to compete with growing advertising and propaganda programs for public attention and funds. As a result, we are now exposed to attacks. Those attacks would be less effective if people were well informed about the purposes and values of education.

2. *We have explained the purposes and values of education poorly.* In spite of our understanding that a good teacher "starts where the pupil is," we have expected the public to start where we are. Too often, in public statements, we have used complicated technical language that means little to untrained laymen.

No competent advertiser would present his client's product to the public with the technical terms used by the chemists and engineers who produce the product. No experienced speaker addresses laymen with laboratory language. We do. We often excuse such language on the grounds that our work is too complicated to be described simply. Our excuses have not created public understanding. They have exposed us to misinterpretation and attack.

3. *We have involved ourselves in needless and artificial controversy.* In our enthusiasm to develop better school programs we have created the false impression that we are neglecting long accepted objectives. For example, during this generation in which we have made unprecedented improvements in the teaching of reading, we are accused of teaching reading poorly. That is largely because in our enthusiastic, but maladroit, efforts to explain new objectives, we have left impressions that we somehow were replacing the old accepted objective of literacy. Nothing could be further from the truth. But by

awkward presentation of our interests in additional objectives we have unintentionally created impressions that we propose to neglect reading.

4. *We have been defensive.* Many of us have attempted sincerely to correct public misunderstandings. We have often been successful. Too often, however, we still react to criticism with comments that the criticism is unjustified or that the critic obviously does not understand the complexities of education. Both comments may be true. Neither helps correct the public misunderstanding upon which unfair criticism is based.

Likewise many of us have been antagonistic or unresponsive to fair criticism. We interpret many honest criticisms as attacks. By failure to consider or clarify the complaints of honest critics, we have alienated the support of many individuals and groups who have a genuine interest in education.

Those are harsh self criticisms. They are not universally valid, but in general, and to a large extent, they are valid. They are not intended as accusations. They are intended as an analysis that can help us maintain an effective school program for the nation's children. We can do little to improve public understanding of complicated public school objectives until we correct the public information inadequacies on which those self criticisms are based.

Now—let's be more positive.

One problem of all who wish to maintain the best possible education for all children is clear. We must do a much better job of helping all citizens understand the educational needs of children and the best known ways of meeting those needs. That has been said many times before. Mere statement of that objective will be fruitless. We must begin now to *do* that job better. It's a big job. We should be realistic and face the fact that we cannot do it all at once. Our first job is to select specific devices and procedures that will enable us to make *the most effective start* and to begin using them. This is everybody's job—teachers and administrators have equal responsibility.

1. *We should maintain and increase our efforts to improve*

education. Results talk. In spite of misrepresentations, the value of educational procedures that result in human development can be made evident to most people.

Improved quality alone will not protect education against attack, but so long as quality is good, attack will be more difficult and defense relatively easy. Even high quality education will need to be defended by skillful information efforts, but it can be defended. Poor quality education is vulnerable. It cannot, and should not, be defended.

Some will point out that it is high quality education which is most frequently attacked. To a degree that is so. But those attacks are effective only because people are poorly informed about the quality. The writer knows of no other product or service that has lost public confidence because its quality has been improved. We need not retreat.

2. *We should be positive; demonstrate the value of the work we do; avoid being maneuvered into artificially defensive positions.* Our first and most important information job is to provide all parents and citizens with plain, understandable facts about the service schools are rendering their children. We must use *plain understandable language.* The services schools render at present are not perfect. We in the teaching profession are rightly making constant efforts to improve education.

But, in spite of its many imperfections, education as it now stands, is one of the best products on the world market. On the whole, the product is worthy of public confidence. If the facts about the work of schools and our efforts to improve that work are understood, our educational program will command public respect and confidence. While continuing our efforts to improve our product we must boldly and aggressively inform people about its present values.

3. *We should be sure that children understand the reasons for the school work they do.* Children are reporters. Whether we like it or not, they deliver more school news to more homes than the Associated Press or 1000 outfits like the National Council for American Education. If they understand the rea-

sons for their work, their reports will be generally satisfactory. Their words will carry much more weight than those of Allen Zoll.

4. *We should do a more thorough job of informing parents and others about the achievements of children.* This is education's most basic means of keeping people informed about the values of education. So far we have used it poorly. The average person measures the value of a school largely in terms of what it does for his children. The average taxpayer has a deep affection for his children. He wants them to succeed. He is proud of their success. He will support teachers and schools that help them succeed. Likewise he will be antagonistic toward teachers and schools that make failures of his children.

Good schools are helping children to be successful in hundreds of ways. Let's be sure that we give the public abundant evidence of those successes. General Fries and Lucille Crain will have a tough time in a home where parents have evidence that schools are making their children successful.

5. *We should speak language laymen understand; avoid the public use of technical terms that can be misunderstood or misconstrued by citizens on Main Street.* On the street—at bridge parties—at organization luncheons—in news stories—in school publications—on radio and television shows—we have many opportunities to speak of the purposes and achievements of our schools. Let's use more of those opportunities—and let's think more about the background of our listeners and speak the language they understand.

Our enemies attack us in terms that appeal to prejudices and convictions which are quite real to many people. We can never build confidence in education by resorting to equally shoddy trickery. We must never descend to that. But we must explain education in terms that untrained people can understand.

6. *We should learn to make effective use of all modern public information techniques.* Purposefully organized school and community committees can make specific plans for using those devices effectively in *every* community. It is high time that they do.

Let's Weigh the Criticisms of Modern Education

By John M. Eklund

(Reprinted from The American Teacher, December, 1951. Used with permission.)

The hysteria that has been created by some of the groups attacking the schools has already been well described.

Certainly the following facts speak for themselves:

1. In some American communities, large sums of money have been subscribed to promote the vilification of school people and school programs.

2. The material disseminated for this purpose is not factual nor accurate—witness the definition given for progressive education: ". . . It emphasizes the adjustment of the child to the group rather than his development as an individual. The acquisition of knowledge, this philosophy holds, is of little or no importance, while the molding of the child to the social order is the principal business of modern schooling."

The groups making these attacks know full well that such a definition is a "phony" and inaccurate. But their method has been to overwhelm parents with half truths such as these, and after the school program has been weakened by their attacks, use their organization to take over the control of the schools and eliminate all modern educational methods and practices designed to meet the needs of the individual child and of the democratic community.

For many years there have been periodic assaults by organized tax limitation groups at both state and local levels. These are the groups that have fought every advance in school services, from the kindergarten through vocational education and special services for exceptional children. The procedure has been

---

John M. Eklund is former president, American Federation of Teachers.

to issue documentation on school costs, preach retrenchment through publications, clubs, and realty boards, and in many cases put tremendous pressure on school boards. Through these methods they succeed all too often in marshaling community opposition to school services.

The schools, however, are not the only objects of such limitation programs; many welfare, protective, and fundamental community services are readied for the axe year upon year.

The tragedy is that at this time, when school budgets should increase in "real" revenue in order to house and staff the schools, the opposition to providing adequate financial support for education is frequently very effective.

The effectiveness of the attacks by tax limitation groups is increased when they join with other groups which are attacking the schools for other reasons. Frequently the groups combine to urge the elimination of "frills"—frills being such fundamental phases of modern education as guidance, special education, reduction of class size, and audio-visual aids.

It would seem that there are two approaches which must be made:

1. The methods and aims of both the hysteria-mongers and the extreme tax-limitation groups must be exposed.

2. The schools themselves must examine their programs and their budgets. Weaknesses must be frankly recognized—and remedied. For there *are* weaknesses.

Let us look, then, at what these groups are criticizing. During recent years nearly every large city in the nation has faced the criticism that youngsters have not been receiving adequate academic training. Parents in many cities have felt a definite uneasiness when the familiar landmarks in child development have not appeared. When children have not revealed traditional academic skills at a particular stage of development, parents have become panicky. In view of the present competitive academic demands at the higher education levels, their fears have been understandable. For it is true the transition to a more realistic and functional education has been far more extensive at the elementary and secondary school levels than it has in the echelons of higher education. Thus it has often been a real shock for a college freshman to come directly from a modern functional secondary school, where the emphasis has been on the needs of the individual child and his community, and to find himself suddenly in a highly academic environment.

It would be well to define what some of the objectives of modern education are and why satisfying results are not always forthcoming. Many definitions of modern education have been made and many more will be attempted. There are, however, at least three statements which appear consistently in most explanations of what modern education is.

1. *"We learn by doing."* The child who merely watches someone else does not profit nearly so much as the child who participates. Hence the emphasis on broad-scale activity in the classroom, on the shaping of jobs at every level so that every child is acting and participating as far as his capabilities permit. On the playground, in the shops, in the classroom, in the assembly, what may appear to be a hopeless jumble of diversified activity may in reality be meaningful experience for the child—sometimes competitive, sometimes cooperative, but always with the emphasis on each child's functioning as an individual being.

2. *"We must consider the whole child."* While we should like to deal constantly with an integrated personality, we realize that a child's mental, physical, and emotional development do not necessarily procced at the same pace. To meet satisfactorily the many variations, each phase of this development must be studied in its own context, though each phase is closely related to the others.

One child may be far advanced mentally, but unable to adjust emotionally to his fellows. Another may be one to three years ahead of other children in his physical development, and yet much retarded in mental skills. A third may be well developed mentally and physically, and yet be emotionally unable to work, to play, to progress with others of his age group. One reason for the complexity of modern education is that it requires recognition of the need for full, rounded development in all phases of growth, and at the same time necessitates determining at what point retardation in one area demands special and specific treatment. Can a child profit mentally if emotionally his normal growth processes in a school environment are thwarted? Or are the best interests of the child served when his growth as whole shows that he is moving adequately and well? He plays, he lives as a social being—and he feels at home with his peers. Are there more impertant criteria than these?

The rate of development varies, depending on the child's total readiness and his all-around environment. Who can gamble that because the development, say in arithmetic, is not average, an overall gain would be made by throwing the child out of the proper social, physical, and emotional environment in order to achieve a specific arithmetic skill—when readiness for this skill may be one or two years away?

3. *"The child lives and works in a complex and changing world."* Most important of all is his orientation as an individual being in that world. The basic learnings are thus not designed as ends in themselves but as aids in the child's search for his place in the social group. How to discover where he can make the greatest contribution to the general welfare and find the most satisfying and fruitful living is "the sixty-four dollar question." It is one which the schools alone cannot answer. Only a well oriented being, aware of community demands and pressures, alive to the many educational forces around him— the radio, films, television, and the daily press, as well as books and magazines—can meet today's demands. The emphasis of his formal education should be not only upon what he is learning in school each day but upon "education as a continuing and life-long process." The goal of the modern school is that the child recognize and use all the life around him as a stimulus to his continued growth.

The most frequent criticism leveled at modern education has been that fundamental skills are ignored. *Where these are ignored, the most severe criticism is justified.* The ability to grow and develop mentally is dependent upon word and number skills. Where these fundamentals are neglected and the schools provide only a bewildering assortment of "happy ex-

periences," a forceful reminder is needed that *without the
essential tools of learning the child is confused and helpless.*
Certainly if parents discover that their children are failing to
acquire the fundamental operational skills; if word knowledge,
reading capacity and interest, numerical proficiency are lacking; if the child seems to find himself in a totally foreign
learning situation—it is time to investigate! For there still are
goals of attainment and measurement devices which can tell
whether the child is reaching the goals. The schools should
define what they expect to accomplish, and when.

Few parents would want their children to leave the schools
these days without being able to take their place in the community as competent, well-adjusted citizens. Under the complex
conditions of modern society, satisfactory social and economic
adjustment becomes difficult if the child is unable to use the
fundamental tools of learning in a fairly competent fashion.

The dilemma that confronts modern education today is that
we must emphasize the human dignity and worth of each
child—and yet we must use the techniques of mass education.
The cheapest and easiest methods in mass education are drill,
well-regimented activity, and having a single set of objectives
for all children. For purposes of control and easy administration
you can't beat a traditional program. In this kind of program
names are unimportant—you deal with groups, assignments,
and passing or failing. The child is a place and a number,
very seldom a person.

But such a program and such methods do not develop the
individual child to the fullest degree. And we have adopted
the philosophy that the child is the all-important factor—not
an administrative technique, not records, not buildings, nor
teachers; these are the means of education, not the ends. The
closer the school comes to meeting the needs of the individual
child, the more teachers there will be, and the smaller the
classes, and the greater the number of auxiliary services.

At this moment, however, there are great gaps in the public
school program, when individual needs—of emotional adjustment, of health, of vocational guidance and other kinds of

counseling, of remedying defects in speech, hearing, and sight, and of providing special services for spastic, crippled, and other kinds of exceptional children—are not being met.

The real difficulty is that the schools know what should be done, but the public seems unable or unwilling to support the kind of program needed. The basic faults in the schools today lie not so much in what they are doing wrong, but in what they are unable to do because of the limitations imposed, largely by the lack of adequate funds.

Can the schools work out of this dilemma? Can such criticisms as "My child can't even read," and "My boy doesn't know how to make change and he is twelve," be recognized and remedies found? The answer depends partly upon the school's ability to share with the community not only the explanation of its program but also the planning.

The school board does not originate the educational philosophy; it accepts it from its employees. But the board is still the responsible agent, and if, after a thorough review of what the schools are doing, the parents decide that changes are needed, the board must respond to the wishes of the people— but that means *all* the people.

Make no mistake, however: it is the administration and application of "modern trends" that are on trial—not the "trends" themselves. There is a mass of data on the effectiveness of the methods now in use. Certainly there are gaps and inadequacies. Certainly some teachers trained in traditional techniques, cannot change over readily. Certainly there are flagrant misuses. It is to these that we as union teachers must turn our attention, to work out cooperatively a fair adjustment, to devise a system of community participation—wider than a seven-man board— and to press constantly for the solution of the problem. The board must realize that they have no special revelation and must welcome community and teacher planning.

There are some admissions, however, which certainly must be made as the beginning point of a real solution:

1. Not all teachers are *immediately* competent or willing to deal with new and modern methods.

2. Up to this time our schools have generally failed to define their objectives adequately.

3. School administration has consistently refused to admit publicly and to face the weaknesses and defects of the program.

4. There has been and still is some feeling of suspicion as to motives on the part of both community groups and school staffs.

5. Frequently no attempt is made to examine carefully and evaluate the success of the entire instructional program at all levels at a given time. (It might be said here, however, that such an evaluation is costly.)

6. Few school boards and school administrative staffs meet freely and openly with all in the community who could contribute to the solution of school problems. Too often board members are not familiar enough with the problems involved.

7. There is need of much greater integration between elementary, secondary, and higher education.

The school is a social institution and, like other such institutions, is at best an imperfect structure. It cannot be efficient in the same way that a business can be efficient, for it deals with lives—not merchandise. But it presents no problems that cooperative, friendly planning cannot solve. Classroom teachers can recommend solutions for many of the problems; and when the community actually turns to teachers themselves for cooperative planning, we shall be headed toward solution.

Now is the time for all groups to make their contribution toward shaping an acceptable and effective educational program for the nation's children. But it must be done in a spirit of good will and trust. This spirit seems to be lacking among most of the groups now attacking the schools.

Crisis in the Public Schools

By Herold C. Hunt

(Excerpted from U.S.A.—The Magazine of American Affairs. Published by the National Association of Manufacturers, copyright 1952, and used with permission.)

Vicious propaganda against the schools is spreading disunity in many American cities from coast to coast. There are demands for a "return to the fundamentals," or the "elimination of socialistic and communistic teaching." Many parents and taxpayers find it easy to support such pleas. As a matter of fact, school superintendents and other educators would endorse them also if there were any substantial basis for their implications.

The criticisms that the schools are negelcting the three R's or that they are un-American in their teaching are simply not in accord with the facts. Repeated investigations by means of standardized tests and the re-use of examinations given generations ago have proved that girls and boys in the public schools of the United States read better today, write more legibly, have greater competency in the arithmetical processes, and can outspell the young people of any other age. Sweeping charges of un-Americanism are equally baseless.

Charges along any of these lines fall flat as soon as all of the facts are known. The only reason that they stand up at all is that children in infinite variety pass through our schools, and adverse critics can always find examples of poor spellers or some other type of exhibit they may need to demonstrate their thesis. The only fair and accurate comparison, of course, would be between groups such as all sixth graders in a typical class of today with all sixth graders in a typical class of years ago. Such comparisons always show that present-day pupils are ahead of their predecessors in the fundamental subjects, and

---

Herold C. Hunt is former general superintendent of Chicago's public schools.

in addition are much better trained in American citizenship and in the other areas of living that are essential to individual happiness and national welfare.

Another frequent criticism of the schools is their cost. It is stated candidly and bluntly that "the schools cost too much money." Large and impersonal organizations interested only in reducing taxes are most likely to press this view, and the average frustrated taxpayer is easily attracted by the catch-phrase, "eliminate frills from the schools," without stopping to consider just what is meant by a "frill" or trying to decide just what—if anything—can really be eliminated.

In addition to those who do not believe in the principle of universality of education and those who are unwilling to pay for it, there are those who prefer private and parochial education. Here in our free America, such is the right and privilege of every American. It becomes equally the responsibility of those who believe in the institution of the public school and who see in public education the great instrumentality of democracy to support and protect it. As long as these freedoms prevail, the public schools will endure and, along with the private and parochial schools, will continue to serve America's girls and boys.

America's public schools are still doing an excellent job in spite of their obstacles. Today's schools and the little red schoolhouse are as far apart as the airplane and the horse and buggy.

Just to survive—not to improve or expand—our public schools must have thousands of new buidings and thousands of new teachers every year. Short-sighted yielding to other current demands is denying the schools the necessary building materials and classroom equipment; equally short-sighted over-concern with costs hampers efforts to entice more young people into the teaching profession. Selfish interests of various types block efforts to surmound these obstacles by creating disunity and confusion in the communities that are endeavoring to save their schools.

Confronted by grave emergencies, Americans have many

time in the past forgotten their minor differences and their private interests in order to band together in joint and victorious conquest. The time is upon us for another such welding of our forces over the nation. Temporizing will invite failure; haggling will jeopardize success; there is no bargain solution to the plight of our public schools.

All agencies in each community, public and private, must bring their full influence to bear on providing buildings, equipment, and teachers for their children, regardless of obstacles. An aroused America will not permit a lack of understanding or a lack of action to deprive the youngest generation of its birthright—its fair chance for an education, American style.

One of the results of criticism is, of course, the type of self-examination called for by Gordon McCloskey and John Eklund. Self-examination may lead to satisfying conclusions too. Here, after listening to the attacks, two teachers look at the American school system and find that occasionally it is a good thing to assess the present strength of our democratic institutions, not with smugness, but with a justifiable pride in achievement.

There's Plenty That's Right with Public Education

By Leo Shapiro

*(Condensed from The American Teacher, April, 1952.
Used with permission.)*

What are the values and practices of the public schools? One way to get a clear view of what American schools are trying to do is by looking at some of the things they are *not* trying to do.

Here, for example, is a poem used in the second grade of a school in Soviet Russia. It is set forth as an exercise and reads:

  (a) Orally and in writing answer each question in words which are meaningfully related.
  (b) Memorize this poem.

About the Brave

Stalin is proud of the brave.
The brave are loved by the people.
Bullets fear the brave one,
The bayonet will not pierce him.

Questions: Who is proud? Of whom is he proud? Who loves? Who is loved? Who fears? Whom do they fear? What does not pierce? Whom does it not pierce?

An exercise like this points up rather dramatically the contrast between Soviet education or, for that matter, any sort of totalitarian education, and the kind of democratic education which the American public schools have been trying to evolve since their inception, and particularly in recent years. In the Soviet poem there is a deification of one man—in this case, Stalin—with the subsequent or consequent dehumanizing of other men and of man in general, so that as one man becomes

---

Leo Shapiro was director of education, Anti-Defamation League of B'nai B'rith, until his death in July, 1952.

suprahuman, all others tend to become subhuman; American education has chosen rather to place its emphasis on the traditional Judeo-Christian value of the integrity of each individual personality and the equality of all in the sight of God. Where the Soviet poem stresses conflict, our schools stress the skills and values of cooperation and working together to solve problems of mutual concern to all. Even on this question of solving problems, the Soviet approach is by rote, the approach of the machine to the automaton; there is nothing here of our educational techniques of critical thinking, scientific method, problem-solving, objective analysis. (One can just imagine what would happen to the educator in Russia who would append an exercise, American-style, to the above poem reading something like this: "The statements are made here that 'Stalin is proud of the brave,' and 'The brave are loved by the people.' Are these statements true? How do you know?") Finally, the Soviet poem reflects the cleavages and exclusivism of the society, the great and awful chasm separating those loved by Stalin and those less fortunate; American education seeks rather to emphasize the values and skills of participation and of giving to all a sense of belonging.

Here, then, are the emphases of the public schools—equality, cooperation, critical and scientific thinking, participation. Or to put it another way, the schools have been trying to build in each individual child, security without selfishness, problem-solving without problem-manufacturing, realism about domestic and foreign affairs without cynicism, open-mindedness about "different" values or beliefs without skepticism, actionism without the compulsive activism or feeling that you have to beat a drum or make a speech every time a problem arises. These have been the broad goals and objectives of our American schools, and they have resulted in the kinds of skills and techniques which can be found in our schools. But what is much more important is that they are not only appropriate but to a great degree, equivalent to a democratic education. They could flourish in non-democratic schools in a democratic society; they could not flourish in non-democratic schools in a non-democratic society; and if any given school or society is truly democratic, it will inevitably arrive at these skills and these techniques, whether it would be speaking in English or in any other language. This is not to say that what we have suggested is the total content of democratic education. It is to say that they are part of the essential content, a significant part. And they can be found, these values and ideals and techniques, in schools all over the land, in rural areas as well as in metropolitan areas. They can be found in the classrooms, not in all but in a great many, and in the textbooks which our children are using. As traditionally American as the Declaration of Independence and the Constitution, they derive much of their idealism from the Ten Commandments and the Sermon on the Mount.

What's Right with Our Public Schools

By David H. Russell

(Reprinted from the NEA Journal, May 1950.)

Criticism of our public schools raises its voice easily: High-school graduates can't spell. The school doesn't teach enough phonics or grammar or bookkeeping. Delinquency is the result of the failure of our public schools.

More thoughtful critics sometimes say: Cities have slum schools in buildings and equipment. The school doesn't do enough for the gifted pupil. The highschool may crystallize the social stratification existing among its students when they enter school.

These criticisms should be—and are—studied carefully by school people. However, in all fairness, we must not overlook the great strengths of the public schools. The following facts on the credit side of the ledger are given in the spirit of Denis Brogan who, in his perceptive book, *The American Character*, says: "The American school is undertaking to do more than it can (which is very American) and doing much more than it seems to do (which is also very American)."

The public school is the greatest agency for citizenship we now have. In most communities, the public highschool is the only place where all the children of all the people participate in common activities. The school is doing much more than instructing these youth. It is letting them instruct one another in how to live. The public school is the most potent weapon that we have forged for developing the social habits and attitudes that make up good citizenship.

The public schools contribute to the moral and spiritual growth of youth. Our public schools have always held worthy character as one of their principal aims. They leave to the

---

David H. Russell is professor of education at the University of California, Berkeley.

home and the church certain phases of religious education—specific creed or doctrine—and ample time in which to do it. But they work for moral and spiritual values "inextricably associated with human relations, growth, and mental hygiene, and the development of the total personality."

Thru such procedures as cooperative planning, community participation, student government, camping, and other recreational activities, and the use of stories and biographies illustrating high ethical values, the modern public school takes its place as one of the great forces in developing character in a democracy.

The public schools have given the people of this country a very high literacy rate. The record is still not good enough, but it is startlingly good. Never before has such a large percent of our population in the US been able to read. Much of the credit for our steady advance of literacy must be given to the public schools.

There are over 50 million copies of newspapers published daily with an average of two or three readers of each copy. Book sales have declined in the last two or three years but still run far ahead of even a decade ago.

Research suggests that the average reading level of adults in this country has risen appreciably in the last 30 years. Once again, the credit for this rise in general reading ability must go to the public schools. And because people *can* read better things they are beginning to *do* so.

The public schools tend to raise standards of living thruout the communities of the United States. Schools affect more than individuals. They not only make Susan a better reader or Bill a better basketball player, but they affect the living of groups of people. The higher the educational standards of a community, the higher are the productive and consuming capacities of the people of the community. Better education is positively associated with such things as income earned, amounts of rent paid, retail sales, and magazine circulation.

The public schools have helped to improve the physical well being and health and safety habits of the nation. Without detracting from the discoveries of the medical profession, the nutritionists, or the research chemists, I suggest that these groups alone do not build health habits.

Most habits have to be taught, and the schools have been doing a large part of the job. As a result of finding that about one-fourth of the young men drafted in the first World War were physically unfit for service, the schools in 1918 included health as one of their seven cardinal objectives.

Periodic physical examinations and safety education are parts of the regular curriculum, especially in urban areas. Health, hygiene, and safety are now an integral part of our daily living, and to the public schools' teaching belongs much of the credit.

The public schools teach more efficiently now than ever before. Anyone who has consistently visited a modern school knows the miracles accomplished by a skilled primary teacher in reading or a competent seventh-grade teacher in social studies or language or art.

A visit to a good classroom will impress any parent with what children know. And if they have had a chance for varied experiences, they really know they don't parrot back the words in a book.

The commonest complaint about the modern school is that it is not as good as it was a generation ago "when I went to school." Such complaints must not be disregarded even in light of the selective nature of memory.

Actually, most school systems of a couple of generations ago did not have much to commend them. As John A. Sexson has pointed out we can hardly call them efficient when they failed 30% of their enrollments, sent on only 5% of their pupils to highschool and 2% to college. Nowadays, it is common to have about 80% of the youth 14 to 18 years enrolled in highschools.

In the United States, highschool enrollments increased 50% in the 10 years 1930-1940, when the increase for the general population in this age group was only 7%. Comparisons of graduates now and then should take account of highly restricted versus total populations of teenagers. This tremendous growth of the school population is one reason the businessman can always find a highschool graduate who can't spell or add a column of figures correctly.

The next time a parent feels like criticizing the teacher of his child he should recall that in one class of 35 the teacher may have one exceptionally bright child, one or two very dull, and that the others will represent every degree of capaciy, achievement, and interest between these two extremes. In speaking of the accomplishments of the public school, it is unwise to generalize on the basis of one son or daughter or a younger acquaintance. What are the results of public schooling for public-school pupils in general?

Another thing that is right about public education is the willingness of people in it to consider what is wrong with public education. Public education wouldn't be so *right* if people in it didn't know they were *wrong* occasionally.

The desire to improve public education is reflected in the large number of professional organizations with professional aims. Teachers and others support the NEA, for example, 450,000 strong!

It is also reflected in the fact that over 1000 research articles are published in the journals of this country every year, most of them aimed at the improvement of educational practice. More can be done about informing parents about educational problems and much more needs to be done in drawing the community into evaluation and planning, but school people have shown themselves readier than many professions to improve their materials and methods of work.

These seven reasons for continuing and strengthening support of the public school would probably have appealed to Mark Twain. Before public schools were severly criticized, he wrote:

"I remember . . . when I was a boy on the Mississippi River. There was a proposition in a township there to discontinue public schools because they were too expensive. An old farmer spoke up and said if they stopped the schools they would not save anything, because everytime a school was closed a jail had to be built. . . . I believe it is better to support schools than jails."

Is your school trying to accomplish the aims which you cherish for it? It's doing more than you think. And if it isn't, aren't parents, teachers, and citizens all partners in the job of creating better schools?

V.

TO SECURE GOOD EDUCATION

We must have complete acceptance of the idea of school-community planning. While this has long been recognized, it still is accepted with many reservations by administrators. There has come a revolution in community concern and interest in education, as evidenced by the great folk movement of our times, the growth of the National Congress of Parents and Teachers. The working relationships between educational leaders and teachers on the one hand, and parents and other citizens on the other, when established in conformity to the National Congress of Parents and Teachers policy, can bear much fruit. Their statement follows: "What shall be taught and how it shall be taught are the two foremost questions in today's educational policy making. It is not the function of either the school or the home to settle these questions alone. They should be settled cooperatively by the two groups in the interest of a common objective."

—Virgil M. Rogers

Many attitudes must change and new techniques of leadership be acquired if community-wide programs of education—involving the full mobilization of all community resources—are to be developed. Perhaps, as several selections in Chapter IV indicate, no one should change his thinking and practice so much as the professional educator himself. He must become more humble, more willing to listen, more capable in energizing the educational activities of other groups, more skillful in group leadership. And he must be more realistic in his appraisal of the current plight of free institutions in our world and the urgencies they present. It would seem that new programs of preparation for educational leaders are essential if a true community program is to become a reality.

The initiative for community development—the new dynamic in education—may, perhaps, be the job of the citizens themselves. Good lay leadership has often made a more accurate appraisal of the educational needs of a community than its professional leadership. Lay people are less inclined to think in terms of institutions and agencies and more inclined to face the community's real needs and meet them on a community-wide basis. The following selections tell of instances in which working, dynamic school-community relationships have been brought about and how they have operated. Often, you will note, the initiative has been the citizens'.

The Palo Alto Story

By Wilford M. Aikin

(Reprinted from the Saturday Review of Literature, September 8, 1951. Used with permission.)

The 30,000 citizens of this pleasant, rapidly growing California city are not fully content with their public schools. That is all to the good. But they believe in their schools. They have confidence in their Board of Education and the school administration. By overwhelming majorities they vote money to the legal limit for the support of the schools.

But they don't stop there. They say, "The public schools belong to us. We pay for them; the children they serve are our children. Therefore, it is our right and duty to say what we want the schools to do for our children. We provide the grounds, buildings, equipment. We pay the teachers. We are deeply concerned about what happens to our sons and daughters in the buildings we provide."

Obviously, they are right about this. They are right, also in recognizing that they must act in cooperation with the Board of Education, the school administration, and within the framework of education established by the State of California.

In any community citizens could attend meetings of the Board of Education, but they rarely do. They could go and talk to the superintendent or teachers, but they don't except on stated occasions and by special invitation. They could read and think about education, but they are preoccupied with other matters that seem more urgent. So thoughtful consideration of educational matters goes by the board. Parents could make the Parent-Teacher Association a strong force for better

---

Wilford M. Aikin has wide experience as a teacher and administrator in schools and universities throughout the country. He is a resident of Palo Alto.

schools; but they often permit it to dawdle with inconsequential trivia. They could hold meetings and exchange ideas about education and the schools, but they don't unless some row is on.

Now, there must be some way to keep all the people interested in their schools. There must be times and places for them to meet and discuss the work of the schools. And there must be an open channel of communication between the people, on the one hand, and the Board of Education, the school administration, and the teachers, on the other.

To serve these purposes the Palo Alto Education Council was formed about four years ago. The announcement of its formation includes this statement:

> We believe that the people are responsible for the schools; that the quality of education in any community is in direct proportion to the informed intelligent, and active support of the schools by the people of that community. It is the purpose of this council to encourage and crystallize such support.

Whenever an individual or group of citizens expresses an interest in some phase of the work of the schools, the Council encourages study and discussion of the matter. If it is a topic of general interest public forums are arranged in full cooperation with the Parent-Teacher Association. After a busy day in office and homes scores of parents have considered such subjects as these: Current Methods of Teaching the Three R's; How a Community Can Attract and Hold Good Teachers; Counseling and Guidance; Teen-Agers and Their Friends; Is Discpline the Answer to Our Youth Problems?

Believing that boys and girls of high school age want responsibility, the Council fosters their participation with adults in community organizations and projects. Further, when convinced of the soundness of the proposals of the Board of Education for bond issues and increased taxes the Council gives vigorous support. The annual pot-luck dinner to welcome new teachers sponsored by Council and attended by hundreds of citizens is one of the happiest community events of the year.

But the abiding interest of the citizens is in the work of the schools. Obviously, the schools can't do everything. What, then, do the people expect of them?

To find the answer the Council asked the citizens of Palo Alto. "What do you want your schools to do for your children?" The question was answered by the parents of about 90 per cent of all the boys and girls in the public schools.

Here is what they say they want:

Everybody wants the Three R's taught well. The editor of the local newspaper puts it this way: "What we want is education that sends young people out into the world capable of understanding what they read or hear, expressing themselves clearly in either spoken or written words, and making their bank accounts balance."

But that isn't all the people want.

In their responses five characteristics of democratic citizenship stand out above all the others: tolerance, both racial and religious; skill in finding and interpreting facts; the habit of objective study of controversial issues; devotion to the American ideals of freedom; responsibility for the general welfare as the duty of free men and women.

A second group of five goals received only slightly less emphasis: stick-to-it-iveness—the habit of finishing work that is started; clear-cut purpose on the part of each student in regard to his own education; respect and full opportunity for the boys and girls not going to college; intelligent interest in world affairs; skill in planning and working with others in groups.

From 94 per cent to 98 per cent of all returns supported these ten goals of education for the schools of Palo Alto.

Many parents say we expect too much from the schools. This from a lawyer's wife is a typical comment: "When school takes on all these things the parents just lie down on the job. School is to *educate*, not *raise* children."

On the other hand, some parents would have the schools take on more tasks. An attorney's wife states. "We need much more in the arts." Another family emphasizes the importance of developing initiative, independent reasoning, understanding of self and others. In similar vein, an engineer and his wife comment, "It seems to us that the prime function of education, in addition to the fundamental teaching of the Three R's, is to give the child a respect and responsibility toward himself as an individual. In our society so much stress is laid upon what 'they' do, think, and say that differences which make 'individuals' are often neglected."

Hundreds of other families took the time to express their views. As one man wrote, "This is the first time I have been asked what I think our schools should be doing for my children."

But this report should not give the impression that education in Palo Alto is all sweetness and light. Some businessmen complain that high-school graduates can't spell or add correctly. A small group of residents are unhappy because school district boundaries were changed by the Board of Education to avoid overcrowding in some schools. As a result their children were required to change from one school to another and they don't like it.

From time to time criticism of the junior high school reaches considerable volume. Some say that the fault lies in the type of organization; they would go back to an eight-year elementary school and four-year high school. Public discussion of the matter, under the auspices of the Education Council, and open meetings held by the Board of Education revealed strong support for the present six-three-three plan of organization. But just what the junior high school should do for its pupils is still a subject of vigorous discussion.

A good many parents doubt that the senior high school challenges fully the abilities of the most capable students. Others deplore the tendency of students and some teachers to look down their noses at non-academic courses. Many parents feel considerable uneasiness over irresponsible conduct and occasional outbreaks of rowdiness by some high school students.

Nevertheless, education in Palo Alto is in a healthy condition, even though the schools can become better than they now are. At present it would be difficult to point out many superior features of public education in this community. On the other hand, glaring weaknesses are spotty.

There is little likelihood of a school crisis here. There doesn't seem to be much, if any, fear on the part of citizens that subversive teaching finds any place in the schools. Nor does there seem to be any question about the complete loyalty of the teachers. Since everybody has a chance to say what he thinks and to say it openly to his fellow citizens, there is no reason for bottling up dissatisfaction. Secret whispering in a corner just doesn't fit into the picture.

The people have told the schools what they want for their children. They stand ready to help the administration and teachers in any way possible. As appropriate plans for action are made, there is every reason to expect that the people will continue to work together in mutual confidence.

The Organization and Work of the National Citizens Commission

By Roy E. Larsen

(Reprinted from The School Executive, January, 1952. Used with permission.)

More than four years ago, President James B. Conant of Harvard University and six members of a joint committee appointed by the Educational Policies Commission of the National Education Association, together with the Problems and Policies Committee of the American Council on Education, came to a small group of laymen, of whom I was one, and suggested the idea of a National Citizens Commission for the Public Schools.

These distinguished educators had felt a growing undercurrent of questioning among thinking Americans about the goals and end results of our public school system. They believed that our great American system of education was in urgent need of reappraisal by citizens at the local and national level. They propounded the view that our public school education cannot be left to the professionals, any more than government can be left to a professional governing group.

It was time, these farsighted men said, that laymen took the lead in encouraging all citizens to become actively interested in the public schools. Good public schools benefit every American, they emphasized, and the efforts of all citizens are needed to create good schools. The professional educators cannot be expected to do the job alone.

We accepted their thesis and their challenge. We felt there was room for an organization like the old American Lyceum of the nineteenth ceuntry which stressed the importance of

---

Roy E. Larsen is chairman of the National Citizens Commission for the Public Schools and president of Time, Inc.

education for the safety of the nation and for the prosperity of each community, in addition to other reasons. We felt that history was re-creating (or, again presenting) the reasons the old Lyceum worked for better schools, again illustrating the timelessness of Thomas Jefferson's warning that a nation cannot hope to remain both ignorant and free.

Over a period of two years, the group of laymen who had been thus challenged by the educators met for frequent exploratory discussions to determine whether such a Commission could make any real contribution toward the improvement of our vast and complex public school system. The decision was that we could. It was decided that the Commission should be a national Commission, not because we believed that there was any national solution to public school problems—on the contrary, we were convinced that the solutions everywhere must be found by citizens at the state and local level—but because, as a national organization, we could bring to the school improvement campaign greater objectivity and also serve as a coordinating agency for the existing, contributing agencies and the hitherto scattered volumes of information.

Our financial backing comes from the General Education Board, the Carnegie Corporation and the New York Community Trust. Our members have come together from all parts of the country and from many fields of activity. We have just one axe to grind, and that is the improvement of our public schools.

When, in the middle of May, 1949, we launched our National Citizens Commission, I think many of us felt as though we were launching a ship—a deep-keeled ship—into waters of uncharted depths.

This month, the Commission will hold its third annual meeting in St. Louis, Missouri. In the past three years, the course of the Commission—and public school improvement work throughout the country—has become easier to follow and simpler to chart. It has been consistently true that the course is charted by the citizens themselves.

The course of school improvement in the past few years

might be followed by looking at the individual efforts of local communities and the trends they indicate.

Often, the layman begins by being interested in some one specific aspect of education with which his experience has brought him into direct contact. Businessmen often begin by wishing the schools would do more to teach the fundamentals of economics; and it is of course very usual to find persons whose initial concern is that schools teach people to spell better, to read better, or even to use better penmanship. This narrow interest in the schools often plagues professional educators, I know, but I do not think it should be scorned, for we have found it is often the beginning of a long process which can lead to great good.

The mail coming to the Commission in increasing quantity shows that the layman, having begun to concern himself about one immediate goal of education, goes on to try to answer for himself the broader question of the ultimate goals of education: What, in essence, should the schools try to do? How much emphasis should be put on the fundamentals of academic learning? How much emphasis on training for citizenship? How much on acquiring an intellectual and moral sense of values? How much on vocational training?

When the layman begins wrestling with these questions, it isn't long before he begins to get into the further question of how the goals should be pursued. And then the layman often looks around him and realizes for the first time just how great the material difficulties of the schools are. He becomes fully conscious of the overcrowded classrooms and all the other conditions which make talk of the high goals of education almost ironic. Often, I find, the laymen are sincerely shocked and surprised by their belated discovery of such things.

The discovery, however, has not come too late. Citizens, exemplified by more than 1,500 local, country and state committees with which our Commission is in touch, are again accepting their historic role of responsibility for public school education and seeing to it that our children are getting the classrooms they need. When that very real need is attended to, they are going on to study the curriculums, and thus determine and achieve worthy goals for the schools.

This reacceptance of responsibility has led directly to an extension of the Commission's activity. We are now engaged in the preparation of reports on the great issues and immediate problems in education, because the citizens have asked us for these additional tools to do the job. These reports will assemble information and opinion on all facets of many of the pressing questions of the day on education. With these reports in hand, the citizens, on the local level, will measure how well their own schools are doing the job and, if they fall short, correct the deficiencies.

I think history is working on our side. I think the realization is being forced upon the leaders of this country once more that the public schools are urgently needed, not only to offer opportunities to individuals, but to offer opportunities to entire communities and to safeguard the nation. The old motives which inspired the establishment of our schools in the first place are regaining their strength and their validity.

The Relation of Citizens Committees to Other Local Groups

By W. A. Early

*(Reprinted from The School Executive, January, 1952.
Used with permission)*

Thanks to the National Citizens Commission for the Public Schools and other organizations, the spotlight has centered on citizens' participation in the public schools, and interest in the education of our children has been reawakened. That is all to the good. The more of it, the better.

But a sand trap is ahead of us, and before we select our club to aim for the next hole, let's be sure first that we see the sand trap and second, that we clear it.

The sand trap is the danger of allowing citizens committees to fall into a rigid, preconceived organizational pattern. If we try to force it into some special kind of pattern, we may fail in our objective.

Citizen participation in the schools need not and does not follow any specific pattern. It should and does differ in approach from community to community.

We, in Arlington County, Virginia, have undergone what some folks look upon as a sort of community revolution. Our people, dissatisfied with the school situation, rose in justified wrath and proceeded to do something about it. Many improvements have been made. But there is much more work ahead to solve many more difficult problems.

Community interest must not be a one-day wonder, for to be of rich value, it must be continuous. Citizen machinery in Arlington is geared to maintain that interest and constructive participation, but it does not follow precisely a given formula.

W. A. Early is superintendent of schools, Arlington, Virginia.

Since it springs from the people and is spontaneous, it runs in directions that suit the community needs and the character of the people. The important thing is to keep objectives in mind and to discard the notion that there is one way and only one way to win and hold citizen interest.

As we study Arlington's citizens' organization for better schools, we can see not only how one community approaches its problems, but also some of the elements that enter into winning and holding community interest. It is vital to remember that citizen participation is a general concept. What citizens? How do they prefer to organize? In what way can they best concentrate their interest and function?

We have many organized groups in Arlington, many directly concerned exclusively with the public schools, many with varying degrees of interest. All of them together add up to citizen interest.

Three citizen groups may first be cited because they are county- or community-wide in nature.

The Citizens Committee for School Improvement has had a membership as high as 2,500. It organized the School Board Nominating Convention, composed of representatives from all civic organizations in the community having bona fide educational committees. At a recent session of the convention, 590 representatives voted on the nominees to be sponsored for membership in the board of education. Six persons were nominated for three board vacancies. There is, of course, provision for other nominations, but neither political party at present makes nominations for the school board.

The convention does not have legal status, and it need not. It is simply the community's way of expressing its interest in furthering education.

The Citizens Committee for School Improvement has approached another vital avenue. The School board set up a group of exploratory councils in various fields of educational interest. These groups, composed of an average of 21 persons each, function in the fields of art, music, home economics, vocational education, budget procedure, buildings and grounds, special education, school construction, physical education and the like.

They meet regularly, with members of the school professional staff serving as secretaries. Their function is to supply information, to help get the work done, to serve as catalytic agents to crystallize or resolve issues for presentation to the county-wide citizens committee and thence to the school board.

The council on budgetary procedures, for example, to ensure participation of the school staff in budget-making, solicited initial requests by classroom teachers, followed by consolidation of their requests by school principals and presentation of these proposals to the superintendent of schools. Both the lay members and the staff work together in formulating the budget from the beginning. It is then submitted to the superintendent for action.

The second large, county-wide group is the County Council of Parent-Teacher Associations, it representing the individual school. This group is invited to express its views at the monthly board meetings. Machinery exists for the interchange of information, on a basis of mutual confidence Board members are always available and willing to discuss all school issues frankly. There is no bar to parent-teacher participation.

The third county-wide group is the Civic Federation, a composite of all the county civic organizations concerned with the general welfare of the community. Their interest covers a wide range of problems—from roads, water and sewer facilities to playgrounds, police protection and community sanitation. Most of these groups have education committees.

Virginia law authorizes the board of education to appoint a school advisory committee of three persons for every school building. They advise the board on school matters and co-operate in the care of school property and successful operation of the schools. They are media of communication between the small school community and the board. They find problems and causes of irritation or dissatisfaction, and report them to the board.

There are many areas of general interest in which the committees serve and, of course, many peculiar to a given school building. In general, the school committees work with parent-teacher groups, teachers, principals and pupils on such matters as bus transportation, routes, places and time of pupil pick-up, school districting, and protection of school property. Where activities are sponsored on a county-wide basis by other groups, these committees implement the work directly in the individual school.

One of the most helpful services of the school committees is in what we call public communications. When the board contemplates a significant news release, on a step of general community or even of strictly local interest, advance copies may be sent to the school committees. They meet with the parents and teachers, read the proposed statements, consider them, and advise the board of the school reaction to them. This is one way to keep in intimate, sensitive touch with the feelings of the people immediately around the school building.

A somewhat similar two-way communication exists in curriculum matters. The Parent-Teacher county-wide committee on curriculum meets with the profesional staff, discusses curriculum adjustments and reports its views to the board.

What does all this add up to? Is it a complex organizational pattern? Are there inherent conflicts in it? Undoubtedly there are those who, confronted with this active, multicolored fabric of community participation, will wonder how it works. The answer is simple and unqualified. *It works!*

The people, in three successive years, voted substantially larger school budgets in Arlington County. Was there opposition when the budgets were offered? Of course, there was, but by the time the budgets were proposed, the whole school problem had been presented to every nook and cranny of the community. They had been discussed and considered. The board of education had sincerely demonstrated its interest in reflecting community wishes. Mutual confidence existed. The majority of the people recognized the need and voted for the budget.

What, one may ask, happens when someone wants something and the decision is adverse? Obviously, the score is not 100 percent, but the community does not expect 100 percent. As it participates in efforts to solve perplexing problems, it comes to realize that there are many sides, not only two, to a story. There are victories and defeats. There are successes and failures. But the sum total is success, because there is understanding.

Arlington County does it that way. Other communities may pursue other ways, but the basic principles remain. The school system must be close to the people to win their understanding. To the degree that the board achieves this aim, it succeeds.

Some Pointers for Citizens Committees *

(from The School Executive)

Since schools are essentially a local institution and, as such, have their local problems which must be solved on an individual basis, any rule you could set down for citizens committees should be prefaced with: "Though local institutions differ in general, it has been found to be true that . . ." This is not equivocating, but a way of saying at the outset that what works miracles in one community may produce the opposite result in the town fifteen miles down the highway.

In a democracy—which is the only form of government that could permit citizens school improvement committees—the problems of the schools can be solved only by people working together. The tenor of a community will determine the methods used to get people to cooperate.

However, bearing that in mind, some general words of advice and caution can be given, based on the experience of citizens committees throughout the country.

After examining the methods of organization and modes of procedure of some 1,500 local, county and state committees, the National Citizens Commission for the Public Schools points out three common denominators of all effective groups:

1. They are representative of the entire community.

2. They start with fact-finding to make certain their recommendations and actions are based on an objective evaluation of the problems.

3. They work cooperatively with school authorities, but preserve their independence of thought and action.

The handbook for citizens committees, *How Can We Help*

---

* An excellent pamphlet, "How Can We Help Get Better Schools?" describing methods of organization and operation of local citizens' committees is available from the National Citizens Commission for the Public Schools at 2 West 45th Street, New York 19, New York.

Get Better Schools? declares: "The entire success or failure of
a citizens committee is decided when the members are chosen.
If they really represent the whole community or state, it is
very difficult for a citizens committee to do wrong. If they
don't, it's almost impossible for the group to do right."

The authors of the handbook, laymen and educators, asked
themselves questions and pooled their answers on the basis of
their extensive experience. Other groups might find their
ideas adaptable to their own communities.

How do we get members we want?

Several answers were volunteered. It is rarely a good idea
for those who want to start a citizens committee to begin by
holding a mass meeting. A better method is to ask organizations
and community leaders of all kinds to suggest individuals who
might be interested. Newspapermen, councils of social agencies,
and community-wide planning agencies are often helpful in
suggesting names. The names of many community leaders can
readily be found in newspaper files.

*Should people known to be in opposition to the committee's
purpose be asked to join?*

The citizens committee's purpose, of course, should be simply
to improve the public schools. Obviously, people known to be
against the principle of public education should not be asked
to join. Great care should be taken, however, to distinguish
between those who are against the principle of public education, and those who disagree on the nature of good public
education. Probably very few people are against the principle
of public education, but many are accused of it by persons
with differing ideas on the nature of good schools.

Persons who feel schools should put great emphasis on the
arts, for instance, often find themselves in disagreement with
people who feel the schools should greatly emphasize vocational education. Obviously neither group should be excluded
from a citizens committe. In areas where there is controversy
over such subjects as the reorganization of school districts, or
the construction of new buildings, neither faction should be
excluded from a citizens committee. One of the greatest values

of citizens committees is their power to get people of differing opinion together where they can examine facts and reach agreement.

Should local school authorities and school personnel be members of a citizens committee?

The participants in the workshop conference were unanimous in their opinion that school authorities and school personnel should serve as consultants to a citizens committee, but they did not reach agreement on whether they should be members. Those who felt that teachers and school administrators should be members pointed to the great knowledge these people could bring to the group. They said that in addition, the cooperation of schoolpeople and citizens committees would be insured if the former were members of the committee. They added that school personnel and school authorities are, of course, citizens of the community themselves, and should not be excluded from a citizens committee.

Those who believed school personnel and school authorities should serve as consultants, but not as members, felt that because school personnel have such a direct personal interest in the schools it is sometimes difficult for them to preserve complete objectivity. The participants agreed that it would be unfortunate if so many teachers joined that the group became largely professional in character. All agreed that an ideal situation would be one in which teachers were freely invited to join a citizens committee where enough laymen were present to preserve the representative nature of the group, and where the teachers willingly served as citizens rather than as representatives of a profession.

Should public school students be asked to become members of the citizens committee?

The creation of a junior advisory council was thought advisable. Its responsibilities and functions would obviously be governed by the age of its members.

In deciding who should be on a citizens committee, what other factors should be taken into account?

After plans for building a fully representative citizens committee are drawn up, it is sometimes a good idea to examine the list of members with an eye for special abilities. Is there anyone on the list, for example, whose experience will come in handy when the committee studies the financial problems of the schools? Is there anyone who can give the group skilled advice on publicity? If the committee is to study buildings, an architect can be of great help. A lawyer might often be able to explain the laws under which the schools function. Obviously, a citizens committee can profit enormously from the addition of people with special skills, and there is no reason why this can't be done without disturbing the representative nature of the group.

Those in the workshop conference agreed that in general, citizens committees should be organized as informally as possible to perseve spontaneity and to avoid red tape. "When a bunch of people really get interested in doing something for the schools, they haven't got time for a lot of foolish procedure," one participant said. "I always get worried if a citizens committee starts paying too much attention to titles of officers and rules of order."

Nevertheless, everyone concurred that certain usual procedures of organization can facilitate work. Here are some questions on this subject which they considered and the answers they gave:

What officials should a citizens committee have?

A chairman, secretary and treasurer are usually enough.

What standing subcommittees will be needed?

Although this depends greatly on the activities of the committee, most committees usually find it useful to appoint special groups to consider legislation, plans for the committee's long-range program, school finances, membership, research, public relations, and other concerned with major school problems of the area.

Should the citizens committee have written bylaws?

Yes. Written bylaws can make everyone's responsibility clear, help prevent misunderstanding.

How should a citizens committee get the funds it needs to operate?

Those at the workshop conference began by agreeing that most local citizens committees need surprisingly little money to operate. Whatever money is needed can usually be raised by asking members to pay small dues, but the smaller the better. In some cases, money can also be solicited from other organizations in the community. Occasionally, business firms are willing to donate money and if the acceptance of such money is thought desirable by a fully representative committee, there is no reason against it.

The problem of raising funds for state groups is often a little different. They often depend more heavily on donations from other organizations. Sometimes state groups have an opportunity to get funds from governmental agencies, and if they feel their freedom of action won't be impaired, there is no reason not to accept them.

The belief of those at the conference that citizens committees should begin by finding facts has already been emphasized. All agreed that once the local school situation is thoroughly understood, the citizens committee should decide upon a course of action and do everything it can to implement it. After reaching this fundamental agreement, the participants considered these questions.

With what elements of the school system should the citizens committee be concerned?

Although the emphasis would, of course, vary from community to community, those at the conference agreed that a good citizens committee should be concerned with the following: school buildings and equipment, the choice of qualified people for positions on the school board, financial problems of the schools, the possible need for reorganization of school districts, the relationship between the community and the schools, teachers' salaries and the community standing of teachers, long-range studies of school needs, including studies of changes in population and changes in the nature of the community, and the basic problem of what the community wants the schools to provide.

Those at the conference agreed that citizens groups should begin by studying the less controversial and more easily understandable areas, and, after meeting success there, proceed to more difficult problems.

Where can a citizens committee get the facts and information it needs?

From local school authorities, from its own studies and from state and county offices, as well as national organizations.

When a citizens committee is in full possession of all the relevant facts and has decided upon recommendations, what can it do to implement them?

It should begin by submitting its analysis of the facts and its recommendations to the school board. If the board agrees, it will probably suggest specific methods to put the recommendations into effect. If the board does not agree, the citizens committee should find the reasons why it does not and, if necessary, correct its own thinking. If after talking the matter over with the school board, the citizens committee still believes it is correct, the citizens committee after checking again, can undertake a publicity campaign to place the issue before the public. The usual procedure, however, is for the school board and citizens committee to team up to conduct a publicity campaign designed to win public understanding of the facts concerning the schools and public support for the necessary steps.

How can the facts best be placed before the public?

Local newspapers and radio stations are of enormous help. Large public meetings are often good. A speakers' bureau to supply people to talk at meetings of other organizations is useful. Pamphlets and letters mailed directly to residents of the community often have great effect, as do posters, signs on automobiles and telephone calls. Most effective of all are door-to-door campaigns, during which members of the lay group get out and talk with residents of the community.

When a citizens committee has made recommendations, and

the recommendations are put into effect should the committee go out of business?

No—a citizens committee should be a continuing organization. Even when it achieves its goal, there are always plenty more ahead. School systems don't stand still—they're always going up or down hill. Citizens committees can keep them going up.

The workshop participants ended their conference with a note of caution. They pointed out that improving a public school system isn't an easy job. A citizens committee made up by many persons of differing backgrounds and abilities requires tactful and patient leadership. Citizens committees must be careful to avoid friction with school authorities, for their purpose is to *help school* boards, and school administrators create good schools, not to *replace* them.

Do's and Don't for Community School Study Groups

*(Excerpted from "Do Citizens and Education Mix?"
the Report of the Governor of Connecticut's
Fact-Finding Commission on Education.*)*

DO:
Expect the job of organizing a study group to take time. More time spent in the beginning will mean less time wasted in the end. Give the project a chance to grow. Give leadership a chance to emerge.

DON'T:
Be in a hurry or rush others into accepting responsibility before they have a chance to find out how much is involved.

DO:
Start with temporary officers—maybe as temporary as for just one meeting; perhaps a host and/or hostess, instead of a chairman. Take turns keeping notes for the first few meetings. Provide ample opportunity for expression of all views.

DON'T:
Try to elect a slate of permanent officers at the first meeting, or try to choose subjects for study before you know what subjects interest the whole town most.

DO:
Give the Board of Education, Superintendent of Schools, and other school personnel opportunity at the outset to suggest how you can be most helpful

DON'T
Fail continuously to seek cooperation from school authorities. Don't forget that cooperation does not mean domination.

---

* This is a progress report of the commission set up in 1949 by Chester Bowles, then Governor of Connecticut. In 85 towns and cities, school study groups were formed, generally with the purpose of surveying two major areas of the educational apparatus: the actual physical set-up of the school system and the quality of the curricula.

and to join in your activities. If their cooperation is not immediately forthcoming, keep trying. Be sure they receive notices of all meeting dates. Remember that independence doesn't rule out interdependence.

DO:
Seek out for commendation areas in which your schools are setting an example for others, as well as areas in which there is room for improvement. Be a fact-finding, not a fault finding group.

DON'T:
Carp, criticize irresponsibly or involve personalities.

DO:
Make membership represent your town: community and education interests, business, labor, churches, organizations, youth, racial and national backgrounds, and all geographic areas. Keep meetings open to interested groups and persons. Build a cross-section membership big enough to do the job you outline for yourselves.

DON'T:
Try to do a broad job with only a few chosen members.

DO:
"Include the opposition in." Invite those who disagree with you to participate in the group. Try to get them to accept responsibility in the group.

DON'T:
Be afraid of opposition or avoid those who disagree with you.

DO:
Clearly define the purpose, policy, and scope of your group after the first few meetings. This can be amended later, if the interests of the group broaden.

DON'T:
Tackle the job until you have all agreed on precisely what the job is.

DO:
Choose your subjects for study with reference to the preferences of the entire membership of the group, plus town opinion as sampled by the membership.

DON'T:
Have subjects for study chosen by a small committee and foisted onto the rest of the group.

DO:
Determine the number of officers needed, the number of sub-committees, etc., with reference to the scope of the job you carve out, in all its aspects.

DON'T:
Hold committee elections in a vacuum or emphasize *machinery* above *subject matter.*

DO:
Elect a responsible steering committee that will coordinate and stimulate the work of all sub-committees, and will authorize, with reference to the whole group, the work of each sub-committee.

DON'T:
Let sub-committees go off on individual tangents which may duplicate the work of other sub-committees.

DO:
Make liberal use of "live" resources in seeking answers to study-group questions. Consult town and school officials, industry, labor, health and housing authorities, architects, etc.

DON'T:
Rely on printed statistics to provide all the answers.

DO:
Keep the whole town continuously up-to-date on the methods, findings, activities of the group, as you progress. Report to the press. Send speakers to meetings. Hold open forums.

DON'T:
Wait until your study is complete to let others know what you are doing.

DO:
Be sure final recommendations are based on a factual foundation and represent the views of the entire group in relation to the town. Include study of financial resources which can be tapped to support your recommendations.

DON'T:
Make "wishful" recommendations, which are not related to available sources of income, or to the needs of the town.

DO:
Officially share final recommendations with school authorities releasing them generally.

DON'T:
Release final recommendations before school authorities have officially examined them.

DO:
Develop dramatic means of presenting your final recommendations to the entire town. Plan definite avenues of action leading to adoption of recommendations.

DON'T:
File your recommendations and forget about them.

DO:
Consider ways in which a school-community council can be of permanent service to the town.

DON'T
Consider your job as finished when you have completed your first full study.

Our Pledges to America's Children

By George D. Stoddard

*(Reprinted from The National Parent-Teacher,
September, 1951.)*

The seventeen pledges to American children adopted at the
Midcentury White House Conference are not a series of casual
statements. In a very real sense they are the flowering of the
entire conference. They state what American citizens in their
most responsible moments bèlieve with respect to the lives of
children. They record a vision of the better life to come in this
free part of the world.

Before the conference met in December 1950, a hundred
thousand persons were at work fact finding, evaluating, and
studying ways and means to improve conditions for children
and youth in the United States. Four hundred and sixty-four
national organizations and agencies enlisted in this great movement; more than forty-six hundred delegates took part in the
meeting. Formal action was taken on the platform of sixty-seven
explicit recommendations and eight follow-up resolutions.

The White House Conference of 1930, under President
Hoover, dealt with the great issues of the protection, welfare,
and advancement of children. At the 1940 conference President
Roosevelt put his finger on another crucial issue—the damage
that had been done to children in a time of economic depression and the further bad effects to be expected under wartime
conditions. The Midcentury Conference had to do with the
development of healthy personalities in children and youth.
More specifically, its goal was to provide at least partial
answers to these two questions: How can children be helped
to develop the mental, emotional, and spiritual qualities, essential to individual happiness and responsible citizenship? What

---

George D. Stoddard is vice-president of the National Committee for the Midcentury White House Conference.

physical, economic, and social conditions are necessary for this development? On the last day the conference adopted the "Pledge to Children." Every one of the seventeen items in this pledge should be developed explicitly by educational, parent, and civic groups.

The first pledge emphasizes the crucial importance of love in the period of early infancy: *From your earliest infancy we give you our love, so that you may grow with trust in yourself and in others.* The rejected child is certain to be damaged, whether the rejection takes the form of cruelty or of excessive and unnatural sentimentality. I am of the opinion that it is impossible to give children too much genuine love. They need to be reinforced in their relationship with others, especially their parents, at every moment and on every occasion. The father especially should undertake to show his affection and steady regard for his children by spending time with them, by trying to understand their problems and their concepts of the world.

The second pledge is this: *We will recognize your worth as a person, and we will help you strengthen your sense of belonging.* It is closely related to the first and to the third: *We will respect your right to be yourself and at the same time help you to understand the rights of others, so that you may experience cooperative living.* It is also closely related to a sense of democracy and of religious insight. The most deadly condition in any totalitarian system is that it seeks to make of children malleable objects in a political plan and to make of adults hardened work units in the same mechanism. Such a social order does perhaps give a sense of belonging, but it fails to recognize the individual worth of a person. The price of seeming to belong, without a guarantee of personal freedom, is much too high. Men who are truly free belong to a family and a community and country in which the rights, duties, and values of each person are fully sustained.

The fourth pledge reads. *We will help you to develop initiative and imagination, so that you may have the opportunity freely to create.* This should appeal particularly to the teachers of children and youth. On the whole, in my judgment, the schools have not done well in this respect. One finds in them an immense amount of learning of things that have been learned before by others and a strong pressure to conform. Surely we need a large amount of such learning, but it should not have the monopoly. There is in the United States a lack of emphasis upon the imaginative and creative aspects of education, although the preschool and the progressive kindergarten have begun to make a noticeable impact. A child learns by weaving hard fact into a fabric of fact and fancy. Often he is none too sure which is which, but adults who are sure of their facts are frequently unsure what to do with their imaginations.

Unless pushed into the irrational or neurotic, beyond the normal range, children will also separate reality from unreality. The process takes time and should not be forced. Teachers often feel that if something is factual it is therefore desirable. I think the history of civilization shows the narrowness of this view. Even in science the factual elements do not engage our attention or enlist our enthusiasm to such an extent as do hypotheses and theories that leave something undertermined. We need facts as we need bricks and mortar, but we need the imaginative content also, whether we are thinking of the design of a building or the growth of a child. Thus the experience of music, starting early from appropriate choices, dances and marches in and out of our lives.

Our school building and grounds should epitomize the best in architectural design and beauty, through both function and appearance, and they should contrive to bring out the best in children. After all, that is what the schools are for. Similarly the sciences, humanities, and art taught in any school should be the best that the culture can offer.

Of course, all this is related to pledges five and six: *We will encourage your curiosity and your pride in workmanship, so that you may have the satisfaction that comes from achievement. We will provide the conditions for wholesome play that will add to your learning, to your social experience, and to your happiness.*

Children learn by satisfying their curiosity. The activity in which they knit the contents of their lives into a meaningful whole is called play. They work harder at play than some adults work at work. If you doubt this, ask the preschool or kindergarten teacher who has endeavored to equal the perseverance of a child with a hunk of clay, a ball, or a pile of blocks. Most games call for social experience. Through them children learn what it means to be included in a circle and what it means to be left out. They learn that the rules are not made by overly anxious grownups but arise out of the necessities of fair play.

The next pledge, seven, reads: *We will illustrate by precept and example the value of integrity and the importance of moral courage.* And in pledge eight we say: *We will encourage you always to seek the truth.* These two also go together. It is easy to speak the truth when the truth is pleasant and not controversial. It is hard to *seek* the truth when intellectual work is required. The whole process of education is therefore difficult.

Fortunately, learning can be habit-forming. Learning that is adjusted to the mental capacity of children meets, I find, only a reasonable amount of resistance. In adults the blocking effect is more dramatic. Children and youth are refreshingly honest in their expression of opinion. They have a basic moral courage that they exercise until, through bad companions or adult example, they learn about other ways to get what they want in the world.

In pledge number seven we are saying to children. "We will give you good precepts. We will say what we mean. We will fight for the causes we believe in." Children are sensitive to this type of honesty. I have never seen a child who did not at one time or another develop a strong reaction against cruelty, neglect, or unfairness of any type. Our schools are performing a tremendous service in this respect by teaching fair play and personal honesty.

Of course the encouragement to seek the truth is a relative virtue. When a person says he will seek the truth he is assuming that the truth is not known to him, that it is something not previously attained. It is in the process of seeking the truth that we become independent in thought and action, giving every problem and every person full consideration and the full benefit of a just and rational approach.

Pledge nine reads. *We will provide you with all opportunities possible to develop your own faith in God.* This pledge helped to resolve a controversy at the conference. There was a feeling shared by the majority of the delegates that opportunity to develop this faith would be lessened if the child were placed in a school situation involving selection for various types of sectarian religious training.

The final resolution approved by the delegate body reads as follows: "Recognizing that knowledge and understanding of religious and ethical concepts are essential to the development of spiritual values and that nothing is of greater importance to the moral and spiritual health of our nation than religious education in our homes and families and in our institutions of organized religion, we nevertheless strongly affirm the principle of the separation of church and state which has been the keystone of our American democracy and declare ourselves unalterably opposed to the use of the public schools directly or indirectly for religious educational purposes."

Now consider pledge ten: *We will open the way for you to enjoy the arts and to use them for deepening your understanding of life.* Shades of ancient Egypt, Greece, and Rome! Why, you ask, do we have to make an affirmation of this in the middle of the twentieth century? I think I know why. There is a mechanizing drabness and uniformity in the land. We are in danger of forgetting that joy or compassion cannot exist except as human beings transmute the forms of materials into the actions of their everyday lives. For children especially the arts cannot be confined to the casual, museum-best-behavior contact. The arts must penerate their lives.

The eleventh pledge—*We will work to rid ourselves of prejudice and discrimination, so that together we may achieve a truly democratic society*—is inherent in those that have come before, and we might say the same for the pledges that complete the document. The twelfth pledge is this: *We will work to lift the standard of living and to improve our economic practices, so that you may have the material basis for a full life.* A similar thought appears in the fourteenth: *We will protect you against exploitation and undue hazards and help you to grow in health and strength.* Certainly in many cultures and societies people have not considered economic well-being a necessary virtue. As a matter of fact, Americans have been charged with placing too much emphasis on the standard of living. Nevertheless if we regard the health, growth, and orderly maturation of children as crucial to the higher things of life, then we cannot neglect this problem.

It is wrong to expect citizens of our world to talk sincerely about the spiritual qualities of children if those children are hungry, diseased, or neglected. In the long run the socio-economic and the ethical go together. It it a part of our faith to want to feed the hungry, to cure the diseased, to offer hope for the future.

A feature of the 1950 conference that came in dramatically for the first time was the active participation of youth. They were both seen and heard, and some of the best contributions were made by the youngest delegates. It is this participation that explains the last of the pledges to children, which promises that as they develop through youth and adulthood, accepting larger responsibilities, we will help them. Long before they grow up children will have accepted a heavy responsibility in self-dependence. Their pledge to us adults, could they but formulate it, would strengthen our faith in the future.

So let us join forces, attack the real target. American young men are not as healthy and able-bodied as they should be. The trouble stems in part from the conditions of birth and early infancy. Less than ever before in our history is there any excuse for malnutrition in children, of which there is still too great an amount. American families, even in the higher income brackets, can scarcely meet the payments for medical and dental services. An accident or chronic illness in the family usually brings on a financial crisis. In a period of high living costs and heavy taxes it is difficult for most families to build up a reserve.

We know, too, that juvenile delinquency is not a cause but an effect. Unwittingly we produce delinquents and criminals according to the same basic laws of individual and social behavior that will, if properly directed, produce good character. The laws of behavior are not well understood, and some of the necessary guidance must come from organizations. Here again I feel that the National Congress of Parents and Teachers is needed.

Similarly we must do better with the young men now headed for the armed forces. It isn't enough for them to know how to fight. The military will teach them that. But every man must know—and must learn it from his reading, his school, from social organizations—why he is fighting and what he is fighting for. When the time comes to go to the front it is rather late to begin a study of basic history.

Also in the midst of our defense activities we perceive a tremendous lag between purpose and program. We are slow in getting better laws to protect children, slow in getting better schools, hospitals, cultural facilities. Even in the richest nation at the peak of its prosperity there is never enough money to go around, and the reason for this is clear. In our time we have not been free from heavy military burdens that take from us much of the wealth and energy that ought to go toward peacetime reinforcement. Hence we find in the "Pledge to Children" this statement:

Aware that the promises to you cannot be fully met in a world at war, we ask you to join us in a firm dedication to the building of a world society based on freedom, justice, and mutual respect. Surely all of us will join in this declaration that what we want for our children, for the future of the nation and of the race, is a world at peace. In such a world and in no other will the Midcentury Conference "Pledge to Children" become a heartening reality.

CONCLUSION

As the bearers of the only really authentic revolution, the democratic revolution against tyrannies, we in America are only playing our proper roles when we take a genuinely creative outlook on life. We see every human being as a unique organism. This means each person has capacities not possessed by any other individual. To us the good society is therefore the free society, for it alone releases those creative capacities. And the fact is we have released human creative talents to a greater extent than has ever been done before in human history. The productive power of American industry can still be increased through further and more complete release of creative talent and power. We can extend this creative power in the cultural and spiritual areas of life to a much greater extent than we have in the past. We can prove that human brotherhood, under freedom, has more power to fire the imagination of the masses of people than any materialistic outlook which promises to feed men's bodies while putting their minds in chains and suppressing the human spirit.

Into our total educational program should come the practice and the proof of life in a democratic society. It is out of this society and its life that we get the materials of our education. It is in its life that both young and old learn and grow. We thus have all the ingredients for the needed dynamic. We have only to blend them in a vital community life to secure their educational power. This done, we shall have energized our schools—now far too often ineffective because they are isolated from the community like a dynamo without steam or water power. All the resources of the community, lay and professional, together with our total technology, must be harnessed to the task of the hour—that of creating the living proof of the dynamic and the power in our way of life.

Education will have the new dynamic it needs when democ-

racy becomes resurgent, when it recaptures its original moral
and spiritual fervor, when at home and abroad it practices
what it preaches, when it makes of every community a vital,
functioning, educational enterprise. Then also democracy will
win the battle of ideas. Then we can with practicality fight
anywhere on earth for human freedom, for we will be fighting
side by side with men and women who have freedom to win—
and who want to win it because they know it is a working
reality.

Date Due